EUROPE AND THE MIDDLE EAST

EUROPE AND THE MIDDLE EAST

Albert Hourani

University of California Press
Berkeley and Los Angeles

First published 1980 by
UNIVERSITY OF CALIFORNIA PRESS
Berkeley and Los Angeles, California
ISBN: 0−520−03742−1
Library of Congress Catalog Card Number: 78−059452

Printed in Great Britain

To ODILE

Contents

Acknowledgements   ix

Introduction   xi

1 Western Attitudes towards Islam   1

2 Islam and the Philosophers of History   19

3 Muslims and Christians   74

4 Volney and the Ruin of Empires   81

5 Wilfrid Scawen Blunt and the Revival of the
     East   87

6 H. A. R. Gibb: the Vocation of an Orientalist   104

7 Toynbee's Vision of History   135

8 The Present State of Islamic and Middle
     Eastern Historiography   161

   Notes   197

   Index   217

Acknowledgements

Of the essays in this collection, that on *Volney and the Ruins of Empires* has not previously been published. I am grateful to the editors and publishers who have given permission to reprint the others:

Western Attitudes towards Islam: 10th annual Montefiore Lecture, given at the University of Southampton, 5 March 1974, and published by the University, 1974.
Muslims and Christians: Frontier, vol. 3 (1960).
Islam and the Philosophers of History: Middle Eastern Studies, vol. 3 (1967).
Blunt and the Revival of the East: Middle East Forum, vol. 38 (1962).
Toynbee's Vision of History: Dublin Review, vol. 119 (1955), reprinted in *A Vision of History*, Khayats, Beirut, 1961.
H. A. R. Gibb: the Vocation of an Orientalist: Proceedings of the British Academy, vol. 58 (1972), Oxford University Press, 1974.
The Present State of Islamic and Middle Eastern Historiography: L. Binder (ed.), *The Study of the Middle East*, John Wiley and Sons Inc., New York, 1976. © 1976 by John Wiley and Sons Inc.

I must also acknowledge with thanks permission to publish quotations:

Presses Universitaires de France, for the quotations on p. 20 and p. 38 from L. Massignon, *Opéra Minora*, ed. Y. Moubarac.
Editions du Cerf, for the quotation on p. 41 from J. Jomier, *Bible et Coran*.
Macdonald and Jane's Publishers Ltd, for the quotations on p. 102 and p. 103 from the Earl of Lytton, *Wilfrid Scawen Blunt*.

University of Chicago Press, for the quotations on p. 53 and p. 119 from H. A. R. Gibb, *Modern Trends in Islam.* Copyright 1947 by the University of Chicago.

Professor Bernard Lewis, for the quotation on p. 128 from a letter written to him by H. A. R. Gibb.

I am deeply indebted and grateful to those who helped in various ways towards the publication of this book: Sarah Graham-Brown for her editorial work, Patrick Seale my literary agent, and John Winckler and Allan Aslett of Macmillan.

The essays were selected and prepared for publication during a month spent at the Villa Serbelloni on Lake Como in 1975. I must thank the Rockefeller Foundation for making it possible for me to enjoy perfect working conditions at the Villa, and Bill and Betsy Olson for the warm and sensitive friendship and hospitality which turned a study centre into a home.

Introduction

The essays in this book all spring, in one way or another, from a concern with the attitudes of Western thinkers and scholars towards Islam and those who call themselves Muslims, and more generally with the relations of Christians with those who profess other faiths. Some of the essays try to explain, directly or indirectly, the obstacles which confront the Western Christian who has tried to understand Islam, and (in a different form) the Muslim who has tried to understand Christianity: obstacles which have been created both by the nature of the two faiths and by the tangled history of the contacts between those who have professed them. In one of the essays I write of the look of uneasy recognition with which the two religions have always faced each other: neither of them is wholly alien to the other, but each finds it difficult to give an intelligible place within its system of thought to the other, as it has in fact developed and as its adherents interpret it.

The first five essays in the collection all try to illuminate different aspects of this theme. The longest of them, that which I have called 'Islam and the Philosophers of History', took the form it did because of some trains of thought started by my book *Arabic Thought in the Liberal Age*.[1] At the same time, as I was trying to understand how ideas from Europe entered Arab minds, I could not help noticing how some ideas about Islam were expressed by European thinkers. Every now and then a personal contact or literary exchange caught my eye: those of Renan and Jamal al-Din, of Comte and the Ottoman reformers, or of Muhammad 'Abduh and Herbert Spencer.

The roots of this concern lay deeper, however, and in two different places. One of them was an interest of long standing in the relations of Christians with non-Christians. I am conscious of many debts here, not all of them made explicit in the essays: long conversations at different periods with Charles Malik and Jean de Menasce, the writings of theologians like J. Daniélou[2] and C. Journet,[3] and studies of European attitudes such as those of R. W.

Southern, N. Daniel and J. Waardenburg.[4] I have also felt the disturbing influence of two men of genius, Robin Zaehner and Louis Massignon, both known personally; Zaehner as a colleague of many years, Massignon as a revered older scholar whom I met from time to time.

The last essay in the book, that on historiography, may appear to have a different focus of interest. It arises from an attempt to consider how the history of the Middle East should be written in our time; but it also illustrates a certain aspect of my main theme. Any attempt to explain the ways in which historians, and specifically those of Europe and America, have tried to write the history of the Middle East is bound to raise the question, whether the concepts of 'Islam', of 'Islamic society' and of 'Islamic civilisation' can provide the framework of categories within which the history of those regions in which Islam has been the dominant religion can be understood.

Together with this essay I have included one—on Toynbee's *Study of History*—which does not deal mainly with the Near or Middle East, but is not, I think, out of place here, both because Toynbee's ideas about history were moulded by his observations and thoughts on the rise and fall of empires and civilisations in the Near East, and because some of the other essays show clear signs of the influence of his way of looking at history.

The essay on H. A. R. Gibb, too, may seem to have a focus of interest different from the rest. One of its roots is to be found in a persistent curiosity about the way in which ideas are born and grow in the minds of individual thinkers. Certain works read when I was still a student have remained in my mind as models of intellectual biography: Gibbon's autobiography, Keynes's essay on the economist Marshall,[5] and R. W. Chapman's portrait of Ingram Bywater.[6] More recently, E. H. Gombrich's life of Aby Warburg has vividly depicted the pains and triumphs of the scholar's vocation, and that quality of obsession which leads a true scholar to shape his life by thought and research on a single subject.[7] Some reflection of this ideal of scholarship may be found in my study of Gibb, but here too the central theme of the book can be observed, for it was Gibb's constant preoccupation to provide a framework within which the nature and development of Islam, and of those who call themselves Muslims, might be understood.

It may be noticed that sometimes I use the term 'Near East' and sometimes 'Middle East'. It would be a long and profitless task to discuss the origin and precise meaning of these expressions and the advantages of using each of them. I have tried to use the term 'Near East' to refer primarily to the countries lying around the eastern end of the Mediterranean Sea, and the term 'Middle East' when I am writing more generally about countries of Arabic speech or Islamic faith, but it is not possible to be quite consistent in this.

When it is necessary to give a precise transliteration of Arabic words or names, I have used that of the second edition of the *Encyclopaedia of Islam*, with some alterations; diacritical marks have been omitted in the text, but inserted in the notes.

The essays were written at different times and for different purposes, and it would be impossible to bring them up to date without rewriting them. Every now and then I have corrected or modified a statement; I have also added or changed a few bibliographical references, but in general it seemed better to regard the notes as indicating the documentation which I used when writing the essays.

1 Western Attitudes towards Islam

May I begin by thanking the University for asking me to give a lecture, and in particular a lecture named after Claud Montefiore, whom I have held in respect ever since, some forty years ago, I first came upon his writings. While thinking about what I am to say, I have been thinking about him. Most of his work was concerned with the development of Christianity and its relation to Judaism, but one of his books seems to me to be relevant to my own subject. In his lectures on the origin and growth of religion, as illustrated by the religion of the ancient Hebrews,[1] Montefiore is not, of course, writing explicitly about Islam. He is writing within a framework of ideas created by the movement of Biblical criticism in the nineteenth century, and giving an account of the development of Judaism which rests on the reinterpretation and rearrangement of the books of the Old Testament suggested by great scholars who preceded him. Instead of the traditional order—first the historical works, then the works of poetry (Psalms and Proverbs), then those of prophecy—a very different one is proposed. The earliest books, dating from the eighth century BC, are certain of the prophetic ones, Hosea, Amos, parts of Isaiah and Micah; the historical books and the legal codes embodied in them are, except for small parts of them, a later reconstruction of a distant past. From this arrangement there emerges a certain view of the way in which Judaism grew up. The patriarchs before Moses are no more than shadowy figures of legend about whom we can never know anything, except that there may already have been some kind of innate tendency towards worship of one god. With Moses we reach firmer ground, not yet the promised land of monotheism, but at least that of monolatry: although there may be more gods than one, only One is to be worshipped, and worship of Him is directed towards a holy place and linked with respect for a moral code. Then with the Prophets we come to a full assertion

1

that there is only one God, and it is on this firm basis that there is
built the whole structure of ritual, tradition and law which is
historical Judaism.

All this is familiar, and it is not my subject, but I have
mentioned it because this way of looking at the Bible and Judaism
has had an important influence on the way in which western
scholars have looked at the Qur'an and Islam. In Montefiore's
book, as in other books of the same school, we can see an attempt
to throw light on the nature and growth of Judaism by the study
of the nature and development of other monotheistic faiths, and in
particular those professed by other peoples who speak and write
Semitic languages. This implies that while there is a sense in
which Judaism is, for a Jew, unique, just as Christianity is unique
for a Christian, there are other senses in which it should be
regarded as one among several similar manifestations of the human
spirit, one member of a class—the class of all religions, or all
monotheistic religions, or all Semitic religions. Thus there is such
a thing as a 'science of religions', and one religion can be used to
throw light on another. If the Biblical scholars of the nineteenth
century were right, Judaism began with Prophecy, Tradition grew
out of Prophecy, and Law played a special part, both regulating
men's lives in the world and bringing them nearer to God ('it was
law', says Montefiore, 'which made God nearer . . . [and] by which
his sanctifying presence was felt within the heart').[2] Clearly, if the
concepts in terms of which Judaism is to be understood are those
of prophecy, tradition and law, in that chronological and logical
order, then the study of Islam can help us to understand the Old
Testament. Islam is a religion which undoubtedly began with a
Prophet, about whose life and teaching we seem to know a great
deal (I say, 'seem to know', because much of the traditional
biography begins to crumble if one looks at it closely and
critically); it has a vast body of Tradition, the Hadith, recording
the practice of the Prophet and his companions, and gradually
developed and formalised in the first centuries, and an all-
embracing system of law or morality, the *shari'a*, which claims to
be a logical deduction from the Qur'an and Hadith and so to be a
holy law. Awareness of this similarity is one of the roots from
which modern Islamic scholarship has grown. Scholars who began
by studying Judaism went on to study Islam; applying to Islam
methods of criticism learned in their first field of study, they
produced a picture of the early development of Islam very different

in some ways from the picture Muslims themselves had had. To mention two names only, the Hungarian Jewish scholar, Ignaz Goldziher, changed our view of the growth and significance of Hadith, and the German Protestant Julius Wellhausen gave an explanation of the way in which the Prophet's message was embodied in a society and state which has stood for more than half a century, and is only now beginning to be challenged.[3]

But the view of religion which Montefiore expresses is significant in another way as well. This is how he ends his lectures—I cannot resist quoting the whole passage, because it reveals so clearly the faith and hope of a certain generation:

> . . . is any permanent reform of Judaism within the limits of possibility? Can Judaism burst the bonds of legalism and particularism and remain Judaism still? That is a question which it is for the future to answer, and for the future alone. It may be that those who dream of a prophetic Judaism, which shall be as spiritual as the religion of Jesus, and even more universal than the religion of Paul, are the victims of delusion. But, at any rate, the labour which they may give, and the fidelity which they may show, to this delusion, cannot be thrown away. They will not be the only men who have worked for a delusion, and have yet benefited the world. For their devotion to the cause of an imaginary Judaism remains devotion to the cause of God. They are the champions of Monotheism, herald-soldiers of a world-wide Theism which, while raising no mortal to the level of the divine, can yet proclaim the truth of man's kinship and communion with the Father of all. To that religion let the future give what name it will.[4]

Such a statement as this implies that monotheism is the true religion, but the way in which men have thought about God and worshipped Him has been moulded by their human characteristics—their racial character, as some thinkers of the nineteenth century would have said, or their language, or their social structure; that these ways change as human society develops; and that we may look forward to a time when the vision of God is freed from the elements of legend and fantasy with which it has been adorned or obscured, and no longer expressed in terms coloured by the self-conscious pride of limited human communities.

The way in which Montefiore writes of this world-wide theism of the future may be a modern one, but the idea itself is not. It has a long and respectable ancestry, among Jews, Christians and Muslims alike, and has provided one of the ways in which each of the three groups can look at the others. It is easy to see the historical relationship of Christians and Muslims in terms of holy war, of Crusade and *jihad*, and there is some historical justification for this. The first great Muslim expansion in Christian lands, Syria, Egypt and North Africa, Spain and Sicily; the first Christian reconquests, in Spain, Sicily and the Holy Land; the spread of Ottoman power in Asia Minor and the Balkans; and then the spread of European power in the last two centuries: all these processes have created and maintained an attitude of suspicion and hostility on both sides and still provide, if not a reason for enmity, at least a language in which it can express itself. Bismarck, encouraging the French to occupy Tunisia, told the French Prime Minister, 'You cannot leave Carthage to the barbarians'; Allenby making his entry into Jerusalem, evoked the memory of the Crusaders; and Bidault, explaining why he had deposed the King of Morocco, said he had done it because he preferred the Cross to the Crescent. On the other side, Palestinians and Algerians fighting in a national cause use words—*jihad, mujahid*—which, whether they intend it or not, call back memories of holy war.

But Crusade and *jihad* do not cover the whole reality of political relations between Christendom and the world of Islam, and still less do they explain the attitude of Christians to Islam and of Muslims to Christianity. The communities which profess the two religions have faced each other across the Mediterranean for more than a thousand years; with hostility, it is true, but with a look of uneasy recognition in their eyes.

It is uneasy because neither knows quite what to make of the other. For orthodox Muslim theologians, the uneasiness springs from the difference between what they believe to be the true Christianity and what actual Christians appear to believe. For Muslims, that 'world-wide theism' of which Montefiore speaks, and which he leaves it to the future to name, already exists and already has a name. It is Islam, the full and final revelation of the religion of the one God, innate in the human mind, sealed by a covenant between God and man, and preached by a succession of prophets, sent by God to reveal His words and recall men to their true selves, and ending in Muhammad, the Seal of the Prophets. Both Moses and Jesus are regarded by Muslims as belonging to that succession. Both preached the same message, and Jesus is said by the Qur'an to have had special privileges: he was brought into existence, like Adam, by the creative word *'kun'*—'Be'—he was born of a virgin, worked miracles, and is in some sense the 'word of God' and the 'spirit of God'. There seems no doubt that, in the first phase, Muhammad thought of himself not as founding a new religion but as reviving and completing a perennial one, and it was with surprise that he and his companions found that their attitude to Jews and Christians was not reciprocated. Christians did not accept him as a prophet, still less as the seal of the prophets; they did not regard the Qur'an as the authentic word of God; if they recognised that Muslims believed in the existence of one God, they accused them of rejecting the Trinity and the Incarnation, and so of misconceiving His nature.

This sense of shock, this feeling, one might call it, of being rejected by one's family, has always been there. Medieval Muslim thought tended to come to terms with it in one of two ways. On the one hand, it elaborated a view of Muhammad which placed him on the same spiritual level as Jesus. We can see this process beginning in the traditional biographies and the Hadith, as Goldziher has shown:[5] Muhammad is depicted as a worker of miracles, and teachings are ascribed to him which are closely similar to those of the New Testament—in one tradition, the Lord's Prayer appears almost unchanged. On the other hand, the idea was put forward that Jews and Christians had received authentic scriptures but had corrupted them so as to avoid having to recognise the prophetic mission of Muhammad. This idea of the corruption of the Scriptures—*tahrif*—has a Qur'anic basis and was worked out by the theologians. By some of them, the Christians were accused of actually suppressing texts in the New Testament and introducing new and false ones; by others, of misinterpreting certain texts which both sides accepted as valid. In particular, two sentences in Deuteronomy, and two in the Gospel of St John which speak of the Holy Spirit, were thought by Muslims to announce the coming of Muhammad, if only they were properly understood.[6] In the same way, al-Ghazali tells us that certain texts, which Christians read as asserting that Christ was God, should really be understood as saying that he was man.[7]

Some echoes of this charge of corruption can still be heard in modern times. When faced with attacks from Protestant missionaries of fundamentalist views, Muslim apologists soon learned to reply by distinguishing the religion of Jesus from the latter corruptions of it by St Paul and the Church; as early as 1867 we find an Indian Muslim, Shaykh Rahmatullah of Delhi, showing some knowledge of the Biblical criticism of his time.[8] Later still, a famous group of Islamic writers in Cairo, those connected with the periodical *al-Manar*, made use of the Gospel of Barnabas, an apocryphal work which seems from internal evidence to have been written by an Italian convert to Islam in the fifteenth century, and which certainly gives a Muslim rather than a Christian view of the life of Jesus. Known to European scholars from the beginning of the eighteenth century, it was first published in Oxford in 1907; almost at once it was translated into Arabic and widely used to show what the true teaching of Jesus must have been.[9]

Certainly this is not the whole of the Islamic tradition. There are mystical writers in whose thought the figure of Jesus appears as the human exemplar, *al-insan al-kamil* or perfect man; thus for al-Hallaj Jesus is both prophet and saint, and an example of that union between the divine and human which is the goal of Sufism. But in later Sufi thought, to follow a human teacher or meditate on a human saint is no more than a doorway into a world of mysterious beings in which earthly distinctions and differences are transcended.

Moreover, even for those who gave particular respect to Jesus, it was the Jesus of the Qur'an whom they thought about, not the Christ of Christian theology: a man, a prophet, not in any sense the Son of God, and for most of them not crucified. The orthodox Muslim belief, based on a verse in the Qur'an, was that Jesus did not die on the Cross; either someone else—perhaps, as some versions suggest, Judas—was crucified in his place, or else he was crucified but escaped death. This belief, in a human Jesus sent by God, who went through sufferings but in the end did not fail, seemed to most Muslims to be more in conformity with their concept of God as one, transcendent and all-powerful than the Christian doctrines of the Incarnation and Trinity. In modern Muslim writing, indeed, we often find this put forward as a sign of the superiority of Islam as a religion in the modern world: whereas Christians, it is suggested, cannot hold to their traditional beliefs in the light of modern science, Muslims can preserve theirs, because there is nothing miraculous or irrational in them, and indeed Islam, when restated by modern thinkers, can satisfy the need of modern man to believe.

It is because thoughtful Muslims have on the whole been sure that theirs is the only tenable doctrine of the nature of God and the ways in which He acts in the world, that few of them have shown the same concern to grasp what Christian thinkers say as some modern Christian scholars show for Islam. To the modern interest of some Christians in Muslim doctrine, there corresponds very little Muslim interest in Christian doctrine, and even books where it seems to exist may be different from what they seem. Let us consider for a moment a book which aroused great interest when it first appeared, and even now twenty years later seems remarkable and indeed unique. It is the work of a well-known Egyptian doctor and writer, Muhammad Kamil Husayn, and was published in English translation in 1959 with the title *City of Wrong*, and the sub-title *A Friday in Jerusalem*.[10] In form it is a series of fictional descriptions of what happened on Good Friday, seen from various points of view by those who played a part in it; in content it is a meditation on the meaning of the Crucifixion. The excitement it aroused is not difficult to understand: at last a devout Muslim seemed to be trying to come to terms, in the most reverent way, with the central mystery of Christianity. But if we look closely at the book we shall find that it is a work of quite a different character from what one might have expected. First of all, Jesus does not die on the Cross: 'God raised him unto Him', the author tells us, 'in a way we can leave unexplained'.[11] So he is still writing from the point of view of an orthodox Muslim. Secondly, and this is more surprising still, it does not really matter to him whether Jesus was killed or not. What matters is that those who condemned him intended to crucify him, and Kamil Husayn's concern is with their motives, not with the meaning of the Cross for Christians. The book is not about the Crucifixion so much as about the endless struggle between the individual conscience and the immoral collective will.

This then is what has made orthodox Muslims uneasy in the presence of Christianity: it can only be rightly understood as part of a process which culminates in the coming of Muhammad, yet Christians reject Muhammad. What has made Christians uneasy when thinking of Islam is rather different. For them, the doctrines of Islam contained some truth and much falsehood, so mixed together that even what was true was distorted by its connection with what was false; and even in so far as it was true, it was

difficult to understand why Islam existed and what part it played
in the divine economy.

In recent years a number of considerable historians have written
about the development of Christian attitudes to Islam in the
Middle Ages: M. T. d'Alverny, R. W. Southern and Norman
Daniel.[12] Thanks to them, the main lines of the medieval attack on
Islam are clear enough. First of all, the Christian thinkers could
not regard Muhammad as an authentic prophet. For them, a
universal prophet had his place in the evangelical preparation for
the coming of Christ; a particular prophet foretold future events.
But Muhammad came after the event to which the line of universal
prophets pointed, and he foretold no events in the future. More
than that, a prophet who came after the coming of Christ might be
expected to embody in his message the truths already received, but
Muhammad denied what was the essence of it—the Crucifixion,
the Incarnation and the Trinity. His human character, moreover,
seemed very different from that which Christians would expect to
find in a prophet: he was regarded as one who built a kingdom of
this world by the use of power and violence. For all these reasons,
Islam could not be thought of as carrying further and completing
the Christian message. It might be a form of paganism, or a
Jewish heresy, or a Christian heresy. It was only worthy of study
for the purpose of exposing its errors, or for the secondary purpose
of deciding where exactly it lay on the spectrum of paganism or
heresy.

With dramatic suddenness, the Christian attitude towards Islam
is fully stated before Islam is a century old. One of the great
theologians of the eastern Church, St John of Damascus, lived in
Syria under Muslim rule. He knew Arabic as well as Greek, and,
like his father and grandfather before him, he was an official of
the Umayyad Caliphs before he left the world. He seems to have
been the first Christian thinker to have made a study of Islam: he
knew something of the Qur'an, and something of the first stirrings
of religious thought among Muslims. The work in which he deals
with Islam is not one of political polemics but a serious attempt to
refute its errors; and it is indeed a sign of the age in which he
lived that it was possible to use serious and open theological
arguments. The Umayyads did not try to convert the mainly
Christian population which they ruled; the Christians must have
looked on Islam, not as a sea which would sooner or later engulf
them, but as one of those barbarian movements which had brought

new rulers into the provincial cities of the Roman Empire but had left their essential institutions undisturbed.

St John's main treatment of Islam comes, significantly, in the section on heresies of his main theological work, *The Fount of Knowledge*. Islam for him is a Christian heresy, and it is the one hundred and first heresy he deals with. It shares with Christianity the belief in one God, uncreated, unbegotten, indestructible, maker of all things visible and invisible. But it denies certain essential Christian doctrines: that Jesus was divine, and that he was crucified; and by so doing it denudes of meaning even those parts of the truth which it affirms—its God being deprived of attributes is emptied of essence. On the other hand, it asserts doctrines which a Christian cannot accept: that Muhammad was a prophet and the seal of the prophets, and that the Qur'an was the word of God sent down to him from Heaven.[13] In another work, the *Disputation between a Saracen and a Christian*, which may not have been John of Damascus' own writing but may preserve some of his teaching, the arguments against Muhammad's prophetic mission are put forward in more detail: he was not foretold by the earlier prophets, he worked no signs or miracles to testify to the truth of his teaching, he could not have been a prophet because the line of prophets was completed by John the Baptist.[14]

It was long before the church in western Europe could reach this point of clear and calm understanding. When western Europe first faced the challenge of Muslim power, it did so without any real knowledge of what it was fighting, and the combination of fear and ignorance produced a body of legends, some absurd and all unfair: Muslims were idolaters worshipping a false trinity, Muhammad was a magician, he was even a Cardinal of the Roman Church who, thwarted in his ambition to become Pope, revolted, fled to Arabia and there founded a church of his own. It is only in the twelfth century that we can see the beginnings of serious study of Islam. It came for the most part by way of Spain, where relations across the frontier were closer and more complex than elsewhere; it was encouraged by Peter the Venerable of the abbey of Cluny, under whose patronage was made the first Latin translation of the Qur'an, by Robert of Ketton. From that time, although the legends continued to circulate and be believed, the possibility existed of serious consideration by theologians of the status of Islam, made within a Christian framework of thought and not without charity. Thus for St Thomas Aquinas there are three kinds of unbelief, those of heathens, of Jews and of heretics. To judge by his definitions, Islam falls within the first category, among the forms of unbelief which are the least sinful in one respect, the most grievous in another: less sinful than those of heretics, because Muslims have never accepted the Gospel, more grievous in another because erroneous on more matters of faith. Heathens are not to be forced to become Christians: a man cannot be forced to enjoy his greatest good, and Christian rulers reigning over a large number of heathens should tolerate their manner of serving God.[15]

Something of these medieval attitudes has lingered on until modern times, but in the sixteenth century we can see them being adopted to new purposes. This is the century of the Reformation, and also of the Ottoman advance in central Europe and the long struggle of Turks and Spaniards for control of the western Mediterranean. These two processes were connected with each other in many ways. There were political links, which are not my subject; Protestants from the Holy Roman Empire and Jews from Spain found shelter in the Ottoman domains; Dutch merchants provisioned the Barbary corsairs for their raids on Spanish and Portuguese shipping. In the sphere of religious thought, the connection is more complex. Islam is no longer a theological problem, since it is not relevant to the great controversies about the nature of Christian revelation and the Church. But since it is still present in the consciousness of western Europe, still feared and still, in general, misunderstood, it can be used for polemical purposes in those controversies. When Christian writers speak of Islam, they do so no longer primarily in order to refute its errors, but as a way of refuting each other's errors. In Luther's writings there are many references to Islam and the spread of Ottoman danger. Islam is seen in the medieval way, as a movement of violence in the service of Anti-Christ; it cannot be converted because it is closed to reason, it can only be resisted by the sword, and even then with difficulty. But—and here comes the significant change—it is not the real Anti-Christ; he is found elsewhere. The Pope and the Turk are 'the two arch-enemies of Christ and his Holy Church', and if the Turk is the body of Anti-Christ, the Pope is the head.[16]

From now onwards this is a common theme. Islam is seen with the eyes of inherited fear and hostility, but seen not in itself but as the symbol of some enemy nearer home. Towards the end of the sixteenth century, an English Catholic exile on the Continent, William Rainolds, wrote a book called *Calvino-Turcismus*, in which the doctrines of Calvin are compared with those of Islam, on the whole to the benefit of Islam:

> Both seek to destroy the Christian faith, both deny the Divinity of Christ, not only is the pseudo-Gospel of Calvin no better than the Qur'an of Muhammad, but in many respects it is wickeder and more repulsive.[17]

Inevitably a Protestant (also an Englishman, the Anglican Matthew Sutcliff) wrote a reply, and called it *De Turcopapismo*.[18] A century or so later, one of the first Arabic scholars in England, Humphrey Prideaux, used the same weapon against another enemy. The title is significant: *The true nature of imposture fully display'd in the life of Mahomet. With a discourse annex'd for the vindication of Christianity from this charge*. There is a sub-title as well, and that is no less significant: the book is *Offered for the consideration of the Deists of the present age*. Prideaux's work is not directed against the Muslims. What he is really trying to do is to point the contrast between the origins of the two religions and the character of their founders, and in so doing to defend Christianity against the attacks of deists who wish to retain nothing of it except 'the common principles of natural religion and reason': with the aid of those principles we cannot rise above a certain point, Christianity is so elevated that we must seek its origin elsewhere.[19]

A generation later, Voltaire wrote a play with a similar title, *Fanaticism, or Muhammad the Prophet*. Muhammad appears as the paradigm of the theocratic tyrant, who uses the sentiments and beliefs of human beings in order to serve his 'affreux desseins'.[20] But in a later age the enemy changes. Islam is not used so much by one group of Christians to attack others, as by those who believe in human progress to attack the forces of unreason and tradition which stand in its way. In 1883, for example, Ernest Renan published a famous lecture on Islam and science, in which he maintained that they were incompatible with each other:

> Anyone [he declares] who has been in the East or in Africa will have been struck by the hidebound spirit of the true believer, by this kind of iron circle which surrounds his head, rendering him

absolutely closed to science, incapable of learning anything or of opening himself to a new idea.[21]

Renan was explicitly criticising Islam, and seems indeed to have thought that Islam more than other religions held men in this circle of iron; but in what he writes there is an implicit rejection of other 'Semitic' faiths, and 'the impossibility of believing in religious traditions which have grown up independently of the critical spirit'.[22]

The idea that Islam is a barrier against progress, a faith which obstructs the growth of certain virtues necessary for individuals or peoples who want to live in the modern world, is still put forward from time to time, but not so much in the terms used by Renan, for whom Islam (or all revealed religion) was opposed to science, rather in other terms: Islam (or any kind of faith which justifies a traditional order) is opposed to social and economic development. The idea was given this modern form largely by a specifically modern experience, that of imperial rule. To be powerless in the hands of others is a profound and conscious experience; to have power over others may affect people as deeply, but without their being conscious of it. Those who found themselves ruling Muslim peoples, whether Englishmen or Frenchmen, could easily take up an attitude which in some ways continued those older ones I have been talking about. In this attitude we can distinguish a kind of proprietary feeling towards those who lie in one's power, so long as they are willing to accept the pattern of dependence; a sense of superiority which is natural in the circumstances, because the possession of power both depends upon and strengthens certain qualities, whether intellectual or moral, and absence of power may weaken them; and beneath both of these an underlying anxiety, a sense of being in a false position, a fear of the alien masses whose thoughts one cannot know. To take a classic example: in Lord Cromer's *Modern Egypt,* all three elements exist. British rule, he believes, is being used with conscious benevolence for the good of the Egyptians. The case against Islam is put at its strongest. As a religion it is a 'noble monotheism', but as a social system it 'has been a complete failure': Islam keeps women in a position of inferiority; it 'crystallises religion and law into an inseparable and immutable whole, with the result that all elasticity is taken out of the social system'; it permits slavery; its general tendency is towards intolerance of other faiths; it does not encourage the development of the power of logical thought. Thus Muslims can scarcely hope to rule themselves or reform their societies; and yet Islam can generate a mass of feeling which, in a moment, can break whatever brittle bonds the European reformer has been able to establish with those he is trying to help. The fear of the 'revolt of Islam' is never far from Cromer's thoughts.[23]

Such attitudes, as I say, can be regarded as modern forms of older ones. But something new was growing in the nineteenth century, about which I should like to say more. It was created by the vast expansion of the European mind and imagination so as to appropriate all existing things. I shall say nothing about one aspect of this, the romantic cult of what is other and distant, in time or space; what I am concerned with is the growth of universal intellectual curiosity, the desire to know everything, either in order to bring it under man's control, or to contemplate in it the manifold wonders of God's creative work.

So far as the human world was concerned, this movement of the mind led in two directions: towards a study of men, events and processes in their particularity, and towards the elaboration of a system of categories in terms of which all particulars could be explained. I think it is true to say that, in the modern European study of Islam, as a religion, civilisation and society, the second activity came earlier than the first. The nineteenth century was an age of great intellectual syntheses. Philosophers of history or universal historians tried to distinguish various cultures or civilisations, to define the essence of each, and to trace the process of transmission from one to another. Social philosophers, writing under the influence of the biological sciences, tried to classify races, cultures or religions into families and trace the relations of kinship and descent between them. Sociologists tried to work out a typology of social forms, and to classify particular societies in terms of their approximation to various 'ideal types'.[24]

Such systems had to be universal, and therefore had to give some account of Islam. With some exceptions, Islam was not given a high place in them. For Hegel and the universal historians who followed him, Islamic civilisation was of no great value and originality in itself, its historic task was to hand on Greco-Roman civilisation to modern Europe. For theorists of race and language like Renan, Islam was a product of the Semitic spirit, whose contribution to human culture was confined to one thing, the creation of monotheism; 'once this mission had been accomplished,

the Semitic race rapidly declined, and left it to the Aryan race to
march alone at the head of the destinies of humanity'.[25]

To some extent, perhaps, this difficulty in seeing Islam clearly
sprang from that uncertainty about its nature and status which
Europe had always had. But it was also caused by simple
ignorance, by the absence of that knowledge which could challenge
the domination of ancient attitudes. This is true even of so great
and careful a thinker as Weber, who died before he was able to
make a special study of the sociology of Islam, as he had done of
other religions and as he intended to do. It is only in the last
century or so that detailed research has begun to modify the broad
outlines of accepted opinions. Wellhausen and Goldziher belonged
to the first generation of scholars who set themselves, as a life's
work, to study Islam in depth, using modern methods of critical
scholarship. The task is so large, the sources are so numerous and
still so little known, and the workers are so few, that even now
there are large tracts of ignorance. But from the work which is
now being done, two broad ideas are emerging which may in time
influence our use of the term 'Islam'. First, the concept of 'Islam'
is not by itself enough to explain everything that exists and
happens in what we call 'Muslim' countries. The idea of a culture
as a totality, of everything which exists as being somehow
determined by the essence of that culture, was one of the seminal
ideas of the nineteenth century, but it is no longer adequate as a
principle of explanation. Let me take some obvious examples. The
Islamic historians of an earlier generation were accustomed to talk
of something called the 'Islamic city', of which the social structure
and even the physical shape were determined by the fact that its
citizens were Muslims. But several scholars in the last few years
have examined this idea and shown that what was specifically
'Islamic' in the cities of the Middle East and North Africa was in
some ways less important than what was common to medieval or
pre-industrial cities.[26] Again, the idea that Islam is an obstacle to
economic development has recently been studied by a French
scholar, Maxime Rodinson, in his book *Islam and Capitalism*, and
once more he has shown that there is nothing in Islamic doctrine
or law which either prevents or encourages capitalist development—if explanations are to be found, they must be found
elsewhere.[27]

Secondly, even when we can use the concept of 'Islam' to explain
something in a culture or society, we must use it subtly and in

conjunction with other principles of explanation. This is the lesson of a small book of great originality, *Islam Observed*, by the social anthropologist Clifford Geertz.[28] Writing of two Muslim countries in which he has worked, Morocco and Indonesia, separated by half the world, he asks whether it has any meaning to speak of them both as 'Muslim'. The conclusion is clear: there is no such thing as 'Islamic society', there are societies partly moulded by Islam, but formed also by their position in the physical world, their inherited language and culture, their economic possibilities and the accidents of their political history. Before Islam was, they existed, and if Islam has shaped them, they also have shaped it, each in a different way.

This does not of course mean that we must give up the idea that there is something called 'Islam', but simply that we must use it with caution and in its proper sphere. When we have made all the careful distinctions we must make, and recognised that as social beings Muslims act like other men caught in a web of traditions and present needs, there still remains—Islam, a statement about what God is and how He acts in the world, embodied in a book which Muslims believe to be the word of God, and articulated in a system of law and worship by which millions of men and women have lived for many centuries. Perhaps the most surprising, and in the end the most significant, change which has taken place in Europe and America is that this system of beliefs and worship is once more taken seriously. To try to explain the movement of concern for the nature and destiny of other religions which has taken hold of almost all Christian bodies in the last twenty years would, once more, take me beyond my subject. But let me, in conclusion, distinguish three modern Christiam attitudes towards the religion of Islam. They are not the only ones, of course, but they will serve as ideal types through which we can explain most others.

The first is an attitude which can be traced back to Kant and which has become, we might say, one of the orthodoxies of today. It rests on a distinction between the one true religion and the different systems of belief through which men have tried to express it. There is one God, directly accessible to all men through reason or moral conscience, but there are many ways in which men have tried to respond to His revelation—different ideas, different symbols, different kinds of ritual; some of these have been shared by many men over a long period of time, they have accumulated a continuing tradition, and these are what we call the great religions. But in the end all are imperfect attempts to express a single reality, and from this, one of two conclusions may be drawn: either that all are roughly equivalent, or that each contains values which are less apparent in the others. From the first conclusion the need for tolerance should be learnt; from the second, the need for dialogue. In Islam, the element of special value is, of course, the uncompromising acceptance of the transcendence of God.

A good example of this way of thought is provided by Wilfred Cantwell Smith, a Canadian Protestant theologian. In one of his books, he poses what in effect is the same question as that asked by St John of Damascus: 'Is the Qur'an the Word of God?' He refuses to answer either 'yes' or 'no', or rather he gives both answers: No, because the Qur'an is clearly the word of a man at a certain time and in a certain place; Yes, because it is a word through which men have come to know God. The implications of such a statement are obvious, and Cantwell Smith draws them: he would give the same answer to a similar question about the Bible and the Incarnation.[29] But against such a view there stands a second one which, starting from what may seem to be the same premise, draws exactly the opposite conclusion. Another theologian brought up in the Calvinist tradition, the Dutchman Hendrik Kraemer, would also begin with a distinction between God's revelation to man and man's response. But Revelation for him means, not the voice of God speaking in silence to the individual conscience, but something public and unique, the Incarnation. And it follows from this that the only authentic response is Christian faith. All other responses, all religious systems, are merely human constructions, 'man-made spiritual worlds'. They are not alternative paths to God, not evangelical preparations by which one can imperceptibly and painlessly arrive at the truth. All in the end are sinful: even 'the mystic who triumphantly realises his essential oneness with God . . . commits in this sublime way the root-sin of mankind, to be like God. In other words: he repeats the Fall.'[30] But precisely because these religious systems have no ultimate significance, it is possible to study them objectively as achievements of human culture which, if they do nothing to bring man nearer God, at least have produced order, art and a kind of social virtue; in Kraemer's writings about Islam there is a certain compassionate understanding of the fragile human achievements of Muslims.

Between these two paths there lies a third one which some

Christian theologians are now taking. They begin with a view of the relations between the natural and supernatural orders very different from that of Calvinism. Islam, like other religions outside Christianity, can be seen, so to speak, as a stopping place on the road towards the Church. Thus in a work on the Church by a famous Catholic theologian, Cardinal Journet, the Muslim community, like the Jewish, is regarded as a body in which a certain spiritual life is possible, but one which by a 'real and ontological desire' looks towards the Church. Islam and Judaism 'may, however accidentally and imperfectly, be sources of light for millions of souls inwardly sustained by the Holy Spirit'.[31]

In the formulations of the Vatican Council we can find, for the first time in Christian history, an effort to define a Christian attitude towards Islam. They recognise fully those elements in Islam which Christians can accept—belief in One God who has spoken to man, in judgement, in Jesus regarded as a prophet—and these are enough to make possible cooperation in the natural order.[32]

In a sense, of course, such a statement does not deal with the problem of Islam at all, at least not of Islam as Muslims see it. It says nothing about the status of Muhammad: was he a prophet, is the Qur'an a witness to the truth? Most cautious Christian theologians would be unwilling to go further; but not everyone should be cautious, and there are Christian writers willing to take a further step and put forward ideas which may be speculative but are signs of an outgoing of the heart and imagination which is new in the long history of the two religions. One of them is R. C. Zaehner, Professor of Eastern Religions at Oxford. In his book *At Sundry Times,* he does not hesitate to call Muhammad a prophet: there *are* prophetic traditions outside Judaism, and Muhammad must be regarded as a prophet:

> there is no criterion by which the gift of prophecy can be withheld from him unless it is withheld from the Hebrew prophets also. The Qur'an is in fact the quintessence of prophecy. In it you have, as in no other book, the sense of an absolutely overwhelming Being proclaiming Himself to a people that had not known him.[33]

More than this, the message of the Qur'an if properly understood does not contradict, it rather affirms that of the New Testament.

By a kind of reversal of the Muslim attitude towards the Bible, Zaehner tries to show how certain passages of the Qur'an can be made to bear a Christian interpretation.[34]

Another thinker no less bold, no less deeply moved by the vision of Christianity as the ultimate meeting-point of all faiths, was the great French orientalist Louis Massignon: clearly a man of genius who, more perhaps than anyone else, has brought Islam back within the range of consciousness of modern Christian thought. In scattered references throughout his works, and in a short and difficult essay on 'the three prayers of Abraham',[35] he took up a theme to be found in some Muslim writers: the Arabs are the descendants of Ishmael, Islam is in the spiritual line of descent from Abraham. Islam, he suggested, was a belated answer from God to Abraham's prayer for Ishmael. But it is more than a consolation given to the excluded brother, it also has some positive role in the economy of salvation. God has spoken through a chain of witnesses, strangers, visitors coming to call us back to ourselves. Muhammad was sent, not only to give knowledge of God to those who had not had it, but also to remind Jews and Christians of the transcendence of God—He is inaccessible in His essence, and comes to us, if at all, only as a stranger. But it is also a challenge: by denying the divinity of Christ, it summons Christians to affirm it, and to redeem Islam by giving their faith to fill what is lacking in that of Muslims. This they can do by trying to live as Christians in the presence of Islam, made more aware of their faith both by what Islam affirms and what it denies; and by common prayer in those shrines and places of pilgrimage where prayer has been valid, above all Hebron and Jerusalem, the sanctuaries of three faiths. What are we to make of this vision of Islam as the reproachful and excluded stranger, and of three faiths turned in prayer towards the same high places? It could not be stated or explained in any terms except its own, but it is disturbing and will not be forgotten in any dialogue of Christians and Muslims, so let me leave it with you.

2 Islam and the Philosophers of History*

To H. A. R. Gibb

The appearance of Islam in the world was no ordinary event. It has not happened very often in history that a religious movement, springing up in a backward region, has within a generation engulfed some of the main centres of power and culture in the known world, and has then proved to be more than a short-lived barbarian incursion, a wave which receded as swiftly as it advanced, but on the contrary has left its mark on thirteen hundred years of history in a quarter of the world, and over the whole range of culture and society. What began as the preaching of a religion led soon to the founding of a state, and when the state

* I acknowledge with gratitude my great debt to the following works: N. Daniel, *Islam and the West: the Making of an Image* (Edinburgh, 1960); J.W.Fück, *Die arabischen Studien in Europa bis in den Anfang des 20. Jahrhunderts* (Leipzig, 1955), and 'Islam as an historical problem in European historiography since 1800' in B. Lewis and P. M. Holt, (ed.), *Historians of the Middle East* (London, 1962), pp. 304-14; A. Malvezzi, *L'islamismo e la cultura europea* (Florence, 1956), R. W. Southern, *Western Views of Islam in the Middle Ages* (Cambridge, Mass., 1962); J. D. J. Waardenburg, *L'islam dans le miroir de l'occident* (The Hague, 1961). (See M. Rodinson, 'The western image and western studies of Islam' in J. Schacht with C. E. Bosworth, (eds.), *The Legacy of Islam* 2nd. ed. (Oxford, 1974) p. 9f.)

The substance of this essay has been given in the form of lectures and seminar talks on several occasions; I am grateful to those who attended them and helped the growth of my ideas by their criticisms and suggestions. A draft was circulated to the members of the Near Eastern History Group at Oxford, and I must thank them too for a valuable discussion of it.

dissolved it left behind a literary culture, a system of law, an organisation of social life and a moral ideal which have helped to mould the nature of regions far beyond those included in the state. Perhaps what is strangest of all is that this vast movement of peoples, of ideas, of laws and institutions should appear to have sprung in the last analysis from a single man, coming from the remote frontier of the civilised world of his time, and who has stamped his image on ages and peoples distant from his own:

> . . . Car c'est bien à un homme, à Mahomet, celui qu'on appelle en arabe Mohammed, que l'on doit ce type d'hommes et ce type de culture. C'est lui qui a fait d'une poussière de tribus arabes une nation, d'un ramassis de clans en dispute, un État, d'un patois à peine écrit, une langue de civilisation mondiale. C'est à lui, à ses premières expéditions militaires, étonnants raids surprises de nuit en plein désert, *sarâyâ,* que remonte cette immense expansion qui a dilaté l'Islam avec la conquête arabe jusque chez les Iraniens, les Turcs et les Balkaniques, dans l'Inde, en Chine, en Malaisie et au Soudan.[1]

Almost from its birth Islam has been a problem for those in western Europe who have tried to find a meaning in human history, whether what they have searched for have been the laws of cause and effect or the intentions of God. The main purpose of this essay is to show how thinkers and scholars have looked at the problem since, at the beginning of the modern age, European thought took all learning for its province and tried to give a systematic account of what had happened in the past. But we should miss a whole dimension in their thought if we failed to grasp that, for the tradition in which they lived, Islam was no new problem, nor one which they could regard with the same detached curiosity as they might bring to the cultures and beliefs of India or China. Islam had always been a major fact of European history, and to the Christian world in which it expanded it posed problems both incidental and essential. In the first place it presented a military challenge: in its early phase of expansion under the caliphs, and then eight hundred years later under the Turkish rulers of Asia Minor and the Balkans, it absorbed regions of Christian belief and culture and threatened the heart of western Christendom. It was important for the Christian peoples thus threatened to form some idea of what it was—the sources of its power, its aims and the probable direction of its policy. But there was more to it than that: the military challenge was rooted in a system of doctrines which Christians did not accept as true, and yet, based as it was on a false belief, it had succeeded in conquering regions which had long been Christian. How could this be? For one brought up in the Augustinian view of history, believing that there is no earthly city which abides, that the righteous may perish and still be righteous, and that worldly triumph and disaster have no essential link with truth and falsehood, the victory of Islam did not of course prove that it was true. It did nevertheless pose a problem: what role, if any, did the victory of Islam over Christianity play in the providential order of the world? Was it a punishment for the sins of Christians, or had it some more positive role in the gradual unfolding of the mystery of salvation? This question inevitably led to another: Islam no doubt was false, but in what precise sense was it false? It could not be regarded by Christians as wholly true: it denied the Crucifixion, the Incarnation and the Redemption, and it asserted the existence of a prophetic tradition after the events to which Old Testament prophecy pointed, the life and death of Christ, had taken place. On the other hand, it could scarcely be regarded as sheer paganism: it believed in one God, in His Revelation through prophets, in moral responsibility and the day of judgement.

In more recent times, this problem has acquired a new depth, as Christians have learnt more about Islam: the authenticity of some of the moral perceptions of the Qur'an, the sense of the majesty of God, of the nearness of the world's end, of the awe and agony of judgement, the purity of the mystics and saints, the *awliya*, 'friends of God', the depth of the mark left by Islam on human history, and behind it all a note of authority in Muhammad's voice—all these seem, on the face of it, to require explanation, and at least it must be asked whether they can be explained in ordinary human terms. To such a question various answers may be suggested. Islam can be seen as a Christian heresy, or a snare of the devil to delude men from belief in the authentic Revelation, or an attempt by the unaided human reason to grasp truths of revelation, or an evangelical preparation for the acceptance by pagans of the Christian truth, or an independent path of salvation alongside those of the Church and Israel, a third religion springing from the same divine source. For an orthodox Christian, these can be no more than suggestions. There has never been a single authentic

and, so to speak, 'official' attitude of the Church towards Muhammad and his prophetic claims, and perhaps there cannot be: for
one of the many causes of the tension and unease which have
marked the relationship of Christians and Muslims is that, while
Muslims regard Christianity as an essential stage of the process
which culminated in the revelation through Muhammad, and
simply by being Muslims are committed to a certain attitude
towards Christianity, this is not so for Christians. Islam came later
than the Christian revelation, it was not implied or foretold in it,
and it added nothing to it. A Christian therefore need not take up
a specific attitude towards Islam. While recognising, as the Second
Vatican Council has now done, elements of truth in the teaching
of Islam, and the possibility of mutual understanding and cooperation in the moral and social order, he can still, if he wishes,
refrain from posing the question of why and how Islam came to
exist in a world already largely Christian; and if he asks the
question, he can answer it in more than one way. Of those we
have indicated, only the last would be difficult to reconcile with
the teaching of the Church.

When Islam first appeared as a challenge to the Christian
world, the attitude of Western Christians towards it was one of
fear and horror. It continued to be so throughout the early Middle
Ages down to the end of the Crusades. In a brilliant study,[2]
Professor Southern has shown that this attitude was rooted in
ignorance; or perhaps it would be more correct to say the opposite,
that it was the fear and horror themselves which were the cause of
ignorance and prejudice, for at a moment of mortal peril it was
natural that men should regard their enemy as a monster in
human form. The first four hundred years of the contact between
Islam and Christendom were, on the side of the latter, an 'age of
ignorance',[3] when Europeans knew virtually nothing of Islam and
tried to interpret it in the light of the Bible alone. Muhammad
was Anti-Christ and the rise of Islam heralded the end of the
world. More direct contact with Islam on a level of military
equality, at the time of the Crusades, did not dissolve this
ignorance. The attitude of Christians may have changed for a time
from one of fear to one of hope and triumph, but this scarcely
increased their knowledge or deepened their understanding. Their
new view of Islam was still an imaginative construction, although
one born in the flush of victory.[4]

There was, it is true, one period in which at least a few

Christians tried to grapple with the problem of the nature and providential purpose of Islam: in the later twelfth century a group of scholars in and around the monastery of Cluny, and inspired by its abbot Peter the Venerable, translated and studied the Qur'an and other texts, and tried to grasp the way in which Muslims themselves understood their faith and the claims they made for it.

In the next century, a new challenge to the western part of the world from the Mongols had various results. Some European writers saw the Mongols as potential Christians and allies against Islam, but others became more aware of what Christianity and Islam had in common against triumphant paganism. Some writers even dared to hope that Islam was ripe for conversion, and the desire to bring the Gospel to Muslims in a persuasive way impelled Raymond Lull and others to a study of Islam and the Arabic language which had seemed unnecessary or even harmful to an earlier age faced with the prospect of unending hostility. But this moment of hope did not last long. The revival of Islamic orthodoxy, in a more intransigent form, and in reaction against its own dissidents as much as against the Christian enemy, led to the squeezing and then the destruction of the Crusading states; while the first probings of Franciscan and Dominican missionaries showed how difficult, humanly speaking, the conversion of even a single Muslim would be. Thus in the fourteenth and fifteenth centuries the impulse to know and understand Islam died out, and for a time no new effort was made to determine its place in the divine order of things.[5]

Although no new advances were to be made for a long time, those made during the 'century of reason and hope'[6] were not lost. Something of the knowledge and understanding acquired by the school of Cluny was preserved and had an influence on later thinkers. Professor Southern's book can be read most profitably together with Mr Daniel's careful study of the achievement and limits of medieval European studies of Islam seen at their best.[7] The body of knowledge built up at Cluny did, as he shows, survive as part of the medieval inheritance; if few made use of it, it was there to be used, and the thought which did take account of it was far superior to the suppositions of the ignorant. Thus, while accusations of idolatry were still hurled at Islam, in the hands of the learned they were literary devices rather than serious and firmly based accusations which could be defended. The learned at least knew that Islam believed in the unity of God, the existence of prophets, the revelation of a book and the divine nature of that book sent down from heaven. If they condemned Islam, they did so on grounds which seemed to them more weighty, and more consistent with what they knew, than earlier writers. In their view, Islam denied the possibility of rational argument, and gave an essential role to force and violence. (This served as the theoretical justification for the attitude which Christians in their turn adopted towards Islam: missionary endeavour, it was generally held, was hopeless unless backed by arms, and the only real solution to the problem was the destruction of Islam by the killing or conversion of Muslims). They thought of Muhammad either as a false prophet or else as no prophet at all. Either he was an evil prophet who taught falsehood, or else he was an ordinary man who did not possess the essential qualities of prophethood. Those qualities, as defined by St Thomas Aquinas, were three: freedom from passions, the working of miracles, and the invariable truth of what the prophet said *qua* prophet. But in the eyes of medieval Europe, Muhammad foretold nothing true, he worked no miracles, and his life was not a model of virtue. At worst he was a 'fraudulent demoniac or magician',[8] at best an impostor who claimed prophetic gifts in order to obtain power, an oppressor when he had power, a man of loose morals and a hypocrite who used religious claims to justify his immorality.

But this picture of sheer opposition should be modified in two ways. Even those who rejected the claims of Islam did not, for the most part, deny it a special theological status. The Qur'an, the immense figure of Muhammad overshadowing the world, the power of the caliphs and the continuing strength of the Muslim states could not be explained away; they at least created a presumption that Islam had a special part to play in the divine economy. It might be a punishment for the sins of Christendom and therefore a sign of God's chastening love; or it could be seen, in spite of its errors, as a reflection of Christian truth and therefore a witness to the truth in its own fashion. The attempt to give Islam a *droit de cité*, a theological status within the framework of Christian thought, went back as far as St John of Damascus who, living in Syria under Umayyad rule, and knowing Arabic as well as Greek, was the first Christian theologian to think deeply about the meaning of Islam. His polemical writings, 'calm and charitable in tone',[9] laid emphasis on the Christian origins of Islam, and later theologians who followed him, in the West as well as the East, saw in Islam 'a superfluous but valid witness to the truth of the Christian faith'.[10] Muhammad had mixed some truths with his falsehood. If the Qur'an denied the divinity of Christ, at least it accepted the prophethood of Jesus and called him 'the word of God' and the 'spirit of God'. If it denied the Trinity, it laid full stress on the unity of God. Thus Islam could not be regarded as sheer disbelief or blind paganism: it could be regarded as a Christian heresy, a schism, or a 'third religion' falsely claiming to have a revelation of its own and in fact reflecting something of the true revelation of Judaism and Christianity.

Moreover even those who were most strongly opposed to the claims of Islam were aware that its existence might bring certain incidental benefits. Christians could learn or profit from it: if it were a punishment for their sins, it could also be an opening for their virtues, providing an occasion for the exercise of loyalty, of penance, and of virtuous activity. But this line of argument could be prolonged in quite a different direction: if those who believed in Christian revelation could use Islam to preach a lesson, so too could those who did not really believe in revelation at all. One of the forms of medieval infidelity was the idea of 'three imposters', Moses, Jesus and Muhammad, who had successively deceived the world.

Such lines of thought, laid down in the earlier Middle Ages, remained open to the traffic of human minds until the nineteenth century. But from the time of the Reformation onwards there took place a gradual change of emphasis. The rise to power of the Ottoman Empire and the renewed threat to the safety of Christian Europe brought once more to the surface the fear of Islam which had been aroused by the first conquest. In a way the fear was greater now because the level of political consciousness in Europe was higher, the lines of division between the two faiths were more sharply drawn, and the sudden rise of a barbarian enemy on the frontier was a more vivid threat to a society more conscious of its growing strength. That force and violence which had seemed to medieval Europe to be inseparable from Islam came to the front of men's minds again.

But the fear went less deep than it had done five centuries earlier. The claims and doctrines of Islam were no longer a threat to the Christian faith, now that the faith had come to terms with Greek philosophy and created intellectual defences; Islam was no longer a heresy which was likely to win supporters nor an intellectual attack against which serious defence was necessary. Christians might be frightened of the Ottoman army, but they could look at the religion whose banner it carried with cool detachment, if not with contempt. At the same time, Christendom was torn by the struggles of the Reformation, and in this context Islam appeared not just as an enemy but as a weapon of controversy and policy. Thus some Protestants thought they had something to learn from Islam; or, it would be more correct to say, thought it useful to write as if this were so. For example, Luther, although his basic attitude was one of horror (the Pope and the Turk were 'the two arch-enemies of Christ and His holy Church'),[11] nevertheless praised the simplicity of Muslim worship and customs, by contrast with those of the Catholics.[12] In the same way, Queen Elizabeth, in a letter sent with her first Ambassador to the Sultan, emphasised the Islamic nature of Protestantism.[13] No doubt the real motive in writing like this was political, the thought that the Turks might be useful allies, for Protestants could, when necessary, argue equally on the other side. The Swiss Protestant P. Vinet could depict Islam as a kind of Catholicism: Muhammad was a Christian apostate who had set himself up as the head of a Church, just as the Pope had done.[14] On the Catholic side too it was possible to reverse the picture and portray Islam as a kind of Protestantism. Thus William Rainolds, in a famous book with the significant title of *Calvino-Turcismus*, drew the parallels between the two false doctrines:

> ... the fundamental principles of Muhammadanism are far better than those of Calvinism. Both seek to destroy the Christian faith, both deny the Divinity of Christ, not only is the pseudo-Gospel of Calvin no better than the Qur'an of Muhammad, but in many respects it is wickeder and more repulsive.[15]

But here too it was possible, in spite of differences of religion, to hope for a profitable alliance with the Turks, and the French King in fact achieved it in 1535.

That Islam could be considered in fundamentally political terms shows both the seriousness of the political danger it presented and a change of attitude in Europe. Political thought was moving away from theological determinants, but theology also was moving away from problems to which the claims of Islam were relevant. When the great subjects of controversy were the nature of Christ and the doctrine of the Trinity, Islam might have something to say; but it had nothing relevant to say about the specifically Christian problems of grace, of redemption, of faith and works. After the Reformation, the theological problem of the nature and status of Islam sinks into the background. When it is raised, it is raised not for its own sake, out of a deep desire to explain, but for polemical purposes, to point a contrast with Christianity. For Pascal, Muhammad is the opposite to Jesus Christ. He killed, whereas Christ's people were killed; he prevented his adherents from reading, whereas Christ's apostles ordered them to read; he succeeded humanly whereas Christ perished; and indeed since Muhammad succeeded, it was necessary for Christ to perish.[16] Nothing he did needs more than a human explanation; 'tout homme peut faire ce qu'a fait Mahomet; car il n'a point fait de miracles, il n'a point été prédit'.[17] He is 'sans autorité . . . il est ridicule'.[18] At the end of the seventeenth century, Prideaux, writing a once famous life of the prophet, calls it 'the nature of imposture fully display'd in the life of Mahomet'.[19] Like Pascal, his object is 'to point the contrast between Islam and Christianity', the one purely human, the other of divine origin; and, by showing how far the human falls short of the divine, to defend Christianity against the fashionable Deism of his time.[20]

But if Islam was regarded as purely human, it could at least attract the interest of the new secular culture which was concerned with human things as such, which took all knowledge for its province, studied the multiplicity of existing things and tried to order them in accordance with principles. In the older study of Islam and things Arabic, the desire to know had been mixed with other motives: to acquire, by the study of Semitic grammar or antiquities, a better understanding of the Biblical texts, or to convert Muslims. Something of this remained, and the old fear and horror of Islam still cast its shadow across Islamic studies when other eastern faiths and cultures were regarded with a new tolerance. But here too the curiosity of the secular intellect made its mark and a new kind of orientalism began to appear. New, more accurate translations of the Qur'an were made: that of Maracci into Latin in 1698, that of Sale into English in 1734. Manuscripts were collected and carefully studied, and painstaking examinations of Islamic history for its own sake were made: Pococke's *Specimen Historiae Arabum*, Ockley's *History of the Saracens*.

The secular thinkers of the new age too could take a new interest in Islam, and some at least of them drew on the works of the orientalists. Muhammad was no longer Anti-Christ but a man who had played a certain part in history; Islam was no longer the work of the Devil but a historical phenomenon of which the causes and nature could be rationally discussed. The creation and maintenance of the caliphate might furnish lessons for those who wished to understand how states and societies were formed and held together.

Thus Islam appears as a minor theme at least in the work of most of the thinkers of the eighteenth century, but there is no consensus of opinion about it. For Voltaire, Muhammad was 'un sublime et hardi charlatan', and the Qur'an, although it gave laws which were good for its time and place, was 'une déclamation incohérente et ridicule'.[21] In his play, *Le Fanatisme ou Mohamet le Prophète*, Muhammad appears as the model of the world-shaking impostor

> . . . né
> Pour changer l'univers à ses pieds consterné[22]

and conscious of the nature of his own aims and deeds:

> Dieu, que j'ai fait servir au malheur des humains,
> Adorable instrument de mes affreux desseins,
> Toi que j'ai blasphémé, mais que je crains encore,
> Je me sens condamné, quand l'univers m'adore.
> Je brave en vain les traits dont je me sens frapper.
> J'ai trompé les mortels, et ne puis me tromper.[23]

In Diderot's *Encyclopédie* also, the triumph of Islam is ascribed to conscious imposture:

> Après avoir connu le caractère de ses concitoyens, leur ignorance, leur crédulité, et leur disposition à l'enthousiasme, il vit qu'il pouvait s'ériger en prophete, il feignit des révélations, il parla
> . . .[24]

But there was an opposing current, of those who thought of the spread of Islam as an extraordinary achievement which needed a more profound explanation. For Leibnitz, Islam spread because it was a form of natural theology, which the followers of Muhammad were able to carry even among the remote races of Asia and Africa, whither Christianity had not been brought, and which destroyed heathen superstitions contrary to the true doctrine of the unity of God and the immortality of souls.[25] Rousseau praised in early Islam the close union between the theological and political systems; it did not possess, as did Christianity, the fatal division of the two powers, although this was to come later when the Arabs were subjugated by the barbarians.[26] Condorcet was more favourable still. The character of Muhammad united burning enthusiasm, astuteness, the qualities of a poet and a warrior. His aim was primarily political, to unite the Arab tribes into a single community; and the creation of a purified religion was the first step to this end. In the State which he founded there was for a time freedom of thought and a revival of the Greek sciences, although later this was extinguished by the rise of religious despotism.[27]

Similarly, the Comte de Boulainvilliers, in a famous life of Muhammad, contrasted the natural religion which was Islam with the claims of Christianity, but gave the founder of Islam full credit for his natural virtues and talents. There is no convincing evidence, he asserts, that Muhammad had the gift of prophecy or that his supposed relevation was a real one. His aims were primarily political, and he chose to create a new religion to carry out his political designs rather than use the Christian religion because of its abuses at that time. The religion which he created was the product of his own mind; but since his gifts were unusual—art, delicacy, resolution, intrepidity equal to those of Alexander or Caesar, and liveliness of imagination—the product was good:

> ... sans la grace de la Révélation Chrétienne, qui nous éclaire bien au-delà de ce que Mahomed a voulu connoître et savoir, il n'y auroit sistème de Doctrine si plausible que le sien, si conforme aux lumieres de la Raison, si consolant pour les Justes, et si terrible aux pécheurs volontaires ou inapliquez.[28]

The laws and practices of his religion he largely drew from the common customs of the Arabians; and, although the Arabs were hard, cruel, and scornful of all those things which other people love, they were also 'spirituels, génereux, desinteresséz, braves, prudents'.[29] His feeling for Islam may even have been more favourable than these statements imply. In spite of a prudent

profession of faith in the Christian revelation, Boulainvilliers'
attitude to religion seems to have been that of a philosophical deist.
Human reason alone is capable of discerning what is true or false,
in the doctrinal as in the moral sphere; the true function of religion
is to satisfy the heart and to prevent the aberrations of human
curiosity. Seen in this light Islam has much to admire, because of
its simple, clear and rational nature.[30]

These thinkers judge Islam as a human, and mainly a political,
phenomenon; and it was fitting that the greatest empire-builder of
the age should pay his tribute to a precursor. Napoleon had seen
Islamic society at first hand in Egypt; he had studied the Qur'an
and the life of the prophet, and had even made profession of faith
in Islam; until the end of his life he liked to think about his
Egyptian episode and all that was connected with it. In exile at St
Helena, he took strong issue with Voltaire's version. Voltaire, he
declared, had prostituted the character of Muhammad and made
a great man who had changed the face of the world act like a vile
criminal. There was much that was legendary in the biographies,
but one thing was certain: the conquest of the world in such a
short time. This had to be explained, and it was not easy to
explain it in terms of fanaticism or of fortuitous circumstances.
There must be, behind all this, 'quelque chose que nous
ignorons'.[31]

In such a statement we can see a reformulation of the mystery
of Islam in secular terms. But statements like this, motivated
simply by the desire to know and understand, were still rare, and
even among writers who made use of the greater knowledge of
Islam now available, there was often to be heard a polemical note,
although polemical in a different way: it was no longer aimed at
Islam itself, but through Islam at enemies nearer home, at the
claims of the Catholic Church or of revealed religion. Thus for
Gibbon Islam was an object-lesson in the way in which reason can
be dominated by fanaticism. At the heart of Islam there lay a
rational system of belief: the God of Muhammad was the God of
the philosophers—

> an infinite and eternal being, without form or place, without
> issue or similitude, present to our most secret thoughts, existing
> by necessity of his own nature, and deriving from himself all
> moral and intellectual perfection.[32]

This idea was conceived by reason, and a 'philosophic Atheist' might subscribe to it. But the descent was easy, and the philosopher became a self-deceived prophet:

> The energy of a mind incessantly bent on the same object would convert a general object into a particular call; the warm suggestions of the understanding or the fancy would be felt as the inspiration of heaven; the labour of thought would expire in rapture and vision; and the inward sensation, the invisible monitor would be described with the form and attribute of an angel of God. From enthusiasm to imposture the step is perilous and slippery ... how the conscience may slumber in a mixed and middle state between self-illusion and voluntary fraud.[33]

Worse still, once the philosopher had become a preacher, the preacher became a prince and a leader of armies, and his character was gradually stained; nevertheless, he showed great gifts as such, and it is to them, rather than to any miraculous element, that his successes must be ascribed. The permanence of his religion too must be explained by human factors: by the skill of the caliphs in keeping the sacerdotal as well as the regal power in their hands and preventing the growth of an independent clergy. On balance the effects of his rule were beneficial; idolatry was replaced by a more human devotion, the spirit of charity and friendship was spread, revenge and oppression were checked.[34]

II

In this thousand-year-long process of thought, there is one factor which is almost constant. The attitude of western Europe towards Islam is one of judgement. Islam is being weighed in the balance against something other than itself, being assigned a place in a scale. The measure of judgement may have changed: as we have seen, there was an undercurrent of European thought, beginning in the Middle Ages but growing more powerful in the eighteenth century, which used its judgement on Islam as an indirect condemnation of Christianity and of all religions which claim to be revealed. But by and large it was the opposite: Islam was judged by believing Christians, and judged as not being Christi-

anity, in fact as being in some ways the antithesis of Christianity.
Even those who, like Condorcet or Napoleon, placed a high value
on the human powers of Muhammad and his human success, also
took it for granted that nothing more than human was there: that
Muhammad's claim to be a prophet and the Qur'an's claim to be
the word of God were false.

In the course of time, as we have seen, this process of judgement
had been permeated by something else: by a process of study and
understanding of what Islam was in itself. By the end of the
eighteenth century, this increased understanding of Islam had
affected the judgement passed on Islam by the secular thinkers.
But it had scarcely yet affected those who thought within the
framework of orthodox Christianity: in other words, those who
accepted Christian doctrine, in its traditional formulations, as
stating the complete and final truth about the universe, and asked
what was the status of Islam inside the Christian system of ideas.
Throughout the greater part of the nineteenth century, those who
thought in such terms either did not consider Islam at all or else
were satisfied to regard it as being not Christianity, or even the
opposite of Christianity, without trying to answer in depth the
question of what it was in itself.

For example, Schlegel in his *Philosophy of History* stated what
was basically a traditional view even if the language in which he
clothed it was the new language of historical 'movements'. He
drew a sharp contrast between the two great tribal movements
which between them broke up the classical civilisation. On the one
hand stood the German tribal movements which accepted Christianity and were essentially conducive to peace and civilisation; on
the other, the Arab tribal movement which expressed itself in the
rise of Islam. This was animated in its early phase by a certain
moral energy and strength of character, but it was directed by the
'tribal spirit' of the Arabs, by their passions of pride and hatred,
of anger and revenge, and these passions were not held in check,
on the contrary they were strengthened and used, by Islam. Islam
was 'a religion of empty arrogance and senseless pride', preached
by a 'prophet of unbelief'. Its positive content was no more than
the 'natural religion' to which all men can attain by reason, and it
missed all the elements of salvation—reconciliation, mercy, love,
happiness. It had therefore produced no civilisation: its system of
rule was 'an anti-Christian combination of spiritual and temporal
authority, which had reduced mankind to a horrible state of

degradation, and in its destructive enthusiasm it had removed all recollection of antiquity in the countries it had conquered and every vestige of a higher and better civilisation'.[35]

In a more subtle way a similar contrast was drawn by Newman in a book deservedly little-known, *Lectures on the History of the Turks*. For Newman, Islam is a religious imposture, but it might have been worse. It is a great improvement on paganism, for it believes in 'one God, the fact of His Revelation, His faithfulness to His promises, the eternity of the moral law, the certainty of future retribution'.[36] Those ideas it had borrowed from Christianity, but with them it had mixed an error of its own, 'a consecration of the principle of nationalism'.[37] In a sense it had denied its own universal mission: its empire built on faith turned in on itself with pride, and what could have been a universal religion became a national one 'closely connected with the sentiments of patriotism, family honour, loyalty towards the past, and party spirit'.[38] It thus stands somewhere between 'the religion of God and the religion of devils'.[39] In the beginning it might have done the work of God. The caliphate indeed was a genuinely civilised state: that is to say, it had as its common good a principle which ordered society, whereas a barbarian state has as its common good something (whether a faith, a dynasty, or the desire for fame) which can generate feeling but cannot order society; and it was built on a common rational discipline able to organise the conscience, affections, and passions. But not so the Turks who succeeded the caliphs: in spite of certain original virtues (valour, truthfulness, a sense of justice, sobriety and gentleness), they were essentially barbarians. They had no interior life, no rational principles and no intellectual discipline. They had added nothing to Islam and given no help to Christianity. They could have placed their barbarian virtues at the service of the truth: in the eleventh century they had to choose whether to turn westwards or eastwards, to oppose God or Satan. They had made the wrong choice, and since the Seljuks the Turks 'have been the great anti-Christ among the races of men'.[40]

In Schlegel's sharp contrast between the two tribal movements we can see an early expression of that racial theory which was to be an important strand in nineteenth century thought; just as in Newman's we can perhaps hear an echo of the conviction of nineteenth century Europe that it was the vanguard of human progress. But fundamentally they were writing as Christians. A view such as theirs is consistent with, although it is not necessarily implied by, the beliefs of Christianity; and it is perfectly compatible with doing justice to the purely human achievements of the prophet and his followers. A responsible Christian scholar, who takes Islam not just as a weapon with which to beat his opponents but as an object of thought in its own right, would probably phrase his judgement with more reservations than Schlegel and Newman, but he would be entitled (although not obliged) to hold a view not fundamentally different from theirs. Thus Sir William Muir, whose books on Muhammad and the caliphate are still not quite superseded, could regard the prophet as the Devil's instrument, and the society he created as barren and bound to remain so. In his view, Islam was stationary; it confounded the secular and the spiritual and so could not know real freedom; it had no middle path between absolute monarchy and the licence of a lawless soldiery; at its highest, its civilisation could be neither stable nor lasting because it had never penetrated the life of the family.[41] In the teaching of Islam there were indeed certain truths, but even they were an obstacle to the penetration of the Truth itself:

> there is in it just so much truth, truth borrowed from previous revelations yet cast in another mould, as to direct attention from the need for more . . . the sword of Muhammad, and the Kor'ān, are the most stubborn enemies of Civilisation, Liberty, and the Truth which the world has yet known.[42]

A greater orientalist, the Jesuit Henri Lammens, could regard Islam, its prophet and the Arabs with a distaste even more total and unmasked. The rise of Islam, in his view, was an unfortunate historical accident which had engulfed the peoples of Syria and other countries, and against which they had struggled with more or less success. At the beginning, the prophet had had a kind of sincerity; if his 'revelations' were the result of auto-suggestion, at least he himself had believed in them. But later even this ceased to be so, and in the Medinese period 'le Qoraisite calculateur'[43] had finally overcome the prophet. But it may have been this harsh judgement which enabled Lammens to distinguish so clearly certain important aspects of early Islamic history: to show for example the part played by the urban and trading milieu in which Islam arose in moulding its development; and to detect beneath the surface of unity the resistance of certain indigenous traditions—a resistance which, in Syria, expressed itself both inside Islam, in the rise of the Umayyads, and outside it in the survival of the Christian personality of pre-Islamic Syria in the valleys of Lebanon.[44]

Such views are typical of the attitude of orthodox Christian thought towards Islam in the nineteenth century. Even when thinkers knew as much about Islam as Muir and Lammens, and still more when they knew as little as Schlegel and Newman, they tended to put it somewhere near the bottom of the scale of human faiths. The human mind, like the conscience, cannot easily be aroused by all problems at all times, and the problems which faced western Christian thought throughout the nineteenth century were not those of the Middle Ages. On the one hand, Islam presented no real political challenge. Politicians, it is true, might sometimes use the language of the Crusades to justify what they proposed to do for other reasons, and even in our own time a French Prime Minister, seeking to justify the deposition of the Sultan of Morocco, did so on the ground that he preferred the Cross to the Crescent; but in general the world of Islam could be regarded as a quaking jelly which would slip into the hands of the European powers without difficulty. Nor was Islam a theological challenge. Its theology was scarcely known and so far as known did not seem formidable; it no longer came to Europe linked, as in the system of Averroes, with philosophical ideas which Christian thinkers had either to disprove or to reconcile with their own faith; it had nothing to say in the great controversies which shook western Christendom in this age, about the nature of the Church, and the reconciliation of Christian doctrine with the claims of modern science.

It was only rarely that Christians thinking in the framework of the traditional formulations of the faith saw that, even if Islam did not help to answer the theological questions which absorbed their age, it did pose questions of its own. One of these rare exceptions was C. Forster who, in *Mahometanism Unveiled,* tried to resolve the problem posed by the close parallels between Islam and Christianity. They were too close, he maintained, to be dismissed as mere coincidence. Both were alike in the abstract nature of their doctrines, the simplicity of their rites, and the supernatural or prophetic character assumed by their founders. Both rose abruptly from obscure origins, faced the same type of obstacle in their early period, but in spite of this spread rapidly and far and

established a permanent domination over the human mind. The
success of neither can be explained in purely human terms, for the
attempt to do so would raise the question:

> by what blind fortune, what mysterious chance, have so many
> independent and unconnected causes been brought thus to
> concur?[45]

For Islam as for Christianity, this question can only be answered
in one way—in terms of

> the interposition ... of the special and superintending provi-
> dence of God ... the agency of a controlling and directing
> Providence.[46]

What can this Providence be, so far as Islam is concerned? It is
the fulfilment of the promise made by God to Abraham in respect
of Ishmael and his descendants. The promises of God to the Jews
came through Isaac, those to the Arabs came through Ishmael, and
while the former culminated in Christ, the latter culminated in
Muhammad. Through Isaac laws and religion were given to a
large part of the world, through Ishmael to an even larger part.

But though the parallel goes so far, it goes no farther. Isaac was
the legitimate son of Abraham and through him came forth the
legitimate faith, while Ishmael the illegitimate son brought forth a
spurious faith. This view might seem to contradict itself: how
could Muhammad have been sent by Providence, but sent to
preach a spurious faith? To this Forster replies that the providential purpose of Islam is a negative one only. It was sent to purge
the world of the evils of idolatry: when Muhammad came,
Christianity and Judaism were both corrupt, Christianity by the
worship of idols and Judaism by the search for an earthly kingdom
contrary to the promises made to the Jews. Islam purged
Christianity of its corruptions, and the temporal goods which the
Jews wrongly sought Islam rightly obtained in accordance with
the promise made to it. Now that this negative purpose has been
fulfilled, what will happen to Islam? In the end, Forster believes,
Muslims will be converted to Christianity, and this should not
even be too difficult: the 'favourable prepossessions and established
doctrines'[47] of Islam will make the approach to their conversion

easy, and the Arabic language, prevalent throughout so much of Asia and Africa, can be an important instrument of conversion—like Greek and Latin, it is providentially designed to prepare the way for the final triumph of the Gospel. But for this a new approach will be necessary, one based on a consciousness of the benefits brought by Islam to mankind—

it is only by fairly acknowledging what they have, that we can hope to make them sensible of what they have not.[48]

Such rare and indeed eccentric thinkers apart, the problem of Islam aroused scarcely an echo in the western Christian mind until the turn of the century, when we can see the beginnings of a new questioning fed from many different sources. One of them was the sheer weight of knowledge about Islam and other religions gradually accumulated by scholars, missionaries, colonial officials and travellers. In the face of this knowledge, it was necessary to admit that there was more to study in Islam than had been thought; if it were to be condemned as falsehood, it could only be in a more elaborate and complex way, and one which understood, evaluated and refuted rather than simply condemning. This gave rise also to a new awareness among Christians of sensitive conscience that those outside the Church could not simply be dismissed, without further qualification, as benighted pagans: to do so was to ignore the positive values which were clearly present in their religions, the human virtues which could spring from them, and the possibilities of salvation they might contain. Such questions must at least be asked, and even if they were answered in the negative, and Islam were treated as wholly false and evil, a further problem remained: the great development of historical thought in this age, reflected in the Christian consciousness, produced a new awareness that the process of preaching the gospel to the whole world was a process in time and one which would only be completed in the fullness of time.[49] The resistance of Islam to Christian penetration—more than that, the strength of Islam as a rival to Christianity—posed not only problems of missionary strategy but one more fundamental, of whether after all the spread and persistence of Islam might not have some meaning or at least be used for some purpose.

To such factors we must however add another, of a kind which cannot be explained in terms of anything except itself: the

disturbing impact of a mind of total originality and unusual force,
that of Louis Massignon.[50] His thought about Islam begins from
that point at which his own life was transformed: a sudden
apprehension of the existence of God and of a debt owed to Him,
at a moment of despair in Iraq in 1908. The experience had come
to him in a Muslim country, through the medium of Arabic, the
language of Islam, and perhaps it was this which gave him the
abiding sense of the divine origin of Islam which posed the
problems to which he remained faithful for more than another
half century of life. If Islam was of divine origin, how could it
have diverged from the fullness of truth revealed in Christ? If it
had diverged, could it still be a channel of salvation?

The beginnings of an answer Massignon found where he found
the whole meaning of history: in those 'hauts lieux de la prière'[51]
where God had revealed Himself and the prophets had spoken.
Islam began where Judaism and Christianity began, with God
speaking to Abraham and Abraham responding to God's call. It
diverged (as Forster had suggested two generations earlier) when
the line of Abraham split between Isaac and Ishmael, with the
exclusion of Ishmael from the covenant given to Abraham and his
seed. But the exclusion could not be complete: the covenant still
stood, the seed of Ishmael could still claim their share of it as
promised in *Genesis,* and Islam was sent as a consolation to the
excluded, an assurance that they were not forgotten. But the
revelation to Muhammad was more than this, it contained values
of its own. Against the corruptions of Christianity and Judaism,
the Qur'an teaches the transcendence of God—the source of all
reality, the destroyer of idols—and the unity of all believers in His
worship:

A sa seconde prière, à Berséba, 'puits du serment,' où Dieu lui
impose l'expatriement 'l'hégire' de son premier-né, Ismael,
Abraham consent à son exil au désert; pourvu que sa descend-
ance y survive, douée par Dieu dans le monde d'une certaine
pérennité privilégiée, marquant cette race, ismaelienne, arabe,
d'une vocation, l'épée, 'le fer à la puissance acérée' (Q. 57,25)
qui suspend sa menace, une fois l'Islam formé, sur tous les
idolâtres; à qui la guerre sainte est déclarée, implacable, tant
qu'ils ne confesseront pas qu'il n'y a qu'un Dieu, celui
d'Abraham: 'le premier Musulman' ... L'histoire de la race
arabe commence avec les larmes d'Agar, les premières dans

l'Écriture. L'arabe est la langue des larmes: de ceux qui savent que Dieu, dans son essence, est inaccessible et que tout est bien ainsi. S'Il vient en nous, c'est comme un Etranger, qui rompt notre vie normale à la manière d'un intervalle délassant du travail; et Il passe. Quelques-uns, approfondissant l'offrande d'Arafât, y trouvent une route vers l'Union, mais seuls, et dans la nuit.

Parce que l'Islam, venu après Moise et Jésus, avec le prophète Muhammad, annonciateur négatif du Jugement de mort qui atteindra tout le créé—constitue une réponse mystér-ieuse de la grâce à la prière d'Abraham pour Ismael et les Arabes: 'Je t'ai aussi exaucé' (pour Ismael). L'Islam arabe n'est pas une revendication désespérée d'exclus qui sera rejetée jusqu'à la fin, et son infiltration mystérieuse en Terre Sainte le laisse entendre. L'Islam a même une mission positive: en reprochant à Israel de se croire privilégié, au point d'attendre un Messie né dans sa race, de David, selon une paternité charnelle. Il affirme qu'il y est déjà né, méconnu, d'une maternité virginale prédestinée, que c'est Jésus fils de Marie, et qu'il reviendra à la fin des temps, en signe du Jugement.[52]

This uniqueness of God is indeed the great abiding message of Islam, just as its art

> ne cherche pas à imiter le Créateur dans ses œuvres par le relief et le volume des formes, mais l'évoque, par son absence même, dans une présentation fragile, inachevée, périssable comme un voile, qui souligne simplement, avec une résignation sereine le passage fugitif de ce qui périt, et tout est périssable 'excepté son visage'.[53]

The Qur'an can therefore be the starting point of a spiritual meditation which may in the end lead the Muslim to the fullness of truth. This indeed is the 'intention maîtresse'[54] of the covenant given to Ishmael, and it must be so, for otherwise the consolation would have been a cheat. It is a way which has been followed by those who, starting from the Qur'an, have sought to interiorise the system of precepts and laws which it contains, and give them a firm root in the heart and mind: above all by the mystics, those who seek for 'la prise de l'homme par Dieu'. In opposition to those who regard mysticism as something brought into Islam from outside, Massignon thought of it as something produced by an inner logic, as being indeed the necessary consequence of taking Islam seriously. It is by the mystics that the potentialities of the Qur'an have been developed, and by them that a new vision of the unity of God and of the union of men with God has been achieved; just as it is by the invisible hierarchy of mystic saints that the coherence of Islamic society has been maintained.

But somewhere on the way which starts from the Qur'an, the seeker after union must pass beyond Islam. If men could reach the fullness of truth through the Qur'an alone, then the death of Christ would also have been a cheat. In reaching the point of mystical vision, Islam becomes something other than itself: the law is superseded, the Ka'ba becomes only a symbol, and the figure of Muhammad is replaced as the norm of sainthood by that of al-Hallaj, the mystic condemned to death at Baghdad in 922, and behind whom there appears that of Christ, *al-insan al-kamil*, the perfect man.[55] In reaching its goal, Islam has also retraced its steps to the point from which it started, to that 'haut lieu' which is at once a place of pilgrimage and a point of return to Abraham to whom God first gave the covenant; and at this point Islam is no longer the excluded brother, it is a part of the alliance with God given in Christ.

This vision of the redemption of Islam, urged in language of great beauty, and not only in words but in acts—of pilgrimage and of political protest, wherever the human dignity of Muslims seemed to him threatened—has left its mark on French life, and on its literature, its theology and its missions as well as its Islamic scholarship. If it is possible for Mr Daniel to say that 'the present phase of Islamic studies is in the hands of active Christian believers',[56] it is partly because of Massignon. After him, a group of scholars have tried, whilst not obscuring the final differences between Islam and Christianity, to disentangle within Islam the secret paths which might lead the Muslim to the fullness of truth. Among them we may name several priests of Arab origin, and for whom therefore there is posed inescapably the problem of 'baptising' the Arabic language and its culture, or, to put it in other words, of creating a Christian culture in a language sacred to another religion, and moulded by that fact. Thus Fr Moubarac, carrying further a favourite theme of Massignon, has interpreted Islam as an attempt to return to the pure monotheistic religion of Abraham the common ancestor, and a conscious attempt, for in the

Qur'an itself Abraham appears as the type of the believer, the founder of true religion.[57] Fr Hayek, following another hint, finds between Islam and Christianity not so much a common ancestor as something of a shared content: Muslims revere Christ and the Blessed Virgin, and look forward to the return of Jesus, 'le justiciare ultime' at the end of time. Although not enough to make Islam a kind of Christianity, this is enough to make friendship possible between Muslims and Christians.[58] In a similar way, Fr Abdel-Jalil, himself not only of Arab but also of Muslim origin, has laid emphasis on the reverence given in Islam to the Virgin Mary.[59] But ideas such as these, if not handled with great caution, may lead to a certain ambiguity of theological position, to a view of Islam as an alternative line of salvation, an authentic prophetic religion, and even a kind of concealed Christianity.[60]

Standing in a rather different relationship to Massignon are two French Catholic scholars, J. Jomier and L. Gardet. Perhaps they would not have written as they have had Massignon not done his work; but what they have written is rooted in a different doctrinal soil, in the revived Thomist tradition of modern France, and is the product of a different and more cautious temper of mind. The work of Gardet, sometimes in collaboration with Fr Anawati, has been devoted primarily to a careful examination of different aspects of Islamic civilisation and thought, bringing out the significant differences from Christianity and relating them to differences of fundamental theological position;[61] while Jomier has made an equally careful and cautious examination of the Biblical elements in the Qur'an and of the very different ways in which Islam understands them. In Christianity, the idea of revelation is linked with that of progress, in Islam not—there is simply an underlying natural religion, recalled by the prophets from time to time; in Christianity, the idea of the supernatural is that of a participation in the life of God, in Islam there remains a separation; the Islamic conception of Jesus contains no idea of Incarnation, of Crucifixion, or of redemption, for salvation comes directly from God. Yet Jomier warns against building on these differences and resemblances either a doctrine of equivalence or one of total rejection:

Certains chrétiens, en effet, préconisent un effort pour inter-préter les passages-clefs de la christologie coranique à une lumière purement chrétienne, afin de mieux montrer toutes les richesses qu'ils pourraient contenir. Et comme des passages isolés supportent facilement une interprétation lorsqu'on les tire de leur contexte, ils pensent qu'une telle entreprise se justifie. Personnellement, pour l'instant, nous ne pensons pas en avoir le droit. Un fait nous frappe: pour des millions de musulmans, le Coran représente un Évangile de salut, bien distinct du nôtre et qui se présente comme achevé dans sa ligne. Ils prennent à la lettre l'enseignement général de Coran et voient la christologie à sa lumière.

Il n'en est pas moins vrai qu'il suffit de voir la réalité une fois pour toutes sans illusions; et, pour éviter de se blesser mutuellement, mieux vaut ensuite rechercher les points sur lesquels nous sommes d'accord. Nous avons en commun avec les musulmans le souci d'obéir pleinement à la volonté de Dieu, de ne rien dire qui aille contre la raison, même si parfois la révélation en depasse les forces; nous croyons à l'Unité de Dieu, au fait qu'Il a parlé par les prophètes. Et c'est déjà beaucoup. Peut-être un des points les plus importants ensuite se trouvera-t-il dans l'explication du message de Jésus tel qu'il a été réellement transmis à ses disciples. Le jour où nos positions sur l'authenticité de la Bible et l'authenticité de son interprétation seront comprises, bien des difficultés pout le dialogue tomberont. Le problème de l'authenticité de la Bible reste jusqu'à nouvel ordre un problème crucial dans la question des rapports entre chrétiens et musulmans.[62]

New ideas of this kind have become, it is not too much to say, the new orthodoxy of the Catholic Church, and their influence is clearly to be seen in the formulations of the Vatican Council, formulations which, while passing no judgement on the claim of Muslims that Muhammad was the mouthpiece of a divine revelation, recognise those elements in what he preached which Christians can accept, and which can serve as a basis for cooperation in the natural order:

L'Église regarde aussi avec estime les musulmans, qui adorent le Dieu Un, vivant et subsistant, miséricordieux et tout-puissant, créateur du ciel et de la terre, qui a parlé aux hommes. Ils cherchent à se soumettre de toute leur âme aux décrets de Dieu, méme s'ils sont cachés, comme s'est soumis à Dieu Abraham, auquel la foi islamique se réfère volontiers. Bien qu'ils ne reconnaissent pas Jésus comme Dieu, ils le vénèrent comme prophète; ils honorent sa Mère virginale, Marie, et parfois même l'invoquent avec piété. De plus, ils attendent le jour du jugement, où Dieu rétribuera tous les hommes ressuscités. Aussi ont-ils en estime la vie morale et rendent-ils un culte à Dieu, surtout par la prière, l'aumône et le jeûne.

Si, au cours des siècles, de nombreuses dissensions et inimitiés se sont manifestées entre les chrétiens et les musulmans, le Concile les exhorte tous à oublier le passé et à s'efforcer sincèrement à la compréhension mutuelle, ainsi qu'à protéger et à promouvoir ensemble, pour tous les hommes, la justice sociale, les valeurs morales, la paix et la liberté.[63]

It is not in the Roman Catholic Church alone that this new approach to Islam is to be found. In the Anglican Church also a similar concern with the theology of missions, and a similar desire for respect and friendship in the truth, have thrown up an analogous movement of thought. In the works of Canon Cragg there is no concealment of difference: Islam is not Christianity, but it can, so to speak, be 'prolonged' in the direction of Christianity. The basic concepts of Islam pose problems which can only be resolved by the doctrine of the Incarnation. In the Islamic notions of *shirk* (the attribution to others of that which God alone possesses), of *islam* (the recognition of God's authority), of the community under divine law, and of the state as the instrument of faith—in all these there lies a gap between God and man which only a divine initiative can bridge.[64]

Such Christian attitudes towards Islam as we have sketched here have become the orthodoxy of today. But they are by no means unchallenged: against the type of thought which originates with Massignon there can be set another which also springs from a man of unusual force of mind, and which denies the bases of the Massignonian view. In a number of works far apart in time, the Calvinist theologian Hendrik Kraemer has looked at Islam from an angle different both from Massignon's and from older formulations against which Massignon reacted.

It is true, Kraemer also begins with the drawing of a line between the Revelation of Christ and the teaching of Islam, but it is a different line. Underlying Kraemer's thought is a Calvinist view of the relations between the natural and supernatural very different from the view of Catholic theology, and the line which he draws does not run between the Islamic and another religious system which is thereby contrasted with it: it runs between all religious systems, including the Christian on the one side and the Revelation of God in Christ on the other. The fundamental distinction is not between the Muslim and the Christian ways of thinking and living, but rather between Revelation and all religious systems constructed by human reason; or, as Kraemer himself expresses it, between what God thinks of men and what men think of God.[65] Revelation is a spontaneous act of God, springing from His sole initiative, and the only authentic response to it is faith. But religions, although they may be rooted in 'a primordial decision and act of faith',[66] are human creations made by human initiative. They *may* contain a reflection of the revelation of God in Christ; they *may* produce order, culture, solidarity, transcendent ideals, and an awareness of man's calling in the world. But fundamentally they still belong to the world of unredeemed man, longing and groping for God but not yet recreated in His image:

> Man wants God, but somehow he wants Him in his own way ... Nowhere do we find a radical repudiation of every possible man-made spiritual world.[67]

It follows from this that there can be no gradual transition from a man-made religion to faith, for faith means a radical break with the past; and the non-Christian religions cannot be regarded as in any sense an evangelical preparation. Even if they contain elements of truth, it is still impossible to be sure that it is precisely those elements which God will use in order to bring men near Him. He may use that which the builders have rejected: and what seems most noble and truthful may in fact be not a step towards faith but a stumbling block:

> The mystic who triumphantly realises his essential oneness with God, or the World-Order, or the Divine, knowing himself in serene equanimity the supreme master of the universe or of his own destiny ... commits in this sublime way the root-sin of mankind—'to be like God'. In other words: he repeats the Fall.[68]

By what may seem a paradox, this total rejection of all man-made religious systems may make it possible to see them with peculiar clarity. They can be seen and studied and understood as products of the human mind, without being set in judgement on one another. For Kraemer, there is no need to condemn Islam because it is not Christianity, or to think of it as an unsuccessful attempt to be Christianity. To some extent indeed it *is* a modified reflex of Judaism and Christianity, but from the beginning it had an independent self-consciousness. It can therefore be regarded as a separate creation of the human mind, and is itself the creator not only of abstract ideas but of a whole way of life, a culture and civilisation, a society and state. As such, it has a special and complex relation with Christian culture, a mixture of 'kinship and deep difference and animosity'.[69] Compared with the 'cosmic naturalism' of the eastern religions, with their search for a harmony of man, nature and cosmos, Islam and Christianity stand together in their belief that there is a gulf between God and the world, and therefore a basic disharmony in the life of man.[70] But although they belong to the same family the meaning they give to what seem to be the same concepts is very different. In Kraemer's view, Islam is a fundamentally simple religion with a superficial understanding of its own concepts. Its idea of revelation is mechanical: the Word became book and not flesh, the content of revelation is 'a set of immutable divine words that take the place of God's movable acts and His speaking and doing through the living man Jesus Christ'. Its conception of sin and salvation is clumsy: there is no drama of salvation between God and the world, only an ethic of obedience to the God of omnipotence. Its unsurpassed apprehension of the majesty of God—Allah, white-hot majesty, omnipotence and uniqueness, whose personality evaporates and vanishes in the burning heat of His aspects —deprives man of his personality: he is personified surrender and nothing else. Islam again, according to Kraemer, has no mysticism of its own, only one brought in by Christian converts. Its intellectual development, which reached its height with al-Ghazali, was strangled by the Muslim view of revelation and by the domination of the 'masses', for one of the special characteristics of Islam is the strength of its solidarity: the aim of Muhammad was not only to preach religion but to found a community, so that Islam from the beginning has been a theocracy, although a secularised one. All this shows that the concepts which Islam affirms are not just Christian 'half-truths'; in spite of the kinship, they have a wholly different character and tendency.[71]

III

Such new views of Islam came late in our period, and are only now beginning to have an influence on those who can accept traditional formulations of the Christian faith. But long before orthodoxy began to see the relevance of Islam, and of other faiths, to the essential problems of Christianity, the existence of non-Christian beliefs had become relevant to another stream of religious thought which, in the course of the century, moved towards a new kind of formulation of Christian faith, or of faith in general. At the basis of this formulation lies a clear distinction between the divine and human elements of religion. There is a God who has created human beings and sustains them, and there is a divine revelation, that is to say, some spontaneous communication of God's will, by God's initiative, to individual human beings. But the concepts, the symbols, the 'metaphors' through which this revelation are publicly expressed are human, are indeed a human response to the reality of the divine intervention. They can and must be judged by human criteria—by whether they express that reality as truthfully and fittingly as human language can; in the end they always fall short—the expression is never perfect, it needs to be reshaped again and again.

Behind such formulation lies a long development of thought. It would be profitable, although difficult, to investigate its origins, but there is no need here to trace it back beyond the beginning of that great movement of the western spirit which took as its task to order all that can be known into systems of thought, and thus produced the great scientific disciplines of the nineteenth century —geology, biology, anthropology, mythology, historiography— but which led also to a radical questioning of the possibility of certainty, springing perhaps from other sources but given its distinctive shape by the vast extension in knowledge of the variety of human beliefs. Already, before the great development of historiography in the nineteenth century, Kant had made the essential distinction between religion and faiths. There is 'only one (true) religion: but there are faiths of several kinds'.[72] True religion consists in establishing the purity of the moral law as the supreme ground of all our maxims; in the idea of a mankind morally perfected and represented in our consciousness in the form of a perfect Man (whether this perfect Man actually existed is irrelevant—what is important is that the idea of him should be present in our minds); and in regarding all human duties as divine commands, coming from God as 'the lawgiver universally to be honoured'.[73] These duties, conceived as laws of God, can be known by reason, and therefore known by all men; but there may be other, less important laws, which cannot be known by reason but only through revelation. These, however, are secondary only and not binding on all men absolutely; they are binding only condition-ally, *if* we wish to honour God in a Church. Whether these conditional laws of particular churches or faiths are really revealed by God is impossible to judge: it cannot be asserted with assurance, but it would be wrong to deny that it may be so. Among such faiths, Kant did not in fact have a high regard for Islam: its paradise, he thought was sensual, and its moral attitude was one of arrogance—it sought to confirm its faith by victories not by miracles.[74]

In the next generation, Hegel, combining with the Kantian distinction between reality and phenomena a vivid sense, drawn from the new science, of the variety and multiplicity of things that exist, put forward

a view of religious dogma as a more or less symbolic represen-tation, in a concrete and historically conditioned form, of the timeless truths of idealist metaphysics.[75]

In the footsteps of Kant and Hegel came a new type of Christian writer and scholar, trying to use the new concepts of German philosophy to explain the structure of the Bible and the develop-ment of the Church. The starting point of this new critical movement was 'a new and more human conception of the mode of revelation'. The texts of the Old and New Testament were regarded as the work of human minds, to be studied and judged in the same way as other written texts; the task of the critic was

to show how the ideas of any particular writer are related to the environment in which they grew, to the spirit of the age, to the life of the people, to the march of events, and to the kindred literary productions of other time, or, it may be, of other lands.[76]

Applied to the development of the Christian faith, such principles produced certain important results which were also to have an influence on thought about Islam. One such was the dissection of the Pentateuch into different strata; the reversal of the generally accepted order of the law and the prophets—the discovery by Duhm that

> the phenomenon of prophecy is independent of every Mosaic law but the moral law written in the heart ... the great Prophets are not the children of the law, but the inspired creators of the religion of Israel. Prophecy is the supreme initial fact which transcends explanation.[77]

Another and perhaps even more delicate aspect of the process was the search for the historical figure of Jesus behind the hero of the gospel narratives. Since what was at stake was a person, not a book or the development of a state, and since all were agreed on regarding the person as the exemplar of human virtue, this activity, for all the care with which it was undertaken, could not but be directed by the individual thinker's view of what human nature was or should be; the result of the work was therefore to produce a variety of different visions of Jesus. Such visions, at their best, could have the compelling and moving quality of the ethical seriousness of the age, but might become a 'literary picture' of which the criteria were no longer moral but aesthetic: Jesus wins converts by 'sa beauté pure et douce', by '[le] charme infini de sa personne et de sa parole'.[78] In the process it might indeed happen that the human personality was 'dissolved' into something else: an element in a system of ideas. In Strauss's *Life of Jesus* the basic concept is no longer that of the revelation of God through Christ, it is that of *religion*, the essence of which is the perception by man that both God and men are spirit, and therefore are not distinct from one another: the infinite spirit is real only when it discloses itself in finite spirits, the finite only when it merges itself in the infinite. Men can perceive this truth either in the form of an idea or embodied in myths; the first is philosophy, the second is religion. But these myths are of human origin, they are produced by 'the spirit of a people or a community', and therefore they vary from one religion to another. In the Christian religion, a man called Jesus, 'a Jewish claimant of the Messiahship', served as the nucleus around which there gathered myths of various kinds—Old Testament myths transferred to him, myths produced by the Messianic expectation, others produced by the impression left by his own life and character. These myths must be interpreted *as* myths: that is to say, as ways by which man returns through his imagination to union with God.[79] It was not so far from this position to that of Bruno Bauer, who showed it to be impossible to prove that the historical personality had ever existed, and unnecessary as well: the only reality of which we could be certain was that of general ideas.[80]

Similar principles led to a further line of inquiry, into the development of the Christian community: an attempt to explain it in terms of normal historical categories, of one thing changing into another under the impact of human factors. Thus for Harnack the growth of Christianity involved a clear change of spirit and content. The gospel of Jesus was preached only to the Jews, the Gentile gospel was the invention of Paul, who 'wrecked the religion of Israel on the cross of Christ';[81] Jesus founded no new sect or school, preached no new religion, taught nothing except the destruction of the Temple and the judgement impending on the Jewish nation; it was Paul who brought the new and consciously different religion.[82]

It has seemed worth while to go into some detail about this new way of looking at Christianity, because it had a profound influence on ways of looking at Islam and other religions. The methods elaborated, and the conclusions to which they led, could be applied to other prophetic leaders, sacred books, and religious communities. In regard to each of the historic religions of mankind it would be possible to ask the same kind of question. How were the texts of its sacred books established? How far did they record a historical process, and how far themselves create a story? What was the human reality of the person of the founder, behind the 'myth' created by the sacred book or the accumulation of tradition? In what ways and under what human impulses did doctrines and institutions develop from the time of the founder? Behind all these there lay another question, which perhaps could not be answered but which had to be asked: what was there of divine, what of human, in this religion? How far did it throw light on the human ways in which religious beliefs and institutions develop, or on the way in which divine providence works?

For those who looked at religions from this point of view, there was perhaps none which offered a greater interest than Islam. It not only had a sacred book, but one which had achieved its definitive form early in the development of the religion. It had a great mass of written tradition which, properly analysed, might

help the religious scholar to understand how doctrines and
institutions had grown up. Its religious leader claimed to be a
prophet, and thus was well-placed to attract the attention of those
who saw in prophecy the key to the development of religion; he
had grown up (or so it seemed) in the light of history, and the
study of his acts and words, as recorded in great detail, might help
to explain how the historical person of the founder of a religion
gradually turned into a mythical figure. The development of the
thought and institutions of Islam had also been fully recorded in
texts and was open to study. It had taken place not by the
authority of rulers or of a church, but by the rational activity of
concerned Muslims, tending towards the elaboration of agreed
opinion; it was likely therefore to throw light on the way in which
the religious consciousness works, and its interaction with political
interests and social needs.

As C. H. Becker put it:

A world-religion, such as Christianity, is a highly complex
structure and the evolution of such a system of belief is best
understood by examining a religion to which we have not been
bound by a thousand ties from the earliest days of our lives . . .
No less interesting are the discoveries to be attained by an
inquiry into the development of Mohammedanism: here we can
see the growth of tradition proceeding in the full light of
historical criticism, a plain man gradually becoming miracle
worker, mediator between God and man, saint, and the collection of his utterances expanding from year to year by the
attribution to him of yet more acts and sayings.[83]

This indeed explains the origin and direction of much of the best
Islamic scholarship of the later nineteenth century. For example,
the seed of the Islamic researches of Julius Wellhausen can partly
be found in his earlier work on the higher criticism of the Old
Testament. In his *Prolegomena to the History of Israel* he drew a
distinction between three phases in the development of Judaism.
The Mosaic phase was essentially that of the creation of a state,
the soil out of which all the other institutions of Israel were later
to arise: a state but not yet a theocracy—that was to come later 'as
the residuum of a ruined State'.[84] The second phase was that of
the prophets, whose role was to develop the doctrine and worship
of Israel: inspired and awakened individuals, needing no support

outside themselves, and so fitted to live in 'the storm of the world's history, which sweeps away human institutions'.[85] Their preaching was of old truths rather than new, and they did not expound or apply the law; that was the role of a third phase and another group of men, the priestly caste which grew up during the exile and continued even after the restoration of the Temple. Their creation was the Priestly Code: but at the same time they destroyed prophecy and the old freedom in the sphere of the religious spirit. They replaced the prophets with a book having authority, and the people of the Word became a 'people of the book'.[86]

The state, prophecy, and the law: these three elements are to be found in Islam too, although the relation between them is of course not quite the same. The state was founded after the prophet had preached, but before the content of prophecy was fully articulated; the law came later and here too perhaps it destroyed religious freedom. Thus a study of Islam could help to illuminate the general nature of religion; but it is typical of the age in which Wellhausen lived, of its belief in the metaphysical importance of the state and in the nation-state as its highest form, that his special attention should have been given to one of the three elements, the Arabian nation-state.[87]

Rather similar preoccupations underlay the Islamic studies of Ignaz Goldziher, even if the intellectual milieu from which he sprang was that of Jewish and not Christian liberalism. His own education was double, both traditional Jewish and modern European: he studied the Talmud, but belonged to the second generation of Jews in central Europe who went to the *gymnasium*. His attitude to Islam was derived perhaps from both these sources. As a Jew of his generation he inherited a certain attitude towards other religions: an attitude in which indifference or hostility might be mixed with something else, the idea (formulated by Maimonides) of 'prophets of the nations' through whom God spoke to the non-Jewish world, communicating the essential truths to it not directly but from behind a veil. As a Jew also he lived the great controversy of his age, between orthodoxy and reform. The reformists did not necessarily deny the special status of the Jews or the validity of revelation, but interpreted them in a new way analogous to that of the liberal Christians. Here also the essential distinction was between divine and human elements. Doctrine was divine, and mediated through the prophets, but law (not only that of the Talmud but that contained in the Torah itself) was a product of historical development and therefore of human factors. Goldziher himself did not belong to the main stream of German-Jewish reformism.[88] Like many Hungarian Jews, he belonged to the group generally known as 'Neologen', and for much of his life indeed was the secretary of their community in Budapest. The 'Neologen' as such had no consistent theological position, but some of them were in sympathy with reformism, and it is clear that Goldziher accepted its main thesis, that of the distinction between divine and human elements in religious systems. He was strengthened in this way of looking at the matter by his secular studies in Germany, where he came into contact with the methods of critical history, as applied to the Near East by such scholars as Nöldeke and Sprenger, and with the science of mythology developed by Max Müller and others: the attempt, that is, to interpret myths as expressions of the collective spirit of an age or a people. His first book indeed was a contribution to this science: *Der Mythos bei der Hebräern und seine geschichtliche Entwicklung.*[89] It is the kind of book which mature men may regret having written in the heat of youth, and he later disowned it, but it helps to explain his way of thinking. At the heart of it lies a distinction between religion and myth. Pure religion is the sentiment of dependence, giving rise to the idea of monotheism pure and unsullied by anything coarse and pagan. In its early phases it has not yet disentangled itself from myths, which are spontaneous acts of the human mind, not inventions of a particular thinker or a truthful record of what happened. As the religious consciousness develops, however, it severs its connection with myths, unites itself with the scientific consciousness, attains the idea of monotheism, and develops a theology. The main purpose of the book was to refute the racial theory of Renan and others that only the Aryans were capable of myth-making and therefore of art; in opposition to this, Goldziher tried to prove that all nations can create myths, Semites as well as Aryans, and that the Hebrew stories contained in the Bible can be given a valid mythical interpretation no less than others.

To one whose interest lay in distinguishing the human from the divine element, and tracing the historical process by which pure monotheism disentangled itself from human creations, the relevance of Islam is obvious. At the origin of Islam there lies an assertion of pure monotheism, a complete break with the past; and this assertion gave rise to a whole process of development, the gradual formulation of a system of doctrine and law by the religious consciousness. This process formed the central theme of Goldziher's studies, and it conformed to his general view of religion that, when writing of the origin of Islam, as in his essay on *Muruwwa*, he should lay emphasis on the 'tension' between Islam and the pagan environment in which it grew up;[90] and that, when studying the subsequent development of religious thought, as in his works on tradition, on the growth of dogma and law, and on the Zahirites, he should treat it as a process subject to historical laws, proceeding from within by the inner logic of the historical consciousness.[91]

Long beyond the time of Goldziher, indeed until the present, this general attitude towards religion, and towards Islam, has continued to be an important motive force in Islamic studies. It underlies such a statement as that with which H. A. R. Gibb prefaces his *Modern Trends in Islam*:

... I make bold to say that the metaphors in which Christian doctrine is traditionally enshrined satisfy me intellectually as expressing symbolically the highest range of spiritual truth which I can conceive, provided that they are interpreted not in terms of anthropomorphic dogma but as general concepts, related to our changing views of the nature of the universe. I see the church and the congregation of Christian people as each dependent on the other for continued vitality, the church serving as the accumulated history and instrument of the Christian conscience, the permanent element which is constantly renewed by the stream of Christian experience and which gives both direction and effective power to that experience.

My view of Islam will necessarily be the counterpart of this. The Muslim church and its members constitute a similar composite, each forming and reacting to the other so long as Islam remains a living organism and its doctrines satisfy the religious consciousness of its adherents. While giving full weight to the historical structure of Muslim thought and experience, I see it also as an evolving organism, recasting from time to time the content of its symbolism, even though the recasting is concealed (as it is to a considerable extent in Christianity) by the rigidity of its outward formulas.[92]

In this careful statement, a balance is kept between what

distinguishes religious traditions and what they have in common: all grow up in conformity to the laws of human nature and society, but what they produce is different in nature and may differ in value—'the metaphors in which Christian doctrine is traditionally enshrined' are seen as 'expressing symbolically the highest range of spiritual truth'. But it would also be possible to develop this line of thought in another direction: towards a final equivalence of religious systems, each containing something of value, each a more or less inadequate expression of what cannot be fully expressed, all to be regarded with respect and without judgement, for— whether or not they differ in value in the eyes of God—they cannot be judged objectively by men each of whom is bound by his own tradition.

Such a concept of religion has been worked out by Wilfred Cantwell Smith. Once more he starts with a distinction, between 'inner faith' and 'outward system'.[93] Faith is 'a well-nigh universal human phenomenon', [94] but outward systems change, and not only forms of worship but doctrines as well. They change because they are human, the expression of different cultures, 'the religious forms of a people';[95] and for the same reason they will continue, for mankind is inescapably divided into different cultural groups, each with its own religious tradition enshrining certain values. What are the values and distinguishing marks of the Islamic religious community? They are to be found in the special ways in which Muslims talk of God, or rather of His actions in the world: He reveals not Himself but something about Himself, and does so through a book, not a person, and a book revealed to a human prophet; the content of that book is first of all a command, to worship God alone, and therefore also a rejection, of polytheism, of human tyranny, of 'the false Gods of the heart'.[96] These should be regarded more as the values of a community than of a religion, for the concept of 'religion' or of 'religions' is a false reification, itself the product of the modern phase of the Judaeo-Christian tradition of thought. It falsely confounds two underlying realities: on the one hand, the vitality of personal faith; on the other, the cumulative tradition of the different human cultures in which men have embodied their faith through history.[97]

IV

In such writings we can see implicit a view of Islam which, while remaining within the bounds of Christianity (or, with Goldziher, of Judaism) has come to concede to Islam an existence in its own right, if not as a separate mode of divine revelation, at least as a separate type of human response to the divine call, and one which expresses itself in all aspects of life and contains certain values of its own. But there was another line of thought which looked on all religious systems and all civilisations as products of the human spirit. The very extension of knowledge and change of view which led to that 'new and more human conception of the mode of revelation' could lead also to a denial of the distinction between what was known through revelation and what was known by reason: in the last analysis, religions like other human phenomena could be seen as products of mind, whether by that was meant the individual human mind or something universal and absolute.

This was a conclusion implicit in one of the seminal ideas of the nineteenth century, that of Process or Development: the idea that all which exists is part of a continuous, self-creating, self-maintaining process, changing in accordance with principles contained within itself, through the operation of some 'force' which works upon matter to produce ever more complex forms; and that the goal of the process is not something beyond it, but its own last and highest stage. Seen in this light, every stage of the process has a unique importance, each has contributed something, and if we are to understand the whole we must distinguish what that something is. When applied to human history, this conception gave importance to the idea of a 'period' or 'civilisation' in which all events and institutions had a unity, since all were expressions of one 'force', whether it were defined in terms of religious belief, or 'spirit', or race, or class. History as such assumed a new importance: it was the working out of the nature and destiny of the universe, and the study of history was the attempt to define the laws by which that working out took place, and to give a rational explanation of why everything happened as and when it did, and what it contributed to the process.

Thus the Islamic phase of civilisation like all others took on a new meaning, and it became necessary to ask new questions about it, or at least to ask old questions in a new way. Islam was seen not only as a religion but also as a civilisation in which religious belief was only one (and perhaps not the basic) element; and the problem to resolve was not whether the beliefs of Islam were true or false but what was the nature of this civilisation, what distinguished it from others. What was the underlying 'force' which had given it this nature—was it the religion of Islam or something else? Again, what was the relationship between it and what came before and after, what did it take from the one and transmit to the other? In the light of this, what was its role in the whole process, what did it contribute which no other civilisation did?

For the first great thinker of this line, the role of Islam was secondary but not without importance. The thought of Hegel was open, as we have seen, to a 'religious' interpretation, but also to an immanentist or humanist one. For him, Reason was both the matter and the active formal principle of the historical process. History was the progressive self-realisation of Reason, it was Reason making itself actually what it was potentially, an embodiment of its own idea, and this idea was Freedom: Reason is fully itself when free and conscious of being so, and when embodied in a free society and state in which the private and general wills are in harmony. In this process there have been four main stages: the oriental world, where law existed, but as an external force of compulsion; the Greek world, where Spirit became conscious of itself; the Roman world, where Spirit realised its freedom but only in the realm of individual faith, while society and state remained the domain of tyranny; and finally the German world in which freedom is embodied in the state. The role of Islam had been to help this fourth world into existence. The barbarian peoples who occupied the Roman world were free, as the Romans had not been free, but they were free only to follow their particular aims: there was no common aim, no single principle or law to order particular wills, and therefore their public life had been the domain of 'chance and entanglement'. Islam had come as the antithesis to correct this particularity: it was essentially the worship of the One, the absolute object of attraction and devotion. But this excess of devotion had also its defect: for Islam all men were as nothing compared with the One, the only object of secular existence was to be subject to the One. Islam, therefore, lacked the special relationship which, in Judaism, existed between the One and at least some human beings, and which in Christianity had led the human spirit back from the One to the human world, in a self-conscious return on itself. On the contrary, Islam had no interest in the human world except that it presented the pure adoration of the One, and recognised no purely natural bond between human beings, only that of common belief and worship. Because the object of its worship was abstract Oneness, it tended to enthusiasm and fanaticism, and since the enthusiasm was abstract, it was also destructive (although it could also be magnanimous and heroic). When the enthusiasm died, worldly interests crept in—the love of power and glory—but because of their final belief in the One, Muslims could never give their real allegiance to these worldly things, and sooner or later the enthusiasm would revive. It was this alternation of mood which made Islamic civilisation ephemeral: it flowered quickly but dissolved no less so, for 'on the basis presented by Universality nothing is firm'. Later indeed there was a certain restoration under the Ottomans, but it came too late: the Spirit had moved from Islam to modern Europe, whose historical mission it was to absorb the antithesis into a synthesis, and nothing was left in the Muslim world except sensual enjoyment and oriental repose.[98]

In some sense most of the historians and historical thinkers of the nineteenth century were children of Hegel. But the general concepts which he represented could be developed in many different ways, with differing emphases. If history were a process, divided into different phases, it was possible, when looking at each phase, to lay the main emphasis on either of two points: on its positive value, its contribution as an indispensable step from somewhere to somewhere else, or its defects, as something of less value than that which replaced it. Both these views were reflected in the thought of those who gave serious consideration to Islam.

Among those who, on the whole, took the first path, Auguste Comte regarded Islam, like Christianity, as a necessary phase in the education of mankind. Both indeed belonged, in his view, to the same phase, the 'medieval', with its two principles of monotheism and feudalism. But they differed in various ways: Christianity separated while Islam united the two powers; Christianity was a religion of the governed and taught the discipline of obedience, while Islam was a religion of the rulers and taught the discipline of command. In some ways, Islam was the more conducive of the two to human progress: it had neither a theocracy nor complicated doctrines, and thus it was easier for a man to free himself from it; it gave its subject-peoples, for example the Greeks, a social discipline which they lacked. But in the last analysis neither Islam nor its ancient enemy, Catholic Christianity, could become a universal religion: their long conflict ended in stalemate and common exhaustion, which in turn made possible the coming of the final age of scientific thought, industrial activity and positive religion.[99]

But even if the historical role of Islam was over, something remained behind. The Turks still had the qualities of a ruling people, and would have a special part to play in spreading the ideas of positivism in the East. Comte followed with great interest the progress of the Ottoman reforms. He included in the preface to the third volume of his *Système de Politique Positive* a letter to the former Grand Vizir Reshid Pasha, praising his reforming measures, drawing the attention of Muslims to the positive religion 'comme leur offrant spontanément le dénouement inespéré de leurs principales sollicitudes', and hoping that the East could go directly from Islam to positivism without passing through the stage of metaphysics, that period of 'l'anarchique agitation ... où les philosophes sont forcés de s'adresser aux inférieurs faute de pouvoir être compris des supérieurs'.[100] Later, at the turn of the century, a closer connection was established: the leader of the Young Turk exiles in Paris, Ahmad Riza Bey, was himself a positivist and a member of the Comtean circle in France, and when the news of the Young Turk revolution in 1908 came, he and they regarded it as a triumph for the positive philosophy. In contrast to the Turks, the Persians would be the last people to become positivists: they had no social discipline, and their religion had become a barrier against progress.[101]

Something else remained: the memory of what Islam had done. In the Comtean religion of humanity, human history would take the place of the Incarnate God, and the past would be enshrined forever in the mind of the believer. In the liturgical year of the Church of Humanity, one week would be set apart for the commemoration of Islamic monotheism, the only possible precursor of positivism in the east. In this week, Thursday would be the feast of Muhammad, Sunday the commemoration of Islam in itself, and Monday the feast of the battle of Lepanto, the last great expression of the military instinct, the end of the military era and the beginning of the industrial.[102]

It may be doubted whether the feast of Lepanto was ever observed with great reverence, even by the most fervent believers;

but what we may call in general a 'positivist' way of looking at Islam, as a stage in a purely human process of development, was widespread and was indeed one of the attitudes which inspired the oriental scholarship of the nineteenth century. It began with a number of scholars who, in the middle of the century, tried to give a purely human explanation of the rise and development of Islamic civilisation, in terms of historical factors: among them von Kremer and Sprenger.[103] Later, L. Caetani developed this idea in a more definitely positivist direction, laying stress on psychological rather than religious factors. The rise of Islam for him was not just a sudden upsurge of bands filled with religious zeal, but a phase in the fundamental process which had moulded world-history, the interaction of Asia and Europe. The spirit of Asia is essentially religious, with no idea of race or nation; the European spirit makes a distinction between the secular and religious spheres, hence its great products, Roman law and rational thought. At the time when Islam arose, the Semitic peoples of the Near East were subject to the supremacy of the Aryan race, bringing with it the political institutions of Rome and the Hellenised Christianity of Byzantium. But the Oriental spirit could not permanently accept this moral domination of Europe: even Christianity, although eastern by origin, had been fused with the western soul and had so become European. Hence a violent 'nationalist' reaction by the Near Eastern peoples, giving rise to a spiritual and moral vacuum which was filled first by Christian heresies and then by Islam. Islam was thus a 'symbol' of the revolt of the east: in becoming this, it ceased to be Arab and became a universal religion dominated by the conquered peoples, Syrians, Copts and others; it was they who created Islam as we know it, while the Arabs remained pagan at heart.[104]

For Caetani then, Islam was an expression of revolt against European culture. But to say this was to pose a further problem. If Islam were the product of purely human forces, it could not be regarded as self-generated and self-explanatory, but as a product of factors anterior to itself. Seen in this light, the essential historical problem of Islam became that of its relationship with the Greek civilisation which it replaced; and once the problem was posed, it could not be answered in terms of stark opposition, but rather of interpenetration, of the survival of the Greek spirit in an Islamic form.

Such a line of thought was worked out in some detail by C. H.

Becker. For him there was a sharp distinction between the religion of Islam and the civilisation usually called Islamic. There was, to begin with, a religious impulse, arising from some 'psychological' tendencies in Muhammad himself but influenced by Judaism and Christianity. But this new religion was not by itself the cause of the formation of the State: the fundamental reason for that was economic—the hunger of the Arab tribesmen, directed for Arab political purposes, and using religion as its 'party cry'. The conversion of conquered peoples to Islam also must be explained in mainly political and economic terms, by the desire to join the ruling group and escape from taxation. Once the Arab state and the Islamic community had been formed, there arose a culture which was in essence neither Arab or Islamic. 'Without Alexander the Great no Islamic civilisation':[105] its culture and institutions were a continuation of that which had existed before. 'The Arabs simply continued to develop the civilisation of post-classical antiquity with which they had come in contact',[106] and the process was largely carried out by Jewish and Christian converts who brought into Islam their own habits of thought. Hence the underlying similarity of Christian and Muslim culture, but with one great exception: the European idea of Man was very different from the Islamic, and from this many other differences were to flow—there was nothing in Islam similar to the western concept of the free citizen.[107]

In a more reserved and guarded way Levi Della Vida has put forward a similar view. Islamic culture might well be a product of Hellenism, but this is not to deny its originality. Its roots lay in Judaism and Christianity (with a contribution from other oriental faiths), but it was saved from being a mere 'counterfeit Christianity' by the survival of certain characteristics of the culture of pre-Islamic Arabia, transmitted by the Qur'an and the literary tradition. Nevertheless, the value of this should not be placed too high: they are characteristics of a barbarian age, and responsible not only for what is original in Islam, but also for a certain 'crudity' in it.[108]

Thinkers of this type might look harshly on Islam, might deny that it was original, but at least they gave it the credit for having contributed something of value by transmitting the culture of antiquity to the modern world. But when the emphasis shifted, from the relations of Islam with what went before to its relations with what came after, the judgement tended to be harsher, and indeed to be a secular form of that judgement upon Islam, as opposed to Christianity, which was the common attitude of earlier generations. In the work of Renan, for example, that opposition takes the secular form of a contrast between the 'Semitic' and 'Aryan' races. He does not, it is true, deny what Islam has contributed to human civilisation, but he believes that the contribution is over and done with.

For Renan, the motive force of history is the spirit of the race, and the fundamental division is not between religious communities but between races. Christianity and Islam are the products of two different races, each with its own mentality. Islam was the characteristic product of the Semitic mentality. It was a religion which prevented the use of reason and growth of science: all religions, it is true, do this when allowed to go beyond their real purpose of inspiring the human heart with high ideals, and to dominate human thought and action, but Islam did so in a particular way. Its society was based on 'l'idée la plus opposée au progrès: l'État fondé sur une prétendue révélation, le dogme gouvernant la société'.[109] There had never been, there could not be, such a thing as a Muslim scientist: science had indeed existed and been tolerated inside Islamic society, but the scientists and philosophers were not really Muslims. The great age of Islamic thought had been the Abbasid, but the Abbasid caliphs themselves were scarcely believers. The culture of their court and empire was a revived Sassanian culture, produced by men who were not deeply Muslim and were in inner revolt against the religion they were forced to profess. 'Arabic' philosophy and science were Arabic only in language, in spirit they were 'Greco-Sassanian'.[110] The racial theory is so old-fashioned now that it is difficult to understand the force of its impact. But Renan was by no means alone in thinking in this way. Gobineau in his book on the inequality of human races put forward a similar thesis. Islam was created by the Arab race because it could not be absorbed into the civilisations already existing. In the same way, other races were never really aborbed into Islam: they remained true to themselves and in the end reasserted their own culture. The so-called 'Islamic' civilisation therefore did not exist: it was a mixture of the civilisations of different races—its religion Arab, its laws Persian and Roman, its sciences Greco-Syrian and Egyptian.[111]

Both the Greeks and Persians, Renan maintains, were Aryans not Semites, and this was not an accident. Science and philosophy

were products of the Aryan mind, moulded by 'la recherche
réfléchie, indépendante, sévère, courageuse, philosophique, en un
mot, de la vérité': while the Semites had 'ces intuitions fermes et
sûres qui . . . atteignirent la forme religieuse la plus épurée que
l'antiquité ait connue'.[112] And just as the Aryans, not the Semites,
had produced science, so they had produced Myth, fertile mother
of the arts. The Semitic spirit was clear but not fecund; its
contribution to the world could be summed up in one word,
monotheism. 'Le desert est monothéiste':[113] its religion is simple,
patriarchal, without mysticism or theology (except such as it has
borrowed from outside), without mythology, without a sense of the
creative richness of life, hence also without epic or the plastic arts,
and without political civilisation—'l'anarchie la plus complète, tel
a toujours été l'état politique de la race arabe'.[114] Once monotheism
was established, the Semites had made their great contribution to
human culture and handed on the torch to the Aryans. Sprung
from the same stock, the two 'grandes races nobles' had comple-
mented each other for a time. The essential task of the Semites
had been 'de bannir le polythéisme et les énormes complications
dans lesquelles se perdait la pensée religieuse des Ariens'. But

> une fois cette mission accomplie, la race sémitique déchoit
> rapidement, et laisse la race arienne marcher seule à la tête des
> destinées du genre humain.[115]

This thesis had an immense impact when it was first put forward.
As we have seen, the desire to refute it inspired Goldziher's first
book, and the same motive led the famous Muslim publicist Jamal
al-Din al-Afghani to write a reasoned reply—a reply of which
Renan acknowledged the strong points, while ascribing them to
the fact that Jamal al-Din, being an Afghan (or more likely a
Persian), was himself an Aryan.[116]

Jacob Burckhardt went further than Renan. He could not even
find that Islam deserved credit for what it had done. Its civilisation
was not only less advanced than that of modern Europe, it was
also a retrogression from what had gone before. Its triumph could
be explained by two factors: first, the Arabs, 'a brilliant people,
capable of self-denial, with boundless self-reliance of individuals
and tribes . . . summoned to a new faith and to world-hegemony in
the name of this faith';[117] and secondly the nature of that faith
itself. Muhammad was a radical simplifier, hostile to 'all idolatry,

... all the multifarious ramifications of the hitherto existing faith',[118] and this was both his strength and his weakness. Islam succeeded because it was 'a triumph of triviality, and the great majority of mankind *is* trivial'; but for the same reason, once it had succeeded it destroyed over wide areas two more profound religions, Christianity and dualism.[119] It had the peculiar power of abolishing in the minds of those who accepted it their previous history, of giving them an arrogance in the light of which they grew ashamed of what they had been.[120] In place of the richness of their past it installed dryness and unity. It knew only one kind of state, despotism: all Islamic states were 'mere replicas of the world-empire on a small scale', and the only change was the alternation between rulers who lived for a cause and the ordinary despots who succeeded them.[121] Similarly, it had only two ideals of life, the ruler and the *darwish*; no patriotic feeling, only religious pride; no epic, drama or comedy, and a literature which exalted grammar and speech over content. Its faith lacked inwardness, and such genuine devotion and mysticism as it had came from outside.

V

To place civilisations or societies on a temporal line, passing from the lower to the higher, as these theories do, is not the only way of thinking about them. The impact of the natural sciences on all modern thinking has been so strong that many attempts have been made since Montesquieu to work out a science of societies analogous to the natural sciences in its purpose and methods. Its purpose would be, not to judge but to classify, and to formulate general laws covering classes of wider or more limited extension; and its method, to abstract from the individual members of the classes some general nature which they share. Seen in this light, what would be most interesting about Islam would be not what distinguished it from all other societies, but what it had in common either with a limited group of other societies or with all societies as such; but of course many different views might be held about what the common characteristic was.

In the nineteenth century many such classifications of society were attempted, and Islam was relevant to some of them. Marx and Engels, for example, in an exchange of letters shortly before the outbreak of the Crimean War, when the future of the Ottoman

Empire was being much discussed, tried to explain the rise of
Islam within the framework of a materialistic theory of history,
and did so by dividing Asiatic from other societies. Using an idea
of which the origin can be found in the writings of Adam Smith
and the Mills,[122] the two correspondents make a broad distinction
between oriental and western history and treat the rise of Islam as
a phenomenon typical of the first. The basic fact which provides
the key to all oriental history, Engels suggests, is that there is no
private property in land. Climate and the condition of the soil in
the vast desert regions stretching from the Sahara to East Asia
make agriculture impossible except by means of artificial irriga-
tion works, and these can only be created and maintained by the
government. In other words, agriculture depends on political
factors: a single war can ruin a whole civilisation. In Arabia and
the surrounding countries there took place during the seventh
century a weakening of governments, because of the displacement
of trade-routes from Arabia northwards to Iraq and Persia; when
government weakened, settled society also grew weak, and it was
easy for the nomads to move in and dominate it.

This coming in of the nomads was only one of numerous such
invasions throughout history, which had led to the rapid creation
of empires and new cities. The Jewish occupation of Palestine had
been another such, for the Jews were nothing but a Beduin tribe
differentiated by local circumstances from others. It was a process
which in itself needed no complex explanation, and the only
problem it raised was that of 'the religious swindle': of why in the
Orient social and economic phenomena took a religious form—
why the history of the East *appears* to be one of religions. No
clear answer emerges from the letters, but the problem itself is
defined in clear and vigorous terms: the nomadic reaction against
a weak and decadent settled life expressed itself in a pretended
new religion, which was in fact a reassertion of an older 'national'
religious tradition in its pure form against an amalgam of that
tradition with a decadent Judaism and Christianity. Here too the
rise of Islam was only one manifestation of a recurrent theme in
Near Eastern history: the pretended Holy Book of the Jews had
also in its time been no more than a transcription in a modified
form of the old religious tradition of the Arab tribes.[123]

Carlyle too can be regarded as one who made an early and
rather crude attempt to classify historical events. In a famous
lecture he depicts Muhammad as an example of a type of mind

which has appeared again and again in human history, the 'prophetic' type. The prophet is a certain kind of human hero who carries certain human qualities to the limit: 'a silent great soul . . . one of those who cannot *but* be in earnest'; austere, intuitive, looking 'through the show of things into *things*', convinced and propagating Islam through conviction not through the sword, and above all sincere. Whether he was in fact inspired by God is not to be known; perhaps Carlyle himself has doubts of it, for he describes the Qur'an as 'a wearisome, confused jumble, crude, incondite . . . Nothing but a sense of duty could carry any European through the Koran'. But he finds something inspired in the very sincerity of Muhammad:

> The great Mystery of Existence . . . glowed in upon him, with its terrors, with its splendours; no hearsay could hide that unspeakable fact, 'Here am I'. Such sincerity . . . has in very truth something of divine . . . the great Heaven rolling silent overhead, with its blue-glancing stars, answered not . . . The man's own soul, and what of God's inspiration dwelt there, had to answer! . . . Such light had come, as it could, to illuminate the darkness of this wild Arab soul. A confused dazzling splendour, as of life and Heaven, in the great darkness which threatened to be death: he called it revelation and the angel Gabriel;—who of us can yet know what to call it . . . Providence' had unspeakably honoured *him* by revealing it . . . he therefore was bound to make known the same to all creatures: this is what was meant by 'Mahomet is the Prophet of God'.[124]

Yet one more early attempt at a scientific theory of all civilisations is to be found in the writings of Gustave Le Bon, which had a certain fame at the end of the nineteenth century. His general theory of history was a simple one: that there are certain principles of development which have manifested themselves again and again, and will continue to do so. Racial character is the permanent factor in history, moulding institutions, languages, and doctrines in its own image: it can change, but only slowly and because of a change in sentiments and beliefs, and not at will but in accordance with the nature of the race. Among these 'races', Le Bon had a special interest in the Arabs, and spent much ingenuity in fitting them into the framework of his theory. In his view, Islam did not create the institutions or even the moral code of the Arabs: they already existed, and Muhammad could do no more than choose among them and give to those he chose the sanction of a religion. This he did as a political device, to achieve political unity, but he did it at a price:

> C'est l'homme sans doute qui a créé les dieux, mais après les avoir créés il a été promptement asservi par eux.[125]

Islam has slowly changed the racial character of the Arabs, and exercised on them a permanent hypnotic effect:

> Du fond de son tombeau, l'ombre du prophète règne en souveraine sur ces millions de croyants.[126]

But the constitution of other races has not been so much affected: on the contrary, each has remoulded Islam in its own image—for example, the Islam of India has become polytheist like all Indian religions.

Thus there is no Islamic civilisation; there is an Arab civilisation, formed by a combination of the moral and intellectual qualities of the Arab race with the unifying ideal given them by Islam. It is this combination which accounts for its great qualities but also for its defects: the pugnacity of the Arabs was good when there was a world to conquer, but later turned in on themselves and led to internal conflict; the domination of law caused stagnation of mind; autocratic rule again was good for the conquest of an empire, bad because everything depended on the character of the autocrat. Being what they were, the Arabs could never have developed further than they did; they cannot develop further now, and their attempt to Europeanise themselves is doomed to failure because it would involve changing their character.[127]

More elaborate formulations of such naturalistic theories were to come later, in the twentieth century, and to come indeed at a time when philosophers of science were giving a more subtle explanation of scientific method and the nature and status of scientific laws. Belated products of the scientific spirit of an earlier age, the systems of Spengler and Toynbee, doubtful if not desperate as they are about the prospects of western civilisation, are alike in their confidence about the power of human reason to formulate general laws. But their model is that of biology rather than physics, as it might have been a half-century earlier, and for both of them what is important is to discover the 'natural history', the life-cycle followed by all examples of the species called 'cultures' or 'civilisations'.

For Spengler, human history is the record of a number of different cultures each of which can be conceived of as a living being: individual, essentially different from the others, but subject to a similar life-cycle. The essence of a culture is its 'soul', creative of a fundamental symbol or concept of space, through which it views the world, and which is finally incomprehensible to those who do not belong to the culture; but all, however they differ and exclude each other, go through the same phases in the same period of roughly a thousand years. These phases are four: spring, summer, autumn, and winter, distinguished primarily by different attitudes towards the great 'myth' and its corollary, the new 'God-feeling' from which the culture springs, but secondarily by different forms of art and civilisation. Of these various cultures, one of those which most concern him is the Arabian or Magian, of which the fundamental concept is that of the dualism of two mysterious substances, Spirit and Soul, and of the world as a cavern.[128] But this 'Arabian' culture was not created by those whom we usually call Arabs, nor by Islam. The Arabs are themselves a product of it, and Islam is only a phase of something which had begun earlier. The 'Arabian' culture began around the first century AD in the area bounded by Nile, Tigris, Black Sea and South Arabian coast. The myth with which it began was first expressed in the great religious movements of the time: Jewish, Christian, Manichaean and Persian.[129] From that time for roughly a thousand years its history is continuous, and Islam makes no break in it. Its political institutions are unchanged: Diocletian was 'the first of the caliphs'.[130] Its art too continues on a single line: one style is exemplified in Persian fire-temples, Roman basilicas, Christian churches and mosques, and just as Diocletian was the first caliph, the Pantheon as rebuilt by Hadrian was the first mosque.[131] Even its religious ideas remain basically unaltered: Islam is not a new religion, it is the second or 'summer' stage of an older religious tradition, the stage of a puritanism which, like Protestantism in Europe, liberates the forces of popular opposition to the first official formulation of the religious myth. It differs from the similar phase in other cultures by its violence, and of that there are two explanations: the Arabian culture had grown up inside the classical, and it was a slow and arduous task for the Magian soul to liberate itself from the domination of classical thought. It is moreover a culture in which religion has the primacy—its law is an emanation of God, its authority is the consensus of the elect, its community is created by faith, and its inner movements therefore express themselves in violent assertions and denials.[132]

In Spengler's thought some balance is kept between the incommunicable individuality of a culture and the universal nature of its experience in time. In that of Toynbee, the main emphasis is clearly on the second: on the life-cycle of birth, growth, breakdown, of a disintegration which can be checked by the rise of universal churches and empires but then sets in again (unless men take heed in time), and of a new civilisation arising from the ashes of the old. Particular civilisations are only important to him as proving the general truth of the general law, or as possessing characteristics which are not allowed for in the theory and which therefore compel a change in it. For Toynbee as for Spengler, what at first sight appears to be the Islamic civilisation is a favourite object of contemplation: indeed, it is clear that, in very different ways, the two systems have been built on the basis of knowledge of the Near East and its religious cultures. Again, for Toynbee as for Spengler, the history of Islam takes on a new form when seen in the light of the theory. The rise of Islam did not mark the beginning of a new civilisation; like other universal religions, it came to birth at a late stage in the life-history of a civilisation which already existed, had already broken down, was in full disintegration, and from which a new civilisation would arise later. This previously existing civilisation was the 'Syriac', created by the stimulus of the Eurasian nomads on the north-eastern frontier of the Near East; by the tenth century BC it had passed its height and had its breakdown, but its disintegration was then violently arrested by the intrusion of Hellenism.[133] Held, so to speak, in suspended animation within the body of the Hellenic civilisation, when Hellenism decayed it had come to life again at that point of disintegration which it had already reached; and it was at this point that Islam emerged as the universal religion which appears when civilisations decay. Islam therefore did not mark a new birth but a revival of the Syriac civilisation: its religion expressed the alienation of the submerged Syriac proletariat, its caliphate was the universal state of a declining society; it could not stop the decline, it could only arrest it for a time, until it set in once more with the coming of an external proletariat—Turks and Mongols in Asia, Berbers and Beduin in North Africa.[134]

It was only after the death of the revived Syriac civilisation, according to Toynbee, that there emerged between the fourth and seventh centuries AD a specifically Islamic civilisation: at first indeed it would be more correct to speak of two sister-civilisations, the Arabic and Iranic, which only merged into one when the first was incorporated into an Iranic state, the Ottoman Empire. But even then the union was incomplete and forced: the Ottoman Iranic civilisation never flowered, it was flawed at an early stage by the split between Sunnis and Shi'is, and the Ottoman Empire, instead of being a universal state of the whole Iranic world, became an artificial union of half that world with an Arab world forcibly absorbed into it. The Arabs and their rulers never fertilised each other's culture, and the forced union broke down when the Arabs revolted against Ottoman rule, and when both of them underwent a process similar to that of Hellenisation—their violent incorporation into the modern Western civilisation.[135]

Such systems now have a curiously old-fashioned air. Few thinkers nowadays would be so confident that human phenomena can be treated in the same ways as the objects which the natural scientist studies; and even while the ideas of Toynbee and Spengler were being formed other thinkers, and above all Max Weber, were trying to discover some specific and adequate way of thinking about human societies. It is true, in Weber's thought also we find echoes of the past: as Gerth and Mills have pointed out

> Weber's conception of the charismatic leader is a continuation of a 'philosophy of history' which, after Carlyle's *Heroes and Hero-Worship*, influenced a great deal of nineteenth century history writing.[136]

Again, like earlier thinkers Weber tried to see all societies as being what Toynbee would call 'philosophically contemporaneous'; that is to say, abstracted from the temporal relationship of before and after, and laid out on a line to be thought about simultaneously. But in at least two important ways Weber differs from those who went before him: first, in his recognition that each society is unique and that the problem of the sociologist is that of reconciling the 'historicist' approach with the 'positivist', of accepting the uniqueness of each historical event but at the same time making valid general statements about it; secondly, in rejecting any attempt to explain what happens or what exists in terms of a single factor—whether it be 'spirit' or race or class or great men—and insisting that the concrete reality of a particular society can be seen in the light of many different concepts. Societies are unique, but exemplify certain recurrent types, themselves ultimately to be explained in terms of the nature of man. These types are numerous, and subtly described and distinguished from each other; and Weber's view of history allows not only for the influence of the charismatic leader but for the processes which continue once the charisma grows weaker. Moreover, the relationship of types to individuals in the social world is not the same as that of classes and individuals in the natural world. The types are 'ideal types', concepts (whether of a 'state' or of a 'process') abstracted from reality, given an inner logical consistency, and arranged in 'typologies' or scales of alternative types. They can be used to illuminate a concrete reality, but no more than that: for an existent being or historical process never wholly exemplifies an abstract type, seen in different lights it exemplifies many types to some extent, but is always more than the sum of them.

Thus, in the section on the sociology of religion in *Wirtschaft und Gesellschaft*, Islam like other religious systems is formally conceded its unique and separate existence, but an attempt is made to understand it by holding it in the light of several typologies. It is seen, first of all, as corresponding closely to the pure type of a prophetic 'book-religion', and one in which the sacred law is of particular importance.[137] As a prophetic religion, it is 'naturally compatible' with the class-feeling of the nobility: the religious wars which it preached were directed towards the acquisition of large estates.[138] But Weber thinks of it as differing from other prophetic religions, Judaism and Christianity, in the relationship between its ethical system and secular life. Its ethic is 'feudal', oriented— even in its mystical form—towards 'world conquest' and not towards 'world renunciation' as in Christianity.[139] Because of this, its institutions show such marks as the following:

the obviously unquestioned acceptance of slavery, serfdom, and polygamy; the disesteem for and subjection of women; the essentially ritualistic character of religious obligations; and finally, the great simplicity of religious requirements and the even greater simplicity of the modest ethical requirements.[140]

Again, its intellectual life was more restricted than that of Christianity. The development of metaphysics and ethics was in the hands of the 'priesthood', and 'tendencies towards rationalism were completely lacking in the popular dervish faith'.[141] Both because of its 'feudal' character and its 'anti-rationalism', Islam never possessed the characteristics which help to explain the development of modern European (and particularly Protestant) society: a kind of vocational asceticism, the rational control of everyday life, and behind it a moral tension—the tension between an ethics of salvation and an ethics of worldly success, held in uneasy balance by the conception that success is a sign of salvation.[142]

It is enough to state such views for the Islamic scholar to have doubts. That Islam is seen as virtually a pure type of warrior-religion runs counter not only to what is now known and thought about it, but also to Weber's own sense of the complexity of the particular existent being. His Islam is too simple to be true, and this is clearly so because he does not know much about it; his views seem to have been largely derived from Wellhausen and Becker. Islam indeed is the only great religion of which a special and detailed study is not to be found in his *Gesammelte Aufsätze zur Religionssoziologie*. His remarks about Islam are therefore less informed than about other religions; and—what is more important—his typology was never modified to take account of the specific features of Islam.

Nevertheless Max Weber, more perhaps than anyone else, has formulated the problem of how to think about society; his tension between 'historicism' and 'positivism' is still there—everything in history is unique and unrepeatable, but we *must* think about it, and thinking involves general concepts. Where Weber fell short, as other thinkers of secular type had done, was in regarding Islamic society as one among many, and one which in itself offered no important theoretical problem. To some extent this defect may have been accidental: had he lived longer he would no doubt have added a careful study of the sociology of Islam to those he wrote on other religions. But behind such an accident there may lie something else: that peculiar difficulty which thinkers in western Christendom have always had in finding a category in terms of which Islam can be understood, being neither 'east' nor 'west', neither Christian nor unequivocally non-Christian and, wherever one places it, being linked with Europe by a long and intimate, an ambiguous and usually a painful relationship. Jacques Berque has gone further, and suggested that we can see here an example of the 'instrumental' view of other societies which is typical of the modern West: 'le pendant spirituel du commerce d'échelles, ou de l'expansion politique.'[143]

Since Weber wrote there has been a certain change. We can never quite neglect the political motivation of our studies, and no doubt the emergence of a unified world of independent states on the way to modernity has thrown a stronger light on the different paths by which they enter the modern world. But behind this we can discern, as in the nineteenth century, certain general movements of the mind. The great advances in detailed understanding of Islam in the last century were made, as we have seen, by men who came to Islam with certain concepts taken from the new science of religious origins and development; in the present age, few scholars have been untouched by the development of sociology, social anthropology, and social and economic history. Their influence is to be seen in the work of Jacques Berque,[144] so sensitive to the originality of Islamic culture, of von Grunebaum,[145] with his concern for the way in which the Islamic faith served as a 'point of crystallisation' for a new socio-political unity, and what had begun as a religion became a civilisation, and of Gibb,[146] with his classical conception of medieval Islamic society as formed by a continual and unending permeation of matter by form—on the one side, peoples of diverse stocks and traditions drawn into the *umma*, and on the other the unifying force of the social teaching of Islam. From such writings two guiding principles emerge. First, 'Islamic society' is different from others, and only to be understood in its own terms; secondly, it is not a single existing society but an 'ideal type', a group of related characteristics which have embodied themselves in different ways and to different extents in many existing societies. The religion of Islam, its law, and its principles of political and social organisation, injected into different communities, have created a whole class of societies, by no means identical with each other, but all differing specifically from non-Islamic societies in ways only to be understood through a typology formulated for this purpose.

But all this remains an aspiration yet to be fulfilled, and it is only rarely that the detailed work of Islamic scholarship has been fertilised by sociological thought. Watt's *Islam and the Integration of Society*,[147] for all its insight, is perhaps too much affected by an older type of 'generalising' sociology: the rise of Islam is seen as an example of a process which may occur, in some form, wherever certain conditions exist. A new book, Rodinson's *Islam et capitalisme*,[148] springs from a more conscious and mature reflection about sociological method. Accepting in general a Marxist view of the relations between the economic organisation of a society and its prevalent ideas, he nevertheless insists that this does not imply a rigid view of the historical process, a belief that all societies must move through the same sequence of phases; the societies in which Islam has been dominant may in some respects have followed a path peculiar to themselves. But here too it is necessary to make a distinction. Islamic societies have not been formed by Islam alone: it is wrong to suppose

> que les hommes d'une époque et d'une région, que les sociétés obéissent strictement à une doctrine préalable, constituée en dehors d'eux, en suivent les préceptes, s'imprègnent de son esprit sans transformation essentielle, sans qu'ils l'adaptent à leurs conditions de vie et à leurs modes de pensée implicitement suggérés par celles-ci.[149]

But Rodinson's book is rather a programme of research than itself a work of original scholarship. It is in the work of another French scholar, Claude Cahen, that we can find perhaps the most systematic attempt to apply mature sociological concepts to the realities of Islamic society. The guiding principles are explained in an essay in *Studia Islamica*. In the last resort human history is a single process, and the rise of Islam did not by itself create a new world. We cannot in fact understand Islam and its development unless we realise that it took place in 'une société matérielle' which already existed. The adoption of a new religion did not by itself change economic conditions or social structure. In course of time indeed the governments, laws and practices of Islam *tended* to change society, but only up to a point, and the basic problem for the economic or social historian is this: beginning with the ancient societies incorporated in the Muslim political structure, to see what became of them, as compared with those of western Europe and Byzantium.[150] This problem has been explored in a number of detailed studies which have had much influence on the way in which scholars of the present generation look at Islam.[151]

3 Muslims and Christians[1]

In a learned and brilliant book recently published, Professor Zaehner has drawn a distinction between two types of religion, in terms not only of their answers to questions but of the questions themselves. On the one side stand Judaism and Christianity, on the other Hinduism and Buddhism:

> ... whereas the Christian starts with the idea of God, the Hindu and Buddhist do not: they start with the idea of the human soul. Basically they are not interested in what we should call God at all: they are interested in the realization here and now of a state of existence in which time and space and causation are transcended and obliterated; they aim at the realization, the felt experience of immortality ... On the one side you find claims to exclusive truth through revelation, on the other you find a total indifference to so-called dogma and a readiness to admit truth in all and any religious manifestation. On the one side you find prophets claiming to speak in God's name, on the other sages interested only in piercing through to the immortal ground of their soul.[2]

If this division be accepted, it is clear that Islam stands on the same side as Christianity, for it too is concerned with God, revelation, moral responsibility and the Last Things. But, of course, there is a difference. Christianity came before Islam in time, and from the beginning Islam took, so to speak, official notice of Christianity, recognised it as a valid revelation and Jesus as an authentic prophet, one of the line which ended in Muhammad, 'the Seal of the Prophets'. For Christians, however, it is, to say the least, a matter of doubt whether, and in what sense, the Islamic revelation can be regarded as valid: what need can there be for prophecy, when the event to which the line of prophets pointed has already occurred, what purpose in a further evangelical preparation, when that which the ages have prepared has come to pass in the fullness of time? There is also of course another difference even more important: Muslims accept Jesus as a prophet, but do not believe He was Christ, the Son of God. They do not believe in the Incarnation, the Redemption or the Trinity, and some find it difficult to understand that Christians really believe in them.

Thus, quite apart from political and social tensions, which however old are nevertheless accidental, there is an inescapable religious tension between Christians and Muslims, and in a sense it is reflected in a tension inside each religion. Muslims accept Christianity as *they* interpret it and reject it as Christians interpret it, but—to take the matter one step further—in a certain type of mystical theology Islam draws near to Christianity. On the other hand, the Christian attitude towards Islam ranges all the way from utter rejection of the validity and even the sincerity of Muhammad's claims to the acknowledgment, not only that there can be an authentic experience of God in Islam, but that in some sense Muhammad must have been a prophet. To quote Professor Zaehner again:

> The Quran is, in fact, the quintessence of prophecy. In it you have, as in no other book, the sense of an absolutely overwhelming being proclaiming Himself to a people that had not known Him . . . Nowhere else is God revealed—if revelation it can be called—as so utterly inscrutable, so tremendous, and so mysterious. That Muhammad was a genuine prophet and that the authentic voice of prophecy made itself heard through him, I for one find it impossible to disbelieve on any rational grounds . . .[3]

Between total acceptance and total rejection there are innumerable gradations; where among them shall we place Canon Cragg's new book? He is one of our finest Islamic scholars, has lived among Muslims, and is well fitted to write about the Christian presence in Islam. He has given us a difficult, subtly expressed book written out of a fine religious sensibility as well as wide knowledge. It is not easy to define his attitude to Islam in a few words, and in a sense this is a measure of his understanding of the problems involved, and his refusal to resolve the inescapable tension in some mechanical way. Like Professor Zaehner, he emphasises that Christianity and Islam deal fundamentally with the same things— 'prophecy, worship, prayer, mercy, law, scriptures, patriarchs,

God's signs in nature, creation and sin—all . . . religious categories
having to do with the Divine relation to the human situation'. But
he knows also that

> there is a difference between a revelation that contents itself
> with law, and a revelation that brings personality: . . . that
> whereas the Divine mercy in Christ is pledged to man's renewal
> in grace, in Islam it is related in unpledged form to his pardon
> under law.[4]

Canon Cragg walks skilfully on the tightrope between identity and
difference, but every now and then he seems in danger of slipping.
From sheer desire to be fair, to put the case for Islam at its
strongest, he does sometimes seem to come near to reading
Christian meanings into Islamic concepts. Canon Cragg would
reply that he is not describing Islam as most Muslims believe and
live it, but is trying to hint at its 'ultimate dimensions'. It seems to
us that a Christian can write about Islam in two ways. He can
write about it as it exists and has existed (and if he does so it is
only right and charitable that he should, like Canon Cragg,
describe it at its best), or he can write about the truth of Islam,
which in his view will be Christianity; but between the two is
there room for a third entity, an ideal Islam which has a Christian
soul but nevertheless is not Christianity?

Dr Hussein's book may seem at first sight a book of the same
type, written from the other side, an attempt by a believing
Muslim to uncover the Muslim presence in Christianity. This
work is, the dust cover tells us, 'the first ever written in the world
of Islam, which makes a thorough study of the central theme of
the Christian faith', that is to say, the Crucifixion. The reader
who takes these words in their most obvious sense may be
disappointed; for, in that sense, the book is not about the
Crucifixion at all.

Any book about the Crucifixion would surely have to ask
whether the Jesus who was crucified was also the Son of God; and
a book by a Muslim would also have to ask whether Jesus was
crucified at all, for orthodox Muslims, on the authority of the
Qur'an, have believed that, at some undetermined moment in the
process which began with His arrest and ended with the Crucifixion, Jesus was raptured into heaven and someone else was
killed in His place.

To both these questions Dr Hussein gives the orthodox Muslim answer. Jesus for him is a great moral teacher, to be regarded with reverence, as Muslim theology has always regarded Him; but He is the Jesus of Islam—the prophet 'Isa, to give Him His Muslim name—not the Redeemer of Christian doctrine. He was condemned to be crucified but not actually killed; 'God raised him unto Him in a way we can leave unexplained.' This the author asserts in passing, almost casually, and indeed from his point of view it does not matter whether Jesus was killed or not. Since He was an apostle, it is what He said, the content of His message, which is crucial. What He did and how He died have only a derived importance, in that they explain the message or guarantee its authenticity; the Crucifixion, even had it taken place, would have been less important than the Sermon on the Mount. It would even, in a sense, have been unworthy of Jesus, and unworthy of the divine source of prophecy; for it would have shown weakness, and 'when was weakness one of the attributes of God?' This question uncovers a whole world of difference between Muslim and Christian thought.

In another sense however the book *is* about the Crucifixion. As Canon Cragg points out in his introduction, the Cross has two faces:

The Cross is not only a redemptive demand . . . it is also, seen from the manward side, the deed of rejection in which men registered their verdict against the teaching and personality of Jesus.[5]

Dr Hussein's book is first of all a study of that 'deed of rejection', of the collective guilt of those who condemned Jesus. The study is made by means of a series of imaginative reconstructions of what went on in the minds of those who were involved in some way in the tragedy which ended on a Friday in Jerusalem—of Pilate and Caiaphas, Lazarus and Mary Magdalene, the disciples and several symbolic figures whom the author seems to have invented. The bulk of the book indeed consists of this series of soliloquies, dialogues, and narratives, connected by links of commentary. Not all the studies are of equal interest: that of Mary Magdalene has a sort of perverse sentimentalism not unlike a design by Aubrey Beardsley, but there is real depth of insight in that of Caiaphas,

who would have been perfectly prepared to welcome Jesus if He
had only come at a more convenient time:

> Why has this man brought his teaching particularly to us? . . .
> I admire what he proclaims enormously. But I don't want his
> religion established here among us. In our present emergency
> what we need most of all is quietness, inner cohesion and unity.[6]

Dr Hussein is not only writing about the guilt of those who
condemned Jesus, he is writing about all human guilt; the
condemnation of Jesus had its own poignancy, but was not
different in kind from other sinful acts. It is Dr Hussein's purpose
to illustrate two propositions about human nature and morality:
the first, that individuals are morally responsible not only for what
they do but for what society does in their name, and when society
commits crimes to further its interests, every individual member of
it shares the guilt in some way and to some degree; the second,
that such crimes are committed because men go against the dictates
of their conscience.

The principles of conscience, Dr Hussein maintains, are laws of
nature just as are those of physics or biology. All created beings
obey laws, but there is a hierarchy of laws which corresponds to
the order of complexity in created things. The laws of reason are
'higher' than those of biology; but the laws of conscience are higher
still, and give reason its limits and the ends it should pursue.
These laws of conscience differ from 'lower' types of law because
they have no material force to compel men to obey them; man is
free, and only obeys by a 'spiritual compulsion'. Sin arises when
the spiritual compulsion does not work as it should do, and that
may happen in either of two ways: when conscience can no longer
restrain human intelligence within the bounds of morality, and
when, at the other extreme, it grows 'more domineering, while
reason paled and natural vigour dwindled'. When a man or a
society is healthy, the two fulfil their natural roles:

> Reason is constituted by its nature to direct. The nature of
> conscience is to restrain and warn. If each only adhered to its
> natural role the good effects of both would prevail. But to expect
> conscience to be a guide and reason a curb is to ask what is not
> within the nature of either.[7]

Abstract as this may seem, it has practical implications; the book is more of a tract for the times, even more political, than it appears at first sight. Its total denunciation of war reflects the universal problem of our time: 'Man has no right to bring about the death or suffering of anyone on any ground whatsoever.' But it is also a sermon directed specifically at the Muslim community. The distinction it makes between the realm of reason and that of religion may seem a truism to a Western reader accustomed to the Christian distinction of the two realms, and to the concept of Natural Law; but it has quite another significance when drawn within a Muslim community, for the religious law of Islam has claimed to provide a detailed code of ideal morality, social as well as individual. When Dr Hussein says that religion has essentially the negative function of setting limits which reason must not infringe, and that it can only influence the social and political order in this indirect and negative way, he is in fact claiming for society the right to create its own institutions and laws in the light of changing social needs and in disregard of tradition.

He is not, of course, the first Muslim in modern times to make such a claim. To distinguish the sphere of religious doctrine from that of social legislation was indeed one of the purposes of that 'Islamic modernism' of which the greatest figure was another Egyptian, Shaykh Muhammad 'Abduh. The effect, if not the purpose, of the modernist writings was subtly, perhaps not always consciously, to re-interpret the concepts of Islamic thought in the light of the scientific naturalism of nineteenth century Europe. For all the originality of his literary method, Dr Hussein is a belated follower of this school of thought.

Perhaps the most interesting part of his book is the terminal note on the psychology of the disciples, and the effect on them of their failure to strike a blow to save Jesus. It is on this level of human psychology, the author suggests, that the difference between the great religions can be found. The essential teaching of all religions is the same; all reduce themselves to 'the three fundamentals: faith, love and restraint'. But the human response of Muslims, Christians and Jews to the prophetic message was different. It is the author's thesis that there took place, in the early history of each of the three communities, an event which shaped its psychic structure—a 'traumatic' event, to adopt an expression of the psychologist. For the Jews, this event was the Exodus, 'the escape of the Jews from certain and utter annihilation by a most extraordinary miracle', the effect of which has been the coexistence of abject despair and unbounded hope in the mind of the Jews. In the history of Islam, it was the little fight of Badr, when a small number of Muslims defended their prophet successfully against a larger force of the fighting-men of Quraysh. In Christian history, it was the failure of the disciples to save their Master:

> Such a psychological stress could not be without effect on their psyche. Is it not just possible that such effects can be inherited? The best Christian in his most sublime moments is a sad man.

If, as Dr Hussein believes, Islam and Christianity are fundamentally the same, then clearly the only essential difference between them will lie in the human response. But it will seem to Christians that Dr Hussein has misjudged their response because he has not fully grasped what it is to which they believe they are responding. Missing the Crucifixion and the Incarnation, he has missed a whole dimension of Christian psychology, the joy born of

> . . . the good news of peace—the peace of personal wholeness for man and of the acknowledged worship of God . . . If it is the Muslim sense of the adequacy of law alone, and of a mercy that has no Cross at its heart, which makes the Christian faith in Christ crucified so strange an enigma, then by the same token, that faith must be the heart of the relevance of the Gospel of peace to men in Islam.[9]

4 Volney and the Ruin of Empires

Constantin-François Chassebeuf was born in 1757 at Craon in northwestern France; his father was a local lawyer of humble origin, his mother belonged to a bourgeois family which owned land. He studied at the Collège d'Angers in Anjou, which is said to have been Jansenist in spirit, and there he may have acquired that critical attitude towards religious authority which was to mark his writings. At the age of eighteen he went to Paris to study medicine; he began to study Arabic as well, and frequented the salons of d'Holbach and Madame Helvétius, where he met Condorcet, Diderot, Franklin and others. It was in these early meetings that his thought and life found their direction: men must use their reason in order to discover the principle of virtue on which depends the stability and prosperity of human societies, and should study history to understand the origins and nature of religion.

In 1782, having come into a small fortune, he left France for the Near East, partly no doubt from youthful curiosity, but also because he wished to see those parts of the world where the ideas which still governed civilised life had grown up, and to compare the greatness of the past with what was left; his biographer has suggested, but without giving strong evidence, that he may also have had a secret political mission on behalf of Vergennes, then Minister of Foreign Affairs. His journey lasted more than two years. Arriving at Alexandria in January 1783, he spent some weeks there, and then went to Cairo where he remained for several months. At the end of the year he travelled up the Syrian coast to Aleppo, and the first eight months of 1784 he spent at the Melkite monastery of Mar Hanna (St John) in the village of Khanshara in the mountains of Lebanon, studying Arabic and making some short journeys in Lebanon and the interior of Syria. Towards the end of the year he moved southwards to Jerusalem and elsewhere in Palestine, before returning to France by way once more of Alexandria in the spring.

In 1787 there appeared his *Voyage en Syrie et en Egypte;* he used for it, as for his later writings, the pen-name of Volney.[1] The book had a success which was both immediate and lasting, and not only in France; in the same year it was published in an English translation of which a second impression was needed in 1788. It was therefore as a man of some reputation that he went in 1789 as one of the deputies of the Third Estate of Anjou to the meeting of the Estates-General which the King had summoned. He took some part in the discussions of the Third Estate (or, as it was later called, the National Assembly), but before the end of 1790 he had become uneasy about the tendencies towards national enthusiasm and the intolerant exercise of power which were beginning to show themselves; his was the kind of rational spirit and faith in the possibility of creating by general consent a new and juster order which often appear at the beginning of a revolution. He withdrew into silence, and occupied himself with writing his second famous book, *Les Ruines, ou Méditations sur les révolutions des empires,* which appeared in 1791 and was also well received. There followed a period of unsuccessful farming in Corsica, and a few months in prison by order of the Committee of Public Safety (not, it seems, for political reasons but for debts incurred in Corsica). Then in 1795 he started on his second great journey, to the United States of America, where he spent three years. He visited Jefferson (whom he had known in Paris, and who was later to help in translating his *Ruines* into English), met Washington, and travelled inland as far as a French outpost on the Wabash river, left isolated by France's cession of Louisiana to Spain and Canada to England in 1763.

Back in Paris in 1799, he played a certain part in the movement which brought Bonaparte to power as First Consul. He had first met the new ruler as a young officer in Corsica, and his book of travels had been one of the books which Bonaparte took with him on his Egyptian expedition and read carefully (much later it was to form part of his library on St Helena). For some time the relations between the two were close and cordial. Volney was made a Senator, but once more he was disappointed, first by Bonaparte's policy of conciliating the Church and then by his assuming the title of Emperor. There is a story, which may not be true, that Napoleon ended one stormy discussion by kicking the

Senator in the stomach. He tried to resign from the Senate, but his resignation was not accepted, and once more he withdrew into silence, showing his disapproval from time to time by voting against measures proposed by the Emperor. For the rest of his life he occupied himself mainly in writing: a book on the physical geography of the United States, based on his observations while there, and studies on ancient history and the methods of teaching oriental languages. He died in 1820 full of honours. The Emperor had made him an Imperial Count, and the title was confirmed at the Restoration; he was a member of the French Academy, occupying the twenty-fourth *fauteuil,* which had once been that of La Fontaine; he was also a member of the American Philosophical Society of Philadelphia.

Of his works, it is fair to say that only his *Voyage* can now be read with pleasure and profit. Perhaps he himself would have given greater importance to the *Ruines,* but Sainte-Beuve was right to say that its reputation was exaggerated. The *Voyage* however is of lasting importance. This is partly because of its influence during the French occupation of Egypt and on later travellers, but mainly because of its own merits. With his habitual good sense, Bonaparte pointed out where those merits lay. On 26 October 1799, shortly after his return from Egypt, he received Volney and praised his book. According to the note which appeared in the *Moniteur,* he told the author that he was almost the only traveller who had not told lies, and that to the merit of truthfulness he added a remarkable power of observation.

When he wrote his book indeed Volney was consciously going against the habit of previous travellers to exaggerate what they had seen and to indulge their powers of fantasy:

In vain may travellers celebrate the gardens of Rosetta and of Cairo. The Turks are strangers to the art of gardening, so much cultivated by polished nations, and despise every kind of cultivation . . . In vain may they tell us of the orange-trees and cedars, which grow naturally in the fields. Accustomed as we are to combine the ideas of opulence and culture with these trees, since with us they are necessarily connected with them, we do not discover the deception . . . In vain do they describe the Turk softly reposing under their shade, and happy in smoking his pipe without reflection. Ignorance and folly, no doubt, have their enjoyments, as well as wit and learning; but, for my own part, I confess I could never bring myself to envy the repose of slaves, or to dignify insensibility with the name of happiness.

He does not place his own figure in the foreground of the picture. There is almost nothing in the book about his own adventures, and from internal evidence alone it is not even possible to be sure exactly where he went and at what time. He does not express the feeling evoked in him by the contemplation of the monuments of past greatness, in fact he scarcely mentions them at all: he says something about the Pyramids and the temples of Baalbek, he quotes what the English traveller Wood had written on Palmyra, but that is all. His one concern is to give a cool, careful and accurate description of the lands of Egypt and Syria and their peoples, so far as he has seen them.

This description is not only accurate, it is also detailed and full. His power of observation was indeed great, and he noticed and could describe the colours and shapes of the physical world, what people wore and how they behaved, as well as the political events of the day. His analysis of the nature of Mamluk rule in Egypt, and his narrative of the reign of 'Ali Bey, until recently formed the basis of what most historians wrote about eighteenth century Egypt. In the present generation a number of scholars have corrected his picture and filled it in, but what he says can still be used, provided it is used with care. There is not much else in the book about Egyptian society; while in Cairo he did not know enough Arabic to mix freely with Egyptians, and much of what he says seems to have come from European and Syrian merchants. But those parts of Syria which he knew well—the Lebanese mountains, Aleppo, and parts of Palestine—are more fully described, and much can be learned from him still.

Contrasting Volney with another well-known traveller of the day, Gibbon said: 'Of the two modern rivals, Savary and Volney, the one may amuse, the other will instruct.' Sainte-Beuve passed a similar judgement on him. While paying tribute to his scientific accuracy, he regrets that there is so little of Volney himself in the book: 'he has nothing of Montaigne in him, his writing is dry and lacks colour, the book would have been more attractive had it been a simple narrative of a journey and so given the reader the feeling that he was travelling with the author'. A modern reader will probably think better of the work than this. A clear, pointed and easily flowing narrative may by itself please us; besides, as we read we are always conscious of an individual taste and judgement. It is clear that Volney liked Syria more than Egypt, Aleppo more than Jerusalem, the mountains more than the plains, and admired the Muslims more than the eastern Christians:

> The Mahometans . . . though haughty even to insolence, possess however a sort of goodness of heart, humanity, and justice; and above all, never fail to manifest great fortitude under misfortune, and much firmness of character.

In spite of what Sainte-Beuve and others have said, it may be that sometimes the lines are drawn too sharply: was Ottoman rule quite so lawless and destructive, was Lebanese life so free and happy, as he implies? If there is an excess of emphasis, it springs from what he was trying to do. His description is related to a system of clear and firmly held convictions which, in his view, were confirmed and illustrated by what he had seen in the Near East. He was an *idéologue,* a believer in the primacy of reason, and equally opposed to the cult of feeling, the claims of the Church, and the power of absolute rulers. His views were expounded most fully in *Les Ruines.* Happy and prosperous societies are so not because of the working of mysterious supernatural forces, and not primarily because of the physical nature of the lands in which they live, but for moral and social reasons which we can fully understand: the prosperity of empires depends on the existence of governments ruling in accordance with a natural principle of justice, embodied in laws and upheld by general assent. The true enemies of society are the cupidity of rulers unrestrained by law, and ignorance of the principles of rational morality, an ignorance fostered by the priests of false religions. These beliefs explain his political career: his brief hopes in the period of the National and Constituent Assembly and the cult of the Supreme Being, his later withdrawal, his opposition to Napoleon who had brought back the priests and made himself absolute ruler. It explains also why the emphases lie where they do in his *Voyage.* For him, Ottoman and Mamluk rule was a paradigm of lawless tyranny, of a hierarchy of oppression in which each man lords it over those beneath him:

> The bearer of the orders of the Sultan becomes himself, for that moment, the Sultan . . . how numerous must be the abuses of

unlimited powers in the great, who are strangers both to forbearance and to pity, in upstarts proud of authority and eager to profit by it, and in subalterns continually aiming at greater power.

In contrast, Lebanese mountain society at least had a certain natural equilibrium based on the freedom of each man to possess his land in security, and a government which was a not unstable blend of monarchy, aristocracy and democracy.

5 Wilfrid Scawen Blunt and the Revival of the East

In 1885 the creator of revolutionary Pan-Islamism, Sayyid Jamal al-Din al-Afghani, went to London to stay with Wilfrid Blunt, minor poet and amateur of nationalist movements. The purpose of the visit was to discuss with Lord Randolph Churchill, then at the peak of his transient power, a solution for the problems of Egypt and the Sudan. Various suggestions were put forward, but they came to nothing, and the visit ended unhappily: two of Jamal al-Din's oriental friends, so Blunt records,

> seem to have quarrelled over politics or religion and ended by beating each other over the heads with umbrellas. I had to beg them to leave the house, and the Seyyid followed them. One must draw the line somewhere, and I have now suggested to the Seyyid that he should take up his quarters elsewhere . . .

Quarrels over politics or religion, and fights with umbrellas or more lethal weapons, are the stuff of refugee life. The pages of Polish and Russian and Italian history in the nineteenth century are full of such scenes; but this one was given a special poignancy by the complex and masterful characters of the protagonists, and by the vast gap across which their relationship was tenuously stretched. Between the 'wild man of genius' (to use Blunt's own description of Jamal al-Din) and the Victorian squire and man of letters there was indeed a great gulf, only bridged by the wildness and the passion for justice which they shared. It was Blunt's destiny to cross such gulfs, to assure the peoples absorbed by the expansion of his nation's power that one member at least of that nation's dominant class was on the side of the defeated.

Descended from a line of Sussex squires, Wilfrid Scawen Blunt was born in 1840, not at Crabbet Park, his father's house, but at Petworth House, the home of his father's sister and her husband

George Wyndham. Petworth was one of the great houses of England, with its long line of graceful rooms, its matchless collection of pictures, and the great park where the deer grazed and fed out of the children's hands, and it remained all his life 'a vision of mundane stateliness', and not without influence on his own fastidious, splendid and self-willed mode of life. In his early years it was an unattainable vision, for he never knew the safety of a stable childhood. When he was two his father died, and his mother, a brilliant, poetic and restless woman, moved with her three children from home to home. She found rest of another kind: in 1851 she summoned her children to her and told them she had been received into the Roman Catholic Church. They burst into tears, but not for long, and in the next few months all three were themselves received. There were to be aspects of Blunt's life of which the Church could not approve, but it left its mark on him. He went to Catholic schools, Stonyhurst and then Oscott, and at the age of eighteen passed the examination for the diplomatic service. He then served for ten years as attaché in various legations and embassies, and resigned from the service in 1869. The 1860s were a peaceful decade in European politics, disturbed by no great crisis; the duties of a young attaché were not burdensome, and Blunt had much time to give to other matters. An early photograph shows a young man of romantic good looks tinged with melancholy, leaning with careless elegance upon a chair beneath which a dog lies sleeping: he was twenty when it was taken, and just about to plunge into the series of romantic loves which were to form one of the main themes of his life until old age. Indeed, he always thought of himself as having stepped from one life to another when, during a period of service in Paris, he met and fell in love with 'Skittles'—Catherine Walters, a figure who could have been produced by no age except the Victorian, a famous courtesan, mistress of the most elegant young men of the day, but who kept the friendship of her former lovers and many others, holding court in her house in Mayfair and giving parties to which smart and famous men, although not their wives, were pleased to come, and where even Mr Gladstone was sometimes to be seen. Blunt always thought of 'Skittles' as the greatest love of his life, and she was the subject of his early love poems.

During these early years of diplomatic travel and romantic love, indeed, his poet's vocation had revealed itself, and he produced several volumes of poems which had some success. Some of his friends thought him a great poet, but at a hundred years' distance it would be difficult to claim as much for him. He had technical skill, a good ear, the power of expressing feelings and expounding ideas in fluent and moving verse. These qualities made him an excellent translator, and his version of the *Mu'allaqat* can still be read with pleasure:

> Gone are they the lost camps, light flittings, long sojournings in Mina, in Ghaula, Rijam left how desolate.
> Lost are they. Rayyan lies lorn with its white torrent beds, scored in lines like writings left by the floodwater.
> Tent-floors smooth, forsaken, bare of all that dwelt in them, years how long, the war-months, months too of peace-pleasures.[1]

But he lacked the strangeness of the great artist, and neither in his images nor in his words is there the leap beyond the predictable which marks off the major from the minor poet. Still, he was a first-class minor poet, and he had the friendship and respect of other poets, even those of a younger generation and a very different school. In 1914, W. B. Yeats, Richard Aldington, Ezra Pound and four other poets of the new generation travelled down to his country home to dine with him and present him with a poetic address written by Pound and marking their admiration:

> Because you have gone your individual gait,
> Written fine verses, made mock of the world,
> Swung the great style, not made a trade of art,
> Upheld Mazzini and detested institutions
> We who are little given to respect, respect you . . .

No profound meeting of minds seems to have taken place: Blunt confessed that he could not understand what they were talking about, and complained that they had confused Mazzini with 'Urabi. But at least the food (roast peacock served in its feathers) was worthy of the occasion, and he was touched by their gesture.[2]

Beneath the loves and the poetry there was another stream flowing in his life at this time. Darwin's *Origin of Species* was published when he was nineteen. He asked his confessor for leave to read it; permission was refused, but he read it all the same. This was, he later recorded, his 'first deliberate sin'. A little later, he was deeply shaken by his sister's decision to become a nun. These two incidents marked an important stage in his rejection of Catholic teaching and discipline, and opened a period of inner conflict. How could he reconcile what Catholic theology taught about the nature of man and the universe with what Darwin's theories seemed to imply? How to bring the impulses of his own wild nature, his passionate acceptance of the sensuous world, beneath the imperatives of the Church? The conflict was finally resolved, at least to all appearances. He later said that he had 'always since I was twenty-one at the bottom of my mind remained incredulous'. He ceased to be a practising Catholic; in old age he confessed that, try as he might, he could not believe in an after-life; and his will laid down that when he died, he should be buried in unconsecrated ground and without the ministrations of the Church. But he never lost a longing to be able to believe, and a respect for those who had the gift of faith. He knew some of the Catholic 'modernists', including Father Tyrrell, and after meeting him, noted in his diary that 'forty years ago a priest so outspoken would have saved my faith'.

In 1869 he married Lady Anne Noel, a grand-daughter of Byron who had been brought up by the poet's wife, her grand-mother, and shared something of her character. Timid, unworldly, with a scholar's mind but without much insight or humour, uncompromisingly virtuous, unyielding and tough, she was better fitted perhaps to be the companion of his youthful adventures than the sharer of a patriarchal life with a self-centred believer in the claims of romantic love. The marriage broke up in the end: from 1906 they lived apart, and, although the breach was healed by correspondence in 1916, it is probable that they would still, even had she not died soon after, have preferred to live apart, without 'that acute suffering caused by our being in each other's presence'. Their only child, Judith, inherited her father's brilliance and personal beauty and added to them a wilfulness of her own: disputes over property, and her knowledge of his unfaithfulness to her mother, produced in her a profound bitterness against him, removed for a moment on his deathbed, but then renewed to affect the thirty-five years of life that remained to her.

The first years of the marriage, however, were happy and harmonious. The death of his elder brother in 1872 made him lord of his family estates in Sussex. He and his wife spent much time looking after them and enlarging and adorning Crabbet Park, but they also embarked on a series of extended journeys in the Near East. They went in 1873 to Constantinople and Asia Minor, in 1874 to Algeria, in 1875-6 to Egypt for the first of many times. In 1877-9 they made two vast desert journeys such as no European had undertaken before that time: the first took them from Damascus through the Syrian desert to Baghdad; the second, from Damascus down the Wadi Sirhan to Jabal Shammar, thence eastwards to Baghdad and from there to southwestern Persia. Their experiences and observations on these journeys were recorded in Lady Anne's two books, *Bedouin Tribes of the Euphrates* and *A Pilgrimage to Nejd*. Then in 1880-1 they made a second and more extended stay in Egypt to learn Arabic, and travelled from there to Jedda and Syria.

There were several reasons for these journeys: youthful love of adventure; the need to improve Blunt's health, threatened by the consumption which had killed his brother; the desire to buy Arab horses for what later became the Crabbet stud; the longing to escape from the conventions of nineteenth century England into what seemed an ideal world of freedom and fantasy. But the experience went deeper perhaps than they had at first intended: the aristocratic travellers, for whom the outside world and its inhabitants were no more than the background against which their acts and fancies could shine, found themselves taken prisoners by that world's claims.

The Near East that the Blunts first knew was at one of the moments of crisis in its history. Had they visited it ten years earlier, the shape of its problems might not have been clear to them; ten years later, its destinies would have been fixed. But in the 1870s great changes were taking place, and there still seemed something for a man of good will to do in order to ensure that they went in the right way. By this time the movement of administrative and legal reform, started by Mahmud II in Constantinople and Muhammad 'Ali in Cairo, had been proceeding for a generation. It had met with some success both in Turkey and in Egypt, but in both it now found itself faced with three problems, each related to the others. The administration was corrupt, badly trained and ineffective, and could not apply the new measures properly. There was a growing gap between governments and people, for while on the one hand, the government had gone further in reform than the uneducated could grasp or accept, on the other, there was growing up a new educated class which wanted to go further and faster than its rulers, and indeed to impose constitutional limits on the government itself. Most ominous for the future, the influence of Europe was growing and its relationship with the Near East was changing. Ten years earlier the reformers had looked on England and France primarily as the friends of progress, but now they appeared in another light. The Ottoman and Egyptian governments were falling deeply in debt to European bondholders; and in the great 'eastern crisis' of the 1870s the existence of the Ottoman Empire was threatened by one Power and only saved by the intervention of others. A year or two later, the Powers which had intervened to save the centre of the Empire began themselves to nibble at its edges: France occupied Tunisia in 1881, and Britain, Egypt in 1882.

All this process Blunt and his wife observed at close quarters, and much of it is recorded in their books. On their first visit to Asia Minor they saw the corruption of the Ottoman government, and in Egypt two years later they witnessed the extortions practised on the Egyptian peasants by Isma'il's tax-collectors to satisfy his European creditors. They were not much impressed by the attempts at reform. For example, Midhat Pasha, the reforming statesman who had only recently been Grand Vizir during the period of the first Constitution, and who was governor of Damascus when they were there in 1878, disappointed them:

> ... a more essentially commonplace, even silly talker, or one more naively pleased with himself, we had never met out of Europe ... one such reforming pasha as this does more to ruin Turkey than twenty of the old dishonest sort.

But the simple and patient goodness of the ordinary people struck them the more forcibly by contrast with the badness of the governments. As European romantics they were perhaps already inclined to find perfection in what was simple, unspoiled and spontaneous, and we may discount some of their enthusiasm for the Anatolian and Egyptian peasants; but the impact of central Arabia was more profound and more personal, for there it seemed to them that they had found not only a people of primitive goodness but a government of simple justice and freedom. The dynasty of Ibn Rashid, which had established its rule in central Arabia from its capital at Hayil after the collapse of the first Wahhabi kingdom, was not perhaps so virtuous as Blunt thought it; its annals were stained like those of other dynasties, but what Blunt admired in its rule did really exist—the unforced ease in the relationship of ruler and subjects, the existence of a code of justice preserved by the public conscience and which the ruler could not ignore. It seemed to Blunt and his wife to be the form of government most appropriate to the temperament of the Arabs, and most admirable in itself; he was later to write that this experience 'of the ancient system of free government existing for so many centuries in the heart of that wonderful peninsula, was to confirm me in the enthusiastic love and admiration I already entertained for the Arabian race'.

It was perhaps the sight of this flourishing Arab polity which convinced Blunt that, in spite of the decay of the more advanced Islamic countries, Muslim society still contained in itself the seeds of its own revival. From this time indeed the regeneration of Islam became one of his main concerns. When he returned to England in 1879, he plunged into the study of Islam and Islamic politics. He learnt something of them from two unusual men then living in London. The one was Malkum Khan, a Persian of Armenian origin who had introduced into Persia Comte's religion of human-ity, had acquired a certain political influence and then been sent by the Shah into honourable exile as Ambassador to the courts of Europe; the other was Louis Sabunji, a Catholic priest from Iraq who had by this time lost his faith in his own religion and was actively engaged in Pan-Islamic journalism in the interests of the Khedive Isma'il. But Blunt was soon to learn about Islam from more authentic sources. His journey to Egypt in 1880 was undertaken primarily to improve his knowledge of Arabic and of modern Islam, and a fortunate accident led him to the man best able to help him: a young Egyptian shaykh of the Azhar, Muhammad 'Abduh, who was one of Jamal al-Din's closest disciples. Jamal al-Din had spent the years from 1871 to 1879 in Cairo, gathering around himself a group of young Egyptians and imparting to them his own ideas about what Islam really was, how it could be brought back to life, and how the attacks of the European Powers could be repelled. The gist of what Blunt learnt from 'Abduh, and through him from Jamal al-Din, he embodied in one of the best of his books, *The Future of Islam*, published in 1882.

Islamic society was in decay, and the attempts made to revive it had only hastened the decline: to introduce modern secular laws, as Turks and Egyptians had tried to do, was to introduce anarchy, since the new laws weakened the moral basis of society, which was the faith and law of Islam. What was needed was not to ignore religion, but to strengthen it by reinterpreting Islamic law in the light of modern European morality. But for this a law-giver was necessary: in other words, the true caliphate must be restored, with a spiritual function and authority. The Ottoman Sultan did not possess the qualifications needed to exercise *ijtihad*, and the reform of Islam could only come about if the caliphate returned to the Arabs. The Ottoman Empire was dying, and when it finally expired a council of *'ulama* might be held at Mecca to choose an Arab caliph.

Some of these ideas seem more likely to have been Blunt's gloss on the thought of the Islamic reformers than what 'Abduh himself told him. An English romantic was more likely to see the salvation of Islam in the unspoiled Bedouin Arabs, than was a Muslim *'alim* brought up in the tradition of Islamic urban civilisation, with its hostility to the nomads who ruined settled life and whose laws and customs were not in accordance with the *shari'a*. The idea that the Ottoman Sultanate was doomed, and that Islam could only be saved if the Arab caliphate was revived, was to become common among Arab thinkers twenty years later, but at that time it was an idea more likely to occur to an European than to an Arab Muslim with a sense of responsibility for the safety and unity of *dar al-islam*. But even if Blunt's accuracy may be doubted, there is no doubt of the strength of his feelings about Islam and the Muslims, and this he had occasion to show during his stay in Egypt. When he had first been there, five years earlier, he had been inclined to hope that his own country would be able to protect the peasants against the oppression of their rulers, but by 1881 the influence of the bond-holders and the worsening financial chaos of Egypt had drawn England and France deeply into the internal affairs of the country, and not on the side which he believed to be in the right.

The growing influence of the British and French representatives over the Khedive seemed to him to carry with it the danger that a conflict between the Khedive and the nationalist reformers like 'Abduh would become a conflict between the Egyptian nation and Europe. He went out to Egypt once more towards the end of 1881 to do what he could to steer things in the right direction. Shortly after his arrival a group of army officers, headed by Ahmad 'Urabi Pasha and broadly in sympathy with the aims of the civilian nationalists, obtained power. Blunt met 'Urabi, was impressed by him, and with 'Abduh's help drew up a statement of the nationalist aims which was sent to the Prime Minister, Gladstone, and published in *The Times*. For a time he tried to act as intermediary between 'Urabi and the British Consul-General, but the publication in January 1882 of an Anglo-French note, written in threatening terms, brought nearer the danger of European intervention to restore the Khedive's authority and crush the nationalists. Blunt now thought he could be more useful in London. He returned to England, and for the next few weeks worked hard at winning support and bringing pressure to bear on the government. He was received well by Gladstone, but not so well by the Foreign Secretary, Granville, who seemed bent on intervention; at the same time he kept in touch with the nationalists, and passed on to them a warning that, if a British invasion occurred, it would take place from the Suez Canal. But, as the situation worsened, he found himself impotent to help, and his friends dissuaded him from going out again to Egypt, where he could no longer do anything useful. He watched with mounting despair the bombardment of Alexandria, the landing of British troops, the battle of Tall Al-Kabir, the occupation of Cairo, and the restoration of the Khedive's authority. 'Abduh was imprisoned and later sentenced to three years' exile; 'Urabi and the other leaders of the army were also captured, and it was intended to bring them to trial. Blunt knew that the Khedive intended to have them condemned to death, and it seemed likely that the British Government would stand by and do nothing, on the pretext that this was a purely Egyptian matter. Almost single-handed he set on foot a movement to ensure that the trial should be fair and 'Urabi be adequately defended. All his friends and contacts were used; an English barrister was sent out to defend 'Urabi; yielding to pressure, the Foreign Office changed its attitude, and finally a compromise was reached by which 'Urabi pleaded guilty to rebellion and was sent into honourable exile in Ceylon.

From this time until Blunt's death in 1922, the support of movements for national independence against foreign rule was a major purpose of his life. He gave sympathy and help to quite a number of such movements, but his efforts were mainly devoted to three of them, the Irish, Indian and Egyptian. To Ireland he gave several years of hard work in the 1880s, when the Irish question came to a crisis. Those were the years when the Irish nationalist party, given new life and direction by Parnell, was pressing its claim to home rule with more determination than before. His Catholic upbringing inclined Blunt to favour the Irish cause, and in 1885 he began to take an active part in politics as a supporter of home rule. At first he was active on the Conservative side. It was still possible for a Conservative to come out in favour of Irish nationalism, for on this issue party lines were not yet firmly drawn, and the gospel of 'Tory Democracy' preached by Blunt's friend Lord Randolph Churchill held out hopes of a truly progressive conservatism. But Blunt was defeated as a Conservative candidate, and when shortly afterwards Gladstone came out in favour of Irish home rule, he felt obliged to join the Liberal party. He did so reluctantly, since he could never forget Gladstone's part in the occupation of Egypt, and he had no faith in him as a statesman: he called him 'a pedant, a babbler, an impotent old fool'. But the defeat of the Liberals in the election of 1886, fought on the Irish issue, convinced him that nothing could be done through Parliament, and he turned to direct action, to which his temperament was more inclined. At the heart of the Irish question lay the problem of landownership. For the peasants, home rule was important because it alone seemed to offer them the chance of securing ownership of the land they cultivated; the landlords opposed home rule for the same reason, and, since many of the great English families were absentee owners of Irish land, this was one of the causes of the fierce resistance of the Conservative party to the Irish claims. As nationalist activity increased, the tenants took to withholding all or part of their rent; the landlords retaliated by evicting them, with the support of the government. This was an issue on which Blunt saw a clear-cut distinction between right and wrong:

> It is absurd to argue that the landlord, who destroys a hundred families by evicting them, is guiltless because his act is *legal*, and that the peasant who resists or retaliates is a murderer because his blows are illegal. There must be a principle of justice underlying the law, or the law itself is a crime.

He went to Ireland, plunged into the movement against the evictions, and in 1887 defied the new Crimes Act introduced by

Mr Balfour, the Chief Secretary for Ireland, and held a prohibited public meeting. He was arrested, tried and sentenced to two months' imprisonment, which he served. He was not unkindly treated by the prison officials, one of whom told him, 'It is not often we have a gentleman like you here, but when we do we know how to consider him'. But he was to remember for long afterwards the cold and sleepless nights and the 'black discipline' which depressed his normally high spirits.

He had visited India in 1884–5, furnished with letters from Jamal al-Din and others, and with his reputation as champion of Egypt's rights still fresh. He met some of the early nationalist leaders, both Hindu and Muslim, and attended the National Conference at Calcutta; there he made a speech affirming his belief that 'all nations are fit for self-government'. He later embodied his observations in his book *India under Ripon*, but, although he continued to have some contact with Indians, he did not return there or play an active part in its affairs. It was quite otherwise with Egypt however; here he was too deeply committed to withdraw. In 1884–5 he was in the thick of discussions and negotiations about the settlement of the Egyptian and Sudanese problems. He put forward various plans—the Mahdi would release Gordon and undertake not to advance northwards if Britain would withdraw from Egypt; Blunt himself would go to the Sudan, provided with letters from the Sayyid, to negotiate an agreement; Jamal al-Din would go to Constantinople to help Sir Henry Drummond Wolff, then trying to make an Anglo-Turkish agreement about Egypt. It was to discuss such plans that Jamal al-Din made his ill-fated visit to London, but they came to nothing, and indeed it is difficult to believe that any of them could have been carried out.

At this time Blunt was prohibited from entering Egypt, because of the part he had played in the events of 1881–2. But a year or two later the prohibition was lifted and he was free to return. In 1881 he had bought, at Shaykh 'Ubayd near Heliopolis, a garden which Ibrahim Pasha had laid out and which Isma'il's harem had used as a country retreat, and from 1887 for almost twenty years he spent the winter months there. Much of his time was given to the delights of country life, to enlarging the house, tending the garden and travelling in the desert, but he also played an active part in Egyptian public life. He could do so because of two personal contacts. 'Abduh returned to Egypt from exile in 1888, and from then until his death he exerted influence as judge, Mufti of Egypt, creator and reformer of schools, and writer. He and Blunt remained on close and easy terms. Blunt gave his friend a piece of land near Shaykh 'Ubayd; 'Abduh built himself a house there, and when Blunt was in Egypt they saw each other frequently. To some extent their relationship was political: they thought alike about Egyptian politics, and Blunt could help 'Abduh by conveying his ideas to the British Agent and Consul-General, Cromer. Together they tried to persuade Cromer to rely less on the Khedive and his Turco-Egyptian courtiers and to have Egyptians of good talent and character appointed to ministries. But they had another link stronger perhaps than the political. Each, in his own way, was involved in the great nineteenth century problem of Science and Religion. Blunt had lost his faith through reading Darwin, and he suspected that the same was true of 'Abduh: 'I fear he has as little faith in Islam . . . as I have in the Catholic Church'. This was almost certainly untrue, but 'Abduh only saved his belief in Islam by restating it in terms appropriate to the age of biology and progress, and the problem remained alive in his mind. He and Blunt used to talk about it, and once they made a pilgrimage to Brighton together to talk with Herbert Spencer.

With Cromer Blunt had correct and outwardly friendly relations for a number of years after his return to Egypt. They were about the same age and came from the same world; both had inherited the English political tradition that private life should be separated from public; and each could be useful to the other—Cromer could learn from Blunt what Egyptian nationalists thought, and Blunt could only have influence in Egyptian affairs in that he had access to the British representative. They used to meet and talk about politics, but they did not really like each other. Cromer wrote about Blunt with contempt in his *Modern Egypt*, and Blunt, once his attempts to persuade Cromer to change his policy had failed, became ever more opposed to him and what he stood for. As time went on indeed he tended to regard Egyptian politics as a struggle between himself and the British Consul-General, and when Cromer finally left Egypt in 1907 he regarded it as a personal triumph:

I . . . was fast asleep when a telegram was brought me signed by

Meynell containing the joyous announcement of Cromer's resignation. I was at once fully awake and laughing so that the bed shook under me, nor could I stop for several minutes. I sent back in return the single word, Whoo-whoop! I am off to Chapel Street, and Clouds tomorrow, feeling like a huntsman at the end of his day's sport with Cromer's brush in my pocket, and the mask of that ancient red fox dangling from my saddle.

By that time Blunt had already left Egypt for ever. After the death of 'Abduh in 1905 his main human link with the country was severed, and increasing age and the breach with his wife made him more reluctant to go back there. But he remained closely in touch with Egyptian affairs. He spent much time writing a narrative of Egyptian events based on his diaries; it came out in a series of volumes, beginning with *The Secret History of the English Occupation of Egypt*, a lively and indispensable book, although its statements are not to be accepted without question. For a time he was connected with an 'Egyptian Committee' in London, and wrote in their monthly periodical; and he inspired an outspoken criticism of British policy, Theodore Rothstein's *Egypt's Ruin*. Nationalist leaders like Mustafa Kamil came to see him in his Sussex home, and so did Egyptian students; one of them, who later became a distinguished politician of the old régime, still makes the pilgrimage to Blunt's tomb on each visit to England, in memory of kindness received.

This ceaseless political activity took place within the context of a social life which was conventional—even if the conventions of the English landed aristocracy of his time seem strange to our middle-class world. At the same time as Blunt was helping rebellions against his own government, his social life was passed in the midst of the Victorian *beau monde*, which lay much nearer to the centre of power than such groups usually do. He was himself the founder of a not very serious society, the Crabbet Club, composed of clever and witty men of the world who met together at his house once a year 'to play lawn tennis, the piano, the fool, and other instruments of gaiety': they included men later to become famous and important, like Lord Curzon. He was also, by family connection and personal predilection, close to 'the Souls', a

group of clever men and pretty women . . . bent on pleasure, but pleasure of a superior kind, eschewing the vulgarities of racing

and card-playing indulged in by the majority of the rich and
noble, and looking for their excitement in romance and
sentiment.

This position he owed, not to his family (for there were many
families greater and with wider estates), but to the singular charm
of his personality and his great attraction for women. He made
many conquests, although whether his morals were much looser
than those of other men of his time and set, it is difficult to say.
The private lives of men in his position were conducted with great
discretion, and it is only now that a corner of the veil is being
lifted. He himself recorded his own life, as well as what he knew
or thought he knew about the lives of others, in a vast series of
diaries. Some of the political sections he revised and published in
his own lifetime, but the full diaries he bequeathed to the
Fitzwilliam Museum at Cambridge, not to be opened until twenty-
five years after his death. When they were opened in 1947 what
was found led to another embargo of twenty-five years being
clapped upon them.

It may seem difficult to reconcile the fighter for Egyptian
freedom with the old man whom Desmond MacCarthy described
as 'a very handsome vain old man, with a spreading beard and
eagle nose, and a voice sinisterly soft'. It may also seem absurd
and a mark of insincerity that, on the eve of going off to Ireland to
defy Balfour's Crimes Act, he should have been playing tennis
with Balfour at a country-house party. But in fact the two sides of
his life were closely connected with each other. It was because of
his friendships and contacts that he could be of use to nationalist
leaders; he could go straight to the Foreign Office or Downing
Street, as they could not at that time. Moreover, it was because his
closest personal links were with the ruling class of England that
he felt in so intimate a way what he regarded as their denial of the
principles they should respect. It is true, he never thought much of
the Liberals even when he formally belonged to them. We have
seen what he thought of Gladstone; his opinion of Asquith and
Grey was not much higher; the only Liberal who really impressed
him was the young Winston Churchill, who, he recorded in his
diary, 'fills me with admiration and delight ... I should not be
surprised if some day he made the Indian cause his own ... he is
almost converted to the view that the British Empire will

eventually ruin England'. With the Conservative leaders however he was on closer terms. Lord Randolph Churchill had been his friend, George Wyndham was his cousin and the dearest friend of his later years, Salisbury he always respected even when he disliked his policy; Balfour too, although never a friend, he found an agreeable acquaintance.

On the whole they did not take him seriously as a politician. But he took himself seriously, and indeed he suffered something for his political convictions, not only during his brief term of imprisonment but during longer periods when he was estranged from his friends. The Prince of Wales once called him a 'disloyal and eccentric Jesuit'; after his Irish adventures there was a decade during which he was looked at askance by the Tory landed families who formed his own world, and even George Wyndham, who loved him, thought he must be out of his mind. It is worth asking, therefore, what it was which impelled him to persist in a course which brought him little profit and much vexation. In a sense the question need not be asked: his was the kind of passionate and impulsive nature which throws itself into the fight rather than taking up an attitude after careful and rational thought. What he had seen in Egypt and Ireland made it impossible for him to remain inactive; and in Egypt there was also the strong feeling of friendship and loyalty aroused in him by 'Abduh. Perhaps too some part was played by vanity: it was good to feel that, almost alone of the men of his age and class, he knew and cared for the Egyptians and Indians, that they came to him for help, and told him that his name would always be remembered among them.

There was however a motive more important than all these. Beneath the vanity and selfishness of Blunt's character there lay a stratum of firm conviction. He was an English patriot, but after the fashion of his age and class. His England was that of the countryside, of the squire living like a little king among his peasantry, looking after them, loving the land and its ways, only enjoying the fruits of his position because he fulfilled its duties. Beyond England he looked first of all to Europe, and once more to the traditional Europe of the gentry whose family ties, culture and interests knew no national frontiers. He was a 'pre-Imperialist' rather than an 'anti-Imperialist': he belonged to an age which regarded colonies more as a burden than as a privilege, which did not think it necessary to the interests or honour of England to extend her rule, but which could not ignore the obligations of that

rule where it existed. In India, as in Egypt, he believed that the
British presence could be, and indeed had already been, a source
of great benefits:

> The apologists of British rule boast that they have given India
> peace, and peace doubtless is a noble gift; but it has given her
> far more than this. What really deserves all Indian thanks, and
> is indeed an inestimable acquisition, because it contains within
> it the germ of a reconquest of all the rest, is that it has given her
> liberty of thought. This is a new possession which India never
> had, and never perhaps would have had, but for English
> influences . . .
>   I am not one of those who love the East only in its picturesque
> aspects, and I have no quarrel with Europe because it has
> caused the East to change. I note, indeed, the destruction of
> much that was good and noble and of profit in the past by the
> unthinking and often selfish action of Western methods; but I
> do not wish the past back in its integrity, or regret the impulse
> given to a new order there of thought and action . . . To speak
> plainly, the ancient order of Asiatic things, beautiful as it was,
> had in it the germs of death, for the one reason that it did not
> change . . . Asia has been awoke . . . and is slowly informing
> herself with the victorious reason of the West, and assimilating
> to her needs that intellectual daring which is her adversary's
> strength.[3]

But the idea of an intellectual mission seemed to him quite
different from the idea of a right to rule which began to be put
forward by the publicists of imperialism in the last quarter of the
nineteenth century. He despised and disliked the vulgarity of the
new Imperial spirit, the product of the new England of the urban
middle class which was threatening his own England; and he was
shocked by the vainglory, the arrogance and the brutality of its
exponents. There were certain incidents which he could never
forget, because they seemed to him to express in a vivid way this
new spirit: the bombardment of Alexandria, the desecration of the
Mahdi's tomb, and the famous affair of Denshawai. What shocked
him most, perhaps, was the cold brutality with which Arthur
Balfour, a man of his own world, could talk of the Irish
nationalists: 'They will get severe imprisonment with hard labour
—so severe that those who have not strong health will not be able

to stand it. I shall be sorry for Dillon as he has got some good about him. He will get six months' hard labour, and, as he has bad health, it will kill him.' He was so outraged by this statement, made to him in a private talk, that he published it; Balfour denied having said it, and most of Blunt's friends condemned him for making use of a private conversation. But Blunt always insisted that Balfour had in fact said this, and that it symbolised the coldness which lay at the heart of the Imperial spirit:

> . . . the evolutionist creed of man, which in the sixties and seventies imposed itself on the thought of the day as a development of Darwin's *Origin of Species* . . . represented the world of life no longer as an ordered harmony, but as in its essence a struggle for existence where whatever right there was was on the side of might, and where it was a waste of pity to deplore the extinction of less capable races, either of beast or man, before the competition of their more capable rivals. The rule of the survival of the fittest was seized on eagerly by our imperialist politicians as a new argument in favour of their political ambitions, and enabled them to stifle what promptings there might be in them of pity for those they were destroying inherited from a less scientific age. This line of reasoning . . . had the effect of giving to characters naturally kind and just a certain amount of political insensibility, hardening at times into ferocity.[4]

In trying to defend the rights of Ireland or of Egypt, he could therefore think of himself as striking a blow for that conception of 'ordered harmony' in which both as squire and as poet he believed.

6 H.A.R. Gibb: the Vocation of an Orientalist

Hamilton Alexander Rosskeen Gibb was born in Alexandria on 2 January 1895, the younger son of Scottish parents, Alexander Crawford Gibb and Jane Ann Gardner. His father, who was in Egypt as manager of a land reclamation company in the Delta, died in 1897, but his mother remained in Alexandria after her husband's death and taught there in the Church of Scotland Girls' School. He was sent back to school in Scotland when he was five years old. From 1904–12 he studied at the Royal High School in Edinburgh, but spent some summer holidays with his mother in Egypt. In 1912 he entered Edinburgh University and worked for an honours degree in Semitic languages, but the First World War broke out before he could finish his studies. He served first as an instructor in a training unit for artillery officers, then in France and Italy with the South Midland Brigade. When the War ended he did not return to Edinburgh, although he was awarded a 'war privilege' Ordinary MA. He went instead to the School of Oriental Studies, newly established in London. He was appointed Lecturer there in 1921, obtained the degree of Master of Arts in 1922, and in the same year married Helen Jessie Stark (known to her friends as Ella), whom he had first met when he had returned to Scotland as a child; they had two children, a son, Ian, and a daughter, Dorothy.

He remained at the School until 1937, first as Lecturer, then as Reader, and finally as Professor of Arabic. In 1937 he was elected to the Laudian Chair of Arabic at Oxford, and he held it, together with a professorial fellowship at St John's College, until 1955, when he accepted an invitation to go to Harvard as Jewett Professor of Arabic, University Professor and, shortly afterwards, Director of the Center for Middle Eastern Studies. In 1964 he suffered a severe stroke which impaired his powers of speech and movement, and returned to England soon afterwards, although he remained nominal Director of the Center for a little longer. He lived in retirement, at Cumnor Hill outside Oxford until after his wife's death in 1969, then for his last few months at Cherington near Stratford-upon-Avon until his death on 22 October 1971.

He received many honours during his life. His old College, St John's, made him an honorary Fellow when he left Oxford. He was a Fellow of the British Academy, the Danish Academy, and the American Philosophical Society of Philadelphia; honorary Fellow of the American Academy of Arts and Sciences and the Medieval Academy of America; member of the Academy of the Arabic Language in Cairo, the Institut d'Égypte, and the Arabic Academies of Damascus and Baghdad. He was one of the editors of the first edition of the *Encyclopaedia of Islam* in its later stages, one of those who initiated the new edition after the Second World War, and a member of its editorial committee until he went to the United States. He was created Knight Bachelor in 1954, and also held French and Dutch honours.

Such are the bare outlines of his life if seen in terms of acts and achievements; it falls into five periods which can be clearly distinguished—the years of formation, of teaching in London, Oxford, and Harvard, and of retirement. But for a man who lived so much within his mind and imagination as did Gibb, and for his biographer, the intertwined secret histories of his life may be more important. Of certain strands in his private history, he would not have wished me to write even had I been able: his religious faith and his life in a closely knit family. Of two others I can say more: the development of his mind as a scholar and thinker, and his influence on students, colleagues, and friends, on the world of orientalist scholarship and on a wider world of readers of English, to whom he showed the way by which, for a whole generation or more, they would understand the religion of Islam and the society and culture of its adherents. These inner processes can be set within the framework of his external life, for in many ways the moves from London to Oxford, and from Oxford to Harvard, were linked with changes in his work as scholar and teacher.

It is difficult to say how it all began. Sights and sounds half remembered from childhood, chance meetings, words spoken by teachers, books read and perhaps forgotten, can give direction to the lonely impulse of delight from which a scholar's vocation springs:

A door opens, a breath, a noise
From the ancient room
Speaks to him now. Be it dark or bright
He is knit with his doom.

We can only guess at some of the ways in which this particular
vocation may have been formed. Alexandria must have given
something: the city where he was born, where his father died,
where his mother lived until she too died in 1913, and to which he
returned more than once in boyhood, making the long sea journey
from one Mediterranean port to another; by imaginative appro-
priation he belonged to two worlds, that of the eastern Mediterranean as well as Scotland. (His must have been a lonely boyhood:
he rarely spoke of it to his own children, but kept one reminder of
it until he died—an album of picture postcards, many of them sent
him by his mother and with the same sentence repeated on them,
'May you have as happy an Xmas and New Year as the days we
spent at Bad Nauheim'—simple words which unlock a world of
feeling). The Royal High School may have been important in
other ways. Founded by the Augustinians of Holyrood but taken
over by the city magistrates after the Reformation, it remained the
main school of Edinburgh until new ones were founded in the
earlier nineteenth century. It gave boys from modest homes a solid
classical education and sent them out to work in the Empire or the
great world of British trade; there must have been an awareness of
imperial rule over distant peoples, of long trade routes linking
different countries and continents, of varieties of human society,
and on this too the imagination could feed. The most famous
alumnus of the school was Sir Walter Scott, but even had this not
been so, any bookish Scottish schoolboy of the time would have
read his novels, and one of them may have made a lasting mark on
Gibb's mind. It is not fanciful to see in the special interest he
always showed in Saladin, and the unexpected warmth and colour
which came into his prose when he wrote of him, the influence of
The Talisman; fifty years later he was still giving it to students as
a work of art from which they could learn much about Islamic
history.

At the University in Edinburgh he began Hebrew, Aramaic,
and Arabic, and was initiated into the discipline of Semitic
philology by good teachers. This had been one of the great
branches of scholarship in the nineteenth century, rooted as it was

in some of the central intellectual concerns of the age: the attempt to construct a genealogy of languages, races, and cultures, and to understand the Bible through a precise understanding of its words and of the beliefs and practices of the peoples of the ancient Near East. But although he respected it and dutifully sent copies of his first book to his teachers in Edinburgh, it was not his chosen discipline, and he may have learnt more from the University in ways other than through his special studies. In the Scottish academic tradition, general principles should be grasped before details were studied; this was the bent of his own mind, always trying to relate facts to general ideas. The mind should be trained by a balanced study of philosophy, the classics, and natural science: this was to be his ideal, and was one of the things he singled out for praise when he wrote an obituary article on his great contemporary Louis Massignon. Every student had to take at least one course in philosophy. The two brothers who held the chairs of philosophy and provided the teaching available to him, James Seth and A. S. Pringle-Pattison, taught a Scottish variation of the Kantian philosophy and may have played some part (as we shall see) in forming his view of Islam; he is recorded as having taken Seth's course in moral philosophy in his second year.[1]

His studies at Edinburgh were cut short by the coming of war. Had he been in the habit of expressing general moral sentiments, his view of that and other wars would no doubt have been that of any deeply humane and serious person. But he always enjoyed using his mind, and at a certain level his war service interested and satisfied something in him. He never lost his interest in campaigns and battles, and his practical intellect enjoyed learning new techniques and finding new ways of solving problems. (A scholar who went to consult him on a problem in Arabic received a lecture on different ways of growing potatoes, others were instructed in bee-keeping and railway timetables).

It was in the years immediately after the War that he found his vocation. Started only a few years before, the School of Oriental Studies in London was very small when he first went there: in 1920-1 there were only two teachers of Arabic and only six internal students. Even within London University it was marginal, and this was to be important for him; one of his lasting concerns was to rescue oriental studies from their marginal position in the universities, and insert them into the central stream of intellectual life from which they had first emerged. But at the School he found teachers, and that was what mattered most. In these obscure and complicated subjects not everything which is thought or discovered is published at once, and it is important for a young scholar to insert himself into a living tradition of scholarship, to find teachers who will not only give him the technical secrets of their craft but will lead him to the frontiers of knowledge and direct his mind to urgent problems. Two scholars did this for Gibb in different degrees. One was the Director of the School, Sir E. Denison Ross. He was a pleasure-loving man of the world, who would not at first sight have seemed the natural teacher for an austere, unworldly, perhaps over-serious young Scot, but Gibb found in him and respected (as he was to make clear in an obituary article) a total devotion to scholarship, provided only it was living, and inflexible judgement on scholarly matters.[2] Ross gave him at the start of his career kindness and encouragement and a subject for his thesis, the Arab conquest of central Asia, from which he gained a lifelong concern for great historical themes, the conflict and interaction of societies and cultures, and for historical geography.

The other teacher, whose influence went deeper and lasted longer, was Sir Thomas Arnold, whom Gibb was eventually to succeed as Professor of Arabic. Arnold initiated him into a central tradition of European scholarship: he had himself studied at Cambridge with Robertson Smith, who had studied with Wellhausen and others of the great German scholars. But he had added something of his own: a specifically historical concern with the way in which Islam had spread and its institutions been formed, and a moral concern for its present welfare. He had taught for a time at the Anglo-Muhammedan College at Aligarh, and while there is said to have shown his sympathy for his Muslim colleagues and students by appearing in oriental dress; nobody who knew him could have imagined Gibb showing his sympathy in the same way, but the concern was there. Of Arnold's famous books, *The Preaching of Islam* dealt with the continuous, almost invisible expansion of the Muslim community over the world, and *The Caliphate* with the problem of authority in Islam; both were subjects to which his pupil would return.

In those years there was a third person whom Gibb thought of as a teacher and from whom he learnt much: an Egyptian, Muhammad Hasanayn 'Abd al-Raziq, who taught at the School for a time between 1920 and 1923. Gibb was later to call him 'my honoured teacher' and dedicate a book to him.[3] When in later years he went to Cairo he would stay with him, not in one of the quarters frequented by foreigners but in the unfashionable bourgeois suburb of Zahir. It was perhaps through his relationship, which seems to have been personal as well as academic, that he acquired his feeling for the values of the traditional Egyptian Muslim urban life: not the Franco-Ottoman life of the aristocracy or that of the Levantine and European communities, but something simpler, more firmly rooted in the past, and in his eyes more authentic.

During Gibb's fifteen years as a teacher in London he published his first important writings: his MA thesis, *The Arab Conquests in Central Asia* (1923); a translation of selected passages from the traveller Ibn Battuta (1929); *The Damascus Chronicle of the Crusades* (1932), another translation, from a work by Ibn al-Qalanisi, with a perceptive historical introduction; a general survey of *Arabic Literature* (1926); 'Studies in contemporary Arabic literature' (published in the *Bulletin of the School of Oriental Studies* between 1928 and 1933);[4] an essay on the influence of Arabic upon European literature in *The Legacy of Islam* (1931); and *Whither Islam?* (1932), a collection of essays by different hands on the present state and prospects of the Muslim world, edited and provided with a long introduction by him.

A reader who looks through these works with a knowledge of what was to come later will be struck at once by their wide range. They cover almost (but not quite) the whole span of the interests he was to show throughout his life; it was as if he were making a preliminary survey of his whole field of study before taking up each subject in a systematic way. The reader will be struck also by the maturity of thought, taste, and scholarship which these works show—not yet perhaps the writings on Islam, but certainly the historical and even more the literary works. One at least of them sounded a new note in Islamic scholarship: his studies of contemporary Arabic literature were the first attempt by a scholar trained in the European tradition of literary study to apply critical standards to the new writing in Arabic. There were already present that balance and measure which his older contemporary Levi Della Vida singled out as the distinctive mark of his mind, in the *Festschrift* which his colleagues and students gave him on his seventieth birthday.[5]

How should we define the scholarly personality now revealing itself in the 'young Professor Gibb' who so astonished Levi Della

Vida and others when they met him at congresses or elsewhere in his twenties and thirties? At the heart of it lay an abiding concern with the Arabic language. He had a complete knowledge of it in its classical and modern forms, and a sense of its fundamental unity throughout history. (He spoke it with some hesitation, perhaps because he valued it so highly, but given time could say what he wanted in it). He liked teaching Arabic, and told me towards the end of his life that he had taught elementary Arabic to someone or other every year of his teaching career, and every time had learnt something new. (Here too perhaps was a legacy of the Scottish academic tradition, in which the professor gave elementary as well as advanced instruction). But Arabic was important for him not so much for its own sake as because of the literature written in it, and because it had meant so much to Arabs and Muslims. The imagination of the Arabs had expressed itself above all through language, 'the most seductive, it may be, and certainly the most unstable and even dangerous of all the arts'. With that love of general ideas, that desire to link the particular with the general which marked his mind, and which also was not without its dangers, he went on to suggest that the Arabs had a special attitude towards their language:

> upon the Arab mind the impact of artistic speech is immediate; the words passing through no filter of logic or reflection which might weaken or deaden their effect, go straight to the head . . . the Arab artistic creation is a series of separate moments, each complete in itself and independent, connected by no principle of harmony or congruity beyond the unity of the imagining mind.[6]

When writing of the literature expressed in the language, he had that same firm and continuous consciousness of the unity of its development. His little book *Arabic Literature* shows that by the time he was thirty he had read his way through much of it and formed his own personal judgements. His essay in *The Legacy of Islam,* one of the best of his works, shows that he had the same wide knowledge of several European literatures.[7] He read very deeply in English and French, and to a lesser extent in German, Italian, and Spanish; he knew some Russian; his Latin was good, but he once said that his Greek and Hebrew had been casualties of the First World War; he showed surprisingly little interest in the other great Islamic languages, Persian and Turkish; Chinese was what he would really have liked to learn.

Apart from literature, it is difficult to say how much the arts meant to him. He knew the history of European music, and listening to it gave him pleasure. As a student and colleague of Arnold he was certainly aware of the problems of Islamic art, but looking at pictures does not seem to have played a great part in his life, and although he would go a long way to see an important building, what concerned him perhaps was less its beauty than its historical significance or the technical problems involved in its construction. He had no great concern for the elegance of his possessions: he and his wife lived in an orderly, neat, and comfortable way; his clothes, his books, his furniture and his houses were well cared for but were for use rather than display. On the other hand he had very acute visual sensibility. His handwriting both in English and Arabic was beautiful; he could describe the way in which the sunlight fell on the backs of his books at every hour of the day; he had, perhaps as an inheritance from his ancestors, a vivid sense of the land, its shapes and colours, the relations of one region to another, the products and inhabitants of each. The geography of the Muslim world lay near the centre of his interests.

If his intellectual curiosity began with language and literature, it reached far beyond, even in those early years. He was always trying to cross frontiers between disciplines or civilisations, to show unexpected connections or how one thing could help to explain something completely different. In his first book he combined Arabic with translated Chinese sources to illuminate the history of central Asia; if he translated Ibn Battuta, it was because his was a book which could tell us much about the life of vast parts of Asia and Africa; in the same way, Ibn al-Qalanisi could be of help to historians of the Crusades. In all this there was something of the pure self-moving curiosity of the scholar, the mind going its own way at its own pace, but there was something else, the need to impose unity on what he knew, to relate facts to principles and blend them both in a single vision; beneath the surface of this outwardly mild, self-controlled man—almost too mild, almost too much in control of himself—there was a strange and passionate imagination.

He was usually conscious of the danger that imagination and the speculative mind might outrun the need to be loyal to the facts.

His self-control hid (or sometimes did not hide) an inner tension. In his dealings with other people he was just, loyal and affectionate, but always inclined to judge them by high standards. His affections showed themselves in almost hidden ways, by a gesture or an occasional smile of astonishing sweetness; his judgement would express itself more often in impatience than anger. He looked at himself in this way too: he was always trying to hold in a balance the need for scholarly precision and the demands of the speculative intellect and unifying imagination—everything must be linked with everything else, but in a careful and accurate way.

Although he only wrote one passage of explicit self-revelation (to be quoted later), his view of what a scholar should try to do can be deduced from what he wrote about others. Among the obituary articles he wrote is one on his predecessor as Laudian Professor, D. S. Margoliouth, a man of very great learning and complex personality, and known for the elaborate irony with which he expressed or concealed his convictions. Gibb did not find in him the balance he sought:

> ... the ironical tone which informed his observations disturbed many of his European and sometimes infuriated his Muslim readers. The soundness of his judgment was inevitably called in question where insight rather than literary scholarship was demanded.[8]

At the opposite extreme stood Gibb's great contemporary, the French orientalist Louis Massignon, towards whom his attitude was complex. His relations with French scholars were good; he loved their language and its culture, admired the precision and seriousness of their work and the ease with which they could express abstract ideas, and perhaps something in him responded to the formality of French manners. In Massignon he greatly appreciated the vast learning and culture, the intensity of feeling and conviction, the originality of mind, the poetry, in a word, although it is a vague word, the genius; but he had reservations about some aspects of his scholarship, and there is a note of affectionate criticism in what he wrote of him:

> Louis Massignon was too rich a personality, too complex and many-sided to be enclosed within neat formulas and categories. The outstanding character of the man was a web of loyalties:

overt loyalties, to Church, nation, friends, to the pledged word, the dignity of man, the cause of the disinherited and oppressed— and, above all, reconciling what in others might have issued in conflicts and contradictions, an integrity and inner loyalty to the spirit wherever he perceived it. All these were in him bound up together into an inner unity of thought and action, and having taken up a position he remained immovable from it . . .

Oriental studies could not for him be confined to the classical realms of history, literature, or philosophy. The study was not to be dissociated from the field, the ideas from their effects and manifestations in human life and society. In his historical works, as in his analyses of contemporary movements, his presentations were quickened by a perception of enduring Islamic values that had always acted, and continued to act, upon the course of events . . . His writings on these subjects have acquired from the qualities that he brought to them a permanent significance in Islamic studies. But just because of these qualities they are composed, as it were, in two registers. One was at the ordinary level of objective scholarship, seeking to elucidate the nature of the given phenomenon by a masterly use of the established tools of academic research. The other was at a level on which objective data and understanding were absorbed and transformed by an individual intuition of spiritual dimensions. It was not always easy to draw a dividing line between the former and the transfiguration that resulted from the outpouring of the riches of his own personality.[9]

It was perhaps an awareness of some similar tendency in himself which contributed to his self-control. As in his life, so in his writing: once more his ideal was revealed by implication—writing of a favourite author he thus defined his style:

. . . lively, direct, colorful, brilliantly imaginative, exuberantly eloquent Ibn Khaldun, whose ideas stream out in long cascades, sometimes indeed tumbling into excited incohesion, but for the most part held together by a taut and beautifully modulated structure of prose, controlled by precise and refined mechanisms of coordination and subordination, and articulated with a trained elegance that gives to every word the exact degree of emphasis required by his argument.[10]

Gibb's own style does not quite reach this ideal. It is forceful and well-articulated; it can express every shade of his meaning; it never tumbles over into excited incohesion; it flows easily except for a certain clumsiness when, as he was always tempted to do, he tried to express very abstract ideas. But it lacks colour, variety, and fantasy. (There is however at least one joke in his published works: a mock-serious translation from an absurd Spanish-Arabic poem. Extolling a young man's beauty the poet asks:

How do his underclothes not waste away
Since he is a full moon [in beauty] and they are of cotton?

But even this needs a learned gloss to explain that medieval Arabs believed moonlight could dissolve cotton.)[11]

In these early writings one strand, which was to be important later, was only just beginning to appear: concern with the religion of Islam, its past, present, and future. To quote Levi Della Vida once again, at the heart of his view of the Muslim world lay an attempt to grasp 'the specific attitude [of Muslims] towards religion'.[12] He made a first attempt to formulate this in *Whither Islam?*, where he wrote of the lack of harmony between the inner life of the Muslim community and its political development—'a thousand years of jealous autocracy, a thousand years of political quietism'[13]—and the unsettlement and psychological strain brought about in the modern age by the rapid intrusion of new ideas, the change in the balance of doctrine and ethical teaching, and the attempt to transplant new and alien institutions.

But the thought, whether on doctrinal change or its political effects, was still half-formed, and was not to mature until the late 1930s and the 1940s: the creative, self-confident years, his last in London and his first in Oxford, years also of political tension and war. At first, and for obvious reasons, the main sign of inner change was a growing concern with politics. He gave lectures and wrote articles on political problems of the Middle East and on British policy; for the first years of the War he was head of the Middle Eastern section in the wartime organisation set up by the Royal Institute of International Affairs to provide information for the Foreign Office (later to become the Foreign Office Research Department). The responsibilities of power and empire meant something to him, but he was critical of some of the ways in which they were interpreted by the British government: if no satisfactory agreement were made with Egypt on a basis of equality, and if support were given without due caution to the creation of a Jewish national home in Palestine, relations between the Arab Muslim peoples and the outside world would be strained. He had similar fears about French policy in Syria, although he did not criticise it in North Africa, where France was faced with problems different from those of the Middle East, and no British interest was involved. Even before the War ended, however, he had begun to withdraw from these activities. His last major political article, a strong and outspoken one on Anglo-Egyptian relations, appeared in *International Affairs* in 1951.[14] After that, although he would sometimes speak or write about the social or moral factors which might affect political decisions, he seemed reluctant to be drawn into public discussion of questions of policy; only the greatest events—those of 1956 and 1967—could draw from him even a private comment.

This was partly, perhaps, because of a feeling that there was little a scholar could do to solve problems or even bring pressure to bear on those concerned with them, partly because of a certain lack of ease in Egypt and elsewhere in the Middle East as the decades passed. During the 1920s he had travelled widely in North Africa and elsewhere, and in the 1930s he went each year to Egypt as one of the few European members of the Academy of the Arabic Language. He had close friends there; he moved in the world of the liberal intellectuals and parliamentary politicians. But he did not feel quite so much at ease with a new generation and régime; he visited Egypt rarely after the 1940s, and made only short visits to other countries (including, on his last long journey, some in West Africa).

Changes in feeling and habit were linked with changes of intellectual concern and conviction. By the early 1950s British and French power was receding and the Muslim peoples were becoming responsible for their own political destiny, at least within the framework left behind by their former rulers. A European scholar could not take an effective part in their political processes, but he might hope to help them by setting those processes in a long perspective of historical development. As Gibb did so, it became clear to him that modern governments and élites were acting in ignorance or rejection of their own traditions of social life and morality, and that their failures sprang from this. Henceforth his main efforts were given to the elucidation, by careful study of the past, of the specific nature of Muslim society and the beliefs and culture which lay at the heart of it.

Even this problem he tended to see at first mainly in political terms. He approached it from a background of political theory and institutional history. In the early 1930s, after the sudden death of Sir Thomas Arnold, he was teaching Islamic political theory and was much concerned with the rise and decline of states. The articles he wrote on the subject, mainly in this decade, are of great importance, and those who teach or write about it today would still tend to start from the careful distinctions he made between different kinds of theory in terms of which the exercise of power was justified: the theory of the caliphate in its various phases, that of the just sultan ruling within the bounds of the *shari'a*, the Persian idea of the king regulating the orders of society in the light of natural justice.[15] One of his best articles, written in 1932, is that on the Islamic background of Ibn Khaldun's political theory. The aim of Ibn Khaldun, he maintained, was not only to analyse the evolution of states but to reconcile the demands of the *shari'a*, the 'holy law', with the facts of history:

> since mankind will not follow the Shari'a it is condemned to an empty and unending cycle of rise and fall, conditioned by the 'natural' and inevitable consequences of the predominance of its animal instincts.[16]

In this way of looking at the past at this time we can see the influence of Arnold Toynbee, between whom and Gibb there was mutual respect: Toynbee had learnt some Arabic with him at the School, and asked him to read and comment on the passages about Islam in the early volumes of his *Study of History*.[17]

It was no doubt Toynbee's concern with problems of the relations between 'civilisations' which led the Royal Institute of International Affairs (where he was Director of Studies) to commission a number of works about the impact of modern Western civilisation on the ancient societies of Asia. Gibb was asked to write the one on Islam, together with another scholar, Harold Bowen. The two parts of what was intended to be the first volume of *Islamic Society and the West* were not published until much later, in 1950 and 1957 respectively, but the thought and research for them were done earlier, in the 1930s and 1940s. Their purpose was 'to investigate [the] inner mechanism [of Ottoman

Muslim society] and ... the forces at work to maintain or transform it',[18] and the authors began with a detailed study of that society as it was in the 1770s, just at the point where, in their view, new forces began to affect it.

The work was intended to be a survey of published material in order to form some system of categories which might help to direct research in the Ottoman and other material being newly opened to scholars. So far at least as Gibb's share went, it was mainly based on a very detailed use of a small number of important sources: for example, the *Description de l'Égypte*, the chronicle of al-Jabarti, al-Muradi's biographical dictionary. A precise and careful picture was built up of the social and religious structure of Ottoman society, in both the Turkish and Arab parts of the Empire. The work of the two authors is not difficult to distinguish. Bowen was an Ottomanist, minute, careful, rather pedestrian when dealing with the institutions of the central government, the fiscal system, and the Anatolian provinces; Gibb dealt with the nature of civil and religious authority, and with the Arab provinces, and did so in a boldly speculative way. His are clearly the ideas about the Ottoman sultanate. In a chapter which summarises his earlier work on political theory, the sultanate is placed within its Islamic context: not a caliphate, except in the sense given the term by the later jurists, for whom any government which ruled justly and within the *shari'a* could be called a caliphate; deriving less from the tradition of legal thought than from the ancient Persian ideal of kingship as being of divine origin, because it was necessary to keep the world on its axis by making sure that no class transgressed the rights of any other; giving justice to subjects and demanding obedience from them—'sixty years of tyranny are better than an hour of civil strife'.[19]

In the light of this conception of authority, Gibb examined the nature of Ottoman administration in the Arab provinces, and formed a view of it more favourable than that which most historians of his generation would have taken. Faced with the violence of factional spirit among the Arabs, which stirred the deepest passions of the soul even more than personal ambition, the Ottomans at least provided a framework of careful and regular administration, although marred by greed and cynicism, and did not interfere with the life which went on inside the framework: the life of a large number of small groups, defined by a combination of family, local, and vocational links, living under their own heads and in accordance with their own traditions.

In the second part the nature of the religious authority and its relations with government and society were studied. It was respected by the ruler, and in turn recognised his legitimate existence: it could not control him but would not allow itself to be controlled. The fundamental task of the *'ulama* was to ensure that, no matter what political changes might come about, the religious institutions and the intellectual tradition of Islam should be preserved unshaken. This was their vocation, but there was always a tension between it and the natural 'pull' of worldly power and success; the higher *'ulama* at least tended to become too closely connected with the ruling élite.

Many criticisms have been made of *Islamic Society and the West*. The most trenchant is that put forward by N. Itzkowitz, who has cast doubt on certain leading ideas in it: in particular, the idea, derived from the work of an earlier historian, A. H. Lybyer, of the existence of two institutions, the 'ruling' and the 'religious', closely parallel to each other.[20] It may also be that in his sections on the Arab provinces Gibb was too much influenced by certain theories of Massignon about the corporate nature of Islamic society. Nevertheless, the book is still, a generation later, what its authors intended it to be: a stimulus to research and further thought.

Gibb and Bowen never wrote more than the two parts of the introduction; this was partly because it seemed premature to write a work on so large a scale at a time when the Ottoman archives were only just beginning to be explored, but mainly because, even if it had been possible, it would have demanded a more complete concentration of effort, over a longer period, than either author felt able to give. By the mid 1940s the struggle with the book, and the development of Gibb's thought on the subjects with which it dealt, had brought him within sight of a range of problems which could not be tackled on this level of social and institutional history. Reflection on the inadequacy of Muslim political systems and on the historical role of the *'ulama* led him to think about the nature and development of Islam as a religious system. Between 1947 and 1953 he published a series of four works which between them form a coherent body of original thought about Islam, set in the context of his own religious beliefs: *Modern Trends in Islam* (1947), 'The structure of religious thought in Islam' (in *The*

Muslim World, 1948),[21] *Mohammedanism: An Historical Survey* (1949), and 'An interpretation of Islamic history' (in *The Journal of World History*, 1953).[21] They did not in any sense exhaust his energies or interest during these years. Now as at all stages of his career his range was wide, and he continued not only to teach many subjects but to pour out a series of articles on them: in particular, his work as editor of the *Encyclopaedia of Islam* took much time, and some of his longer articles in it were among his major works—the article on history in the first edition, that on Arabic literature in the second.[22] But perhaps the writings on Islam are those by which he will be longest remembered: the book on Mohammedanism, at once simple and profound, easy to read but full of learning, has been for a generation the first book which most teachers recommend to those beginning the study of Islam and its history, and it is still as fresh and valuable as when it was first written.

The key to an understanding of Gibb's thought about Islam is to be found in the preface to *Modern Trends in Islam*, in his one passage of intimate self-revelation—no less intimate for being expressed in a typically tentative, impersonal, and even apologetic way:

One other word must be said, even at the risk of appearing too self-conscious. In these days, when we are enveloped in an atmosphere charged with propaganda, it is the duty of every investigator to define precisely to himself and to his audience the principles which determine his point of view. Speaking in the first person, therefore, I make bold to say that the metaphors in which Christian doctrine is traditionally enshrined satisfy me intellectually as expressing symbolically the highest range of spiritual truth which I can conceive, provided that they are interpreted not in terms of anthropomorphic dogma but as general concepts, related to our changing views of the nature of the universe. I see the church and the congregation of Christian people as each dependent on the other for continued vitality, the church serving as the accumulated history and instrument of the Christian conscience, the permanent element which is constantly renewed by the stream of Christian experience and which gives both direction and effective power to that experience.

My view of Islam will necessarily be the counterpart of this. The Muslim church and its members constitute a similar composite, each forming and reacting to the other so long as Islam remains a living organism and its doctrines satisfy the religious consciousness of its adherents. While giving full weight to the historical structure of Muslim thought and experience, I see it also as an evolving organism, recasting from time to time the content of its symbolism, even though the recasting is concealed (as it is to a considerable extent in Christianity) by the rigidity of its outward formulas. The views expressed by living Muslims are not to be discredited *a priori* by the argument that these views cannot be reconciled with those of ninth century Muslim doctors. It is understandable that modern Muslim theologians themselves should protest against innovations and should seek to tie Islam down to its medieval dogmatic formulations by denying, first of all, the possibility and, second, the legitimacy of the reconstruction of Islamic thought. But it is certainly not for Protestant Christians to refuse to Muslims, either as a community or as individuals, the right to reinterpret the documents and symbols of their faith in accordance with their own convictions.[23]

A number of themes are stated here, some familiar and some less so. The ultimate reality is God speaking directly and of His own initiative to the individual soul, and the soul responding; the 'congregation' is a community of individuals united in a common response which expresses itself in a common symbolism and worship; the 'church' in the narrower sense consists of those individuals in the congregation who act as guardians of the symbols and leaders of the worship. (Since this was what he meant by a 'church', it followed that he could do something which most orientalists would carefully avoid: use the word 'church' in an Islamic context, to refer to the *'ulama*, not as a dangerous analogy but as a literal and accurate description).

Where do these ideas come from? Most deeply, perhaps, they come from his own Scottish Presbyterian tradition, which was a living reality for him: he was a church-goer, although without any narrowness of allegiance—at Oxford he attended services of the Church of England in the College chapel. But he interpreted Christian doctrine in terms of the Kantian philosophy he had imbibed in Edinburgh. In his *Religion within the Bounds of Pure Reason*, Kant had distinguished between 'pure religious faith' and 'ecclesiastical faith'. The former was the religion of reason, which was already working in individuals and would in the end lead to the emergence of a universal religion and ethical state. Until that time should come, most people would live in accordance with 'ecclesiastical faith'; that is to say, some historically revealed faith, itself derived from 'pure faith', about how God wishes to be honoured and obeyed. Such a faith was most stable when based on a scripture as well as tradition; it could lead to the creation of an 'ethical commonwealth' or church, a visible body of men united under authority. These churches could be arranged on a scale of values according to their universality, the stability of their principles, the strength of the moral union between their members, and the freedom of the individual within them. (For Kant, Islam was one of these faiths and churches, but did not stand high in the scale).

Whether or not Gibb read Kant himself, such ideas certainly came to him through his teachers of philosophy. They were well expressed, for example, in Pringle-Pattison's Gifford Lectures, delivered in Edinburgh a few years after Gibb was a student there. The author described the historical religions as different manifestations of a common principle rooted in human nature and giving rise to specific combinations of assent to propositions, feelings, intentions of the will, and a 'religious atmosphere' realised in the collective life of a religious community. Such communities tended to persist over a long period, and to preserve not only their own beliefs and practices but something from earlier ones which they were supposed to have displaced.[24]

The problem of the 'science of religion', then, was to trace the way in which a specific religion emerged from or superseded earlier ones, and in which it developed, but also to explain it as one among a number of possible manifestations of some common principle rooted in human nature. What was this underlying reality? There is some evidence that in the late 1930s and the 1940s Gibb was reading widely in books on religion, philosophy and psychology, not from a desire to be in the fashion, but in a search for categories in terms of which he could explain Islam. Sometimes his search took him into unexpected places; almost the only time I can remember his being angry is when I spoke in what seemed to him a slighting and disrespectful way about Freud's *Moses and Monotheism*. A passing reference in *Modern Trends* shows where he found what he was looking for. He there acknowledged the help he had received in formulating his ideas about religion from the writings of the philosopher R. G. Collingwood, and from internal evidence it is clear which of Collingwood's books had most influence on him: not the later and better known books, but an early one, *Speculum Mentis*, with which the author was himself dissatisfied in later life. (There is a series of extracts copied from this book among Gibb's private papers).

Writing within a broadly Hegelian framework, Collingwood in this book constructs a scale of modes of thought, each of them trying to grasp and express reality and leading in the end to a contradiction which the mind can only resolve by moving to a higher mode. Thus in Art the imagination ranges freely, expressing its own reality in its own symbols. In the mode standing above it, that of Religion, the mind expresses not itself but some reality other than itself, but it still does so through symbols and symbolic action, the rituals of collective worship. At its highest it can lead to a breaking down of the separation between man and that Other. But religious thought ends in contradiction when it tries to express itself explicitly; religion gives rise to theology which interprets the symbols literally and so destroys them. To rise above the contradiction the mind must move to a higher mode, that of Philosophy, in which reality is expressed directly and not in metaphors.

In trying to define the specific nature of Islamic symbols and forms of worship, Gibb drew upon an important tradition of European scholarship, that formulated by I. Goldziher and laying strong emphasis upon the development of Sunnism, the slow accumulation of a tradition through an endeavour to maintain a central position between extremes. One writer of this school had a special influence on him: his fellow Scot D. B. Macdonald, who, after study at Glasgow and with E. Sachau in Berlin, spent his life at Hartford Theological Seminary in Connecticut and the School of Missions attached to it. Macdonald's *Development of Muslim Theology, Jurisprudence and Constitutional Theory*, published in 1903, was an impressive survey of what he regarded as the central path of development. Gibb's copy of it was acquired in 1919, and—something he did rarely—he marked in it a passage which clearly went on echoing in his mind for years: the intellectual unity of Islam, 'for good or evil, is its outstanding quality'.[25] Macdonald's other important book, *The Religious Attitude and Life in Islam* (1909), perhaps had an even deeper influence on Gibb. In it Macdonald dealt with what for him was the essence of religion, the confrontation of the soul with God, the occult phenomena which man has always taken to be signs of the incursion of the invisible into the visible order, the striving of the soul towards God, and the institutions which provided a shared channel for it: 'practically, the conception of the mystical, saintly life and the organization of darwish fraternities cover all Islam and are the stimulants and rationale of Muslim piety.'[26] Although in general Gibb learnt more from reading than from discussion, in the Oxford period, he seems to have received stimulus from two colleagues, both trained in the German tradition: Richard Walzer, whose researches into the absorption of the Greek philosophical tradition into Islam helped to form his own ideas about how elements were transposed from one civilisation to another; and Joseph Schacht, to whose work on Muslim jurisprudence he owed much, although he thought Schacht went too far in his rejection of the information about the Prophet's life contained in the Traditions ('through the mass of all-too-human detail there shines out unmistakably a largeness of humanity ... which contrasts so strongly with the prevailing temper and spirit of his age and of his followers that it cannot be other than a reflection of the real man').[27]

In these works, formed by these influences, there is expounded a view of the development of Islam by a series of responses to challenges; but responses which took the form not of repudiation so much as of the incorporation of new elements into the existing structure of symbols or worship. This was a process which could never cease, because religious vision and experience always broke out of the symbolic framework. At the beginning of it stood the Prophet Muhammad and the Qur'an: an attempt to impose a new symbolic order upon the 'natural' Semitic religion of western Arabia. The Qur'an did not reject the symbols which already existed but gave them a new meaning, and the Prophet himself became a symbol of great force, attracting piety and loyalty. There followed a period in which law and theology were being formed, and when the emerging consciousness of the community was engaged in a battle on two fronts: against the fantasies of the unrestricted religious imagination, and against the attempts of the philosophical mind to dissolve the content of revelation into rational concepts—to turn the God of Abraham into the God of the philosophers. To hold a balance between these two extremes was a delicate matter because of the essential contradiction in theology: we must try to understand, but in the end we must accept what is contained in revelation *bila kayf*, without asking how. To create this delicate balance was the achievement of al-Ash'ari, whose school became the theological 'orthodoxy' of Islam. (This is one of the points at which Gibb's ideas have been much modified by recent work: H. Laoust's researches into the Hanbali school of thought, which have made it more difficult to regard Ash'arism as the main expression of the 'mind of the community'; G. Makdisi's distinction between Ash'ari theology and the Shafi'i school of law; and the publication of texts of al-Ash'ari and others).

Because of its necessary emphasis on the finality of the Islamic revelation and on the independent power of God which was its message, theology tended towards theoretical and rigid formulations of the basic intuitions of the faith. But religious life could not be contained within them, and expressed itself in the organised cultivation of religious experience and a greater emphasis on the indwelling of God. A third phase now began, that of the Sufi challenge, a necessary movement but one which had its dangers. It released 'the inherited religious instincts of the masses'[28] and served as the channel through which the ancient pre-Islamic symbols came back into Islam. Once more the mind of Sunnism had to purify and absorb Sufism into the structure of 'orthodox' thought and worship. On the level of theory this was done by al-Ghazali (although here again, recent work might make us more hesitant in saying what al-Ghazali's real beliefs were), and then by some relatively little-known thinkers in the seventeenth and eighteenth centuries, when 'a succession of remarkable scholars strove to restate the bases of Islamic theology in a manner which broke away from formalism . . . and laid new stress on the psychological and ethical elements in religion'.[29] On the level of organised devotion, it was the work of those Sufi orders which remained within the bounds of the *shari'a*: in them, *'ulama* became Sufis, and legal and mystical thought mingled with each other.

The development of thought was also the development of a community, an *umma*, which shaped and was shaped by it. Gibb would have accepted the famous Tradition, 'my community will never agree upon an error', but only in a special sense: the community tended to accept whatever existed at least in a purified form, and since it was itself the final guardian and judge of truth, what it accepted *was* Islam. But the *umma* is both 'church' and 'congregation', and each has its task in the development of Islam.

The 'church', in other words the body of *'ulama*, is guardian of the symbols. It defines, defends, and transmits them, and the process of transmission from teacher to student is the process by which Islam continues and grows. The concept of a *silsila*, a chain of spiritual and intellectual inheritance, is essential for an understanding of Islam. Hence, as Gibb suggested in a striking essay written a little later, the significance of one characteristic type of Islamic literature, the biographical dictionary:

> ... the conception that underlies the oldest biographical dictionaries is that the history of the Islamic Community is essentially the contribution of individual men and women to the building up and transmission of its specific culture; that it is these persons (rather than the political governors) who represent or reflect the active forces in Muslim society ...[30]

The 'congregation' also are guardians, in another sense. Participating as fully as they do, by piety, concern, and loyalty, they have sometimes had a more correct instinct than the *'ulama* for the reality of Islam and the need for unity. In the deepest sense, they are the creators of symbols and worship; it is their creative and ever growing religious experience which the 'church' tries to formulate and preserve. The interaction of 'church' and 'congregation' within a continuously developing and expanding community, the response of this community to the demands and dangers of life in the world of power and material need, and the evolution of an Islamic culture and society out of these processes: all this forms 'Islamic history' in the real sense of the term. In his interpretative essay on it, Gibb traced the march of the *umma* through the wilderness of religious fantasies, human passions, political conflict, opportunism, and cynicism; or, to be more precise, of the Sunni *umma*, because he had no doubt that Sunni Islam was the orthodox form of Islam. 'Orthodox' was another of the words he applied to Islam with less hesitation than other scholars might have had. Sunnism was orthodoxy for him; he never visited Iran, and had a curious lack of sympathy for Shi'ism. In his view, its 'sterile opposition' had broken the unity of the *umma*; it had 'killed the Persian "humanities" and left no outlet for intellectual activity except in scholasticism'.[31]

The main body of Islam had only just avoided the snares of the world. Sometimes it had been protected or rescued by a just

Muslim ruler. Once more, a movement of Gibb's imagination had to be justified by a general principle. The life of Saladin and the Muslim reaction against the Crusades in the twelfth century, were favourite themes to which he often returned: his contributions to the *Philadelphia History of the Crusades* are among his most important works of detailed research.[32] Saladin was for Gibb the paradigm of the just ruler, his achievement was by good sense and integrity to have ended the political demoralisation of Islam and restored unity under Divine Law.[33] But such rulers came rarely, and what was more important in preserving the community in its right form was a kind of aloofness from power and the world: the achievement on the one hand of the *'ulama* with their refusal to identify the *umma* with any political régime, and on the other of the mystics with their appeal from the visible order of the world to an invisible order ruled by a hierarchy of saints, the *qutb* and *abdal*.

The struggle had to be fought again and again. The world would always strike back: the *'ulama* became subservient to the ruler, Sufi orders turned into armed movements, then into states. In the modern age the struggle was taking a new form. New challenges were being made to established ways of thinking and worshipping, and to study the responses to them was the purpose of *Modern Trends in Islam*. The 'classical' way of meeting the challenges would have been to incorporate new elements into the existing structure. In a lecture given during this period on 'the influence of Islamic culture on medieval Europe', Gibb put forward a theory of the conditions and limits of cultural assimilation, which suggested by implication ways in which this might have taken place in the modern Muslim world.[34] But the Muslim thinkers of the modern age seemed to him to have failed in the task (Julien Benda's *Trahison des clercs* was another book on which he made notes). Instead of seeking the middle ground, they had tended either towards withdrawal from the modern world, or towards an abandonment of the careful, responsible structure of thought they had inherited: the religious sciences of Qur'an interpretation, criticism of traditions, and jurisprudence (*tafsir, hadith, fiqh*). In a kind of denial of responsibility to the history of Islam, a breaking of the *silsila* of teachers and witnesses, they had shown a 'disregard of all objective standards of investigation and of historical truth', and had 'debauched the intellectual insight and integrity of their fellow-Muslims'.[35] By so doing they had destroyed the defence which orthodox Islam had built against the ambitions of rulers, and this was the more dangerous because those rulers were no longer acting within the framework of Islamic justice; they did not recognise the Divine Law embodied in the consciousness of the *umma*, but exploited religious feeling for political ends; by misunderstanding the 'operative factors' in the history of the *umma* they had accepted alien standards.[36] In this gloomy picture Gibb saw one ray of hope. He had a kind of ultimate faith in the good sense and loyalty of the 'congregation', still expanding, still preserving its own mind amidst the disintegration of symbols:

> No one who has ever seen that mile-long procession of brotherhood lodges with their banners, trudging in the dust after the Holy Carpet on its annual progress through Cairo, can fail to be impressed by the vitality of the forces which they represent. Not for the first time, the *ijmaʿ* of the people is opposed to the *ijmaʿ* of the learned.[37]

These works were written during Gibb's Oxford years, the most creative of his life but also perhaps the least happy in a professional sense. He was there indeed at a moment of growth and opportunity. In 1947 a Commission of Enquiry on Oriental, Slavonic, East European and African Studies (the Scarbrough Commission) produced a report recommending the expansion of existing facilities by the creation of strong departments maintaining a balance between linguistic and non-linguistic, classical and modern studies and having firm links with the whole network of the humanities and sciences. Oxford was to be one of the universities where Near and Middle Eastern studies should be helped to expand. Thus Gibb, who for his first ten years had been almost the only teacher of Arabic and Islamic subjects in the University, was able to gather around him a group of colleagues, at a time when good students were coming to work with him— English students who had served in the Middle East during the War, and graduate students from America and the Middle East itself. But, although he was a successful and famous teacher, and although he very much enjoyed the life of his own college, St John's, he was never quite at ease in Oxford. He had not been a student there; its intellectual tradition was not his; he never learnt how to do things effectively and without too much effort in that segmentary society without formal and explicit authority. What was more important, he was always aware how marginal the Faculty of Oriental Studies was, and how difficult it would be to establish close links with other Faculties. He did not find the historians of his time responsive to the idea that the history of Asia was worth studying, and by the 1950s he was coming to feel that this was harming his work. As a scholar he was asking questions to which historians might have helped him to find the answers; as a teacher, he had good students but they were not the students he now wanted, trained in some historical or sociological discipline, and coming to him to acquire not only the Arabic language but an understanding of a society and culture.

Some of his dissatisfaction he expressed in a very interesting and frank letter written at the time to one of his former pupils:

> . . . I should not be leaving Oxford if I thought there was anything more to be done here . . . The real problem is that the big Faculties . . . are dominated by College tutors, who are not interested in anything outside the Schools' syllabuses and dead opposed to any expansion of these, especially into the Oriental field . . . I know therefore, that if I stay here I am condemned to seven years of merely repetitive teaching without any hope of enlarging its scope.[38]

Recollected in tranquillity, this was the starting point of one of his last writings, a lecture on *Area Studies Reconsidered*, given at the School of Oriental and African Studies in London in 1963:

> Almost from the time when I was appointed to the Chair of Arabic in this University, thirty-three years ago, I was conscious of a growing dissatisfaction with the narrow limits in which Oriental Studies were confined at that time. It was largely for that reason that I accepted the opportunity to move to Oxford, imagining, in my innocence, that Oxford would offer a more open field for the broadening out of Arabic and Islamic studies than was possible in the rather tightly-knit and isolated little group which at that time composed the School of Oriental Studies. Deeply as I enjoyed the years at Oxford, I was soon undeceived in these hopes; the jealous rigidity of Faculty and School lines inhibited any attempt to cross them even at the level of graduate study.[39]

Later in the lecture he spoke of the need for 'a new kind of academic amphibian, the scholar whose habitat is in one medium but who is fully at home in another', and who works closely with the orientalist whose task is to relate what the specialists do to a central core, and 'to furnish that core out of his knowledge and understanding of the invisibles—the values, attitudes and mental processes characteristic of the "great culture" . . . the long perspective of cultural habit and tradition'.[40]

Had he waited a few more years, things would have changed in Oxford. A new generation of historians was growing up, and in 1961 another report of another committee (the Hayter Committee) recommended that departments of history and social sciences should be encouraged to give a larger place to the history and societies of the world beyond Europe, that steps should be taken to train the 'new kind of academic amphibian', and that Oxford should be one of the centres of Middle Eastern studies. But he could not have guessed that this would happen, and had he waited for it, he would by then have been near the statutory age of retirement. Long before that, as he approached his sixtieth year, he seems to have decided to leave Oxford early and seek another field of work. A Harvard professor has told how, when consulting Gibb on possible successors to the retiring Jewett Professor, W. Thomson, he was astonished to find a new note creeping into the correspondence: the adviser himself might be persuaded to consider an offer. The offer was made and accepted, and at the age of sixty, the Laudian Professor at Oxford became the Jewett Professor at Harvard.

It was a real entry into a New World, a deliberate choice of a new path in life. But it was a decision he never regretted, although he and his wife felt the separation from children and grandchildren and from close friends. The last time I ever saw him, he spoke with great emphasis of the Harvard years as having been the happiest of his life. He was happy, first of all, in his teaching: he had always loved the art of teaching, and by now his skill in it was fully grown. As a lecturer he was a little hesitant for words, but always found the right ones in the end; he was clear and forceful rather than polished, not witty but lively, never saying things which meant nothing, placing facts and ideas in a logical framework. As a tutor or supervisor, or in private discourse with colleagues, he could be both disconcerting and inspiring: he would sometimes be silent, sometimes follow his own line of thought regardless of what the other had come to talk about; but when the silence and distance vanished, he would try not so much to give information as to help the other to bring out whatever he had in his mind; and when what came out seemed to be of value, particularly if it helped him to carry further the process of thought on which he himself engaged, he would be generous, exciting, himself excited; but then again he would sometimes withdraw his interest. He was best perhaps in a discussion group or seminar, and the American system of graduate education gave him more scope than the English; in such a group or in a conference of scholars, he would exercise an easy authority, as he took some theme, perhaps familiar, and carried his thought about it across the frontiers of knowledge by some unexpected route. It could be most exciting to *see* him thinking. The authority and excitement might continue and there were many former students and colleagues who would always think of him as their master. To his students he was always warm and helpful, just as he was to those who came to him for advice or information on matters on which he felt himself competent to give it; since his death, more than one of his former students has spoken or written about his unfailing generosity and thoughtfulness, which followed them through life long after they had finished their studies with him. He had always had good students both in London and Oxford, but those of his Harvard years played a special part in his life. Some of them had had the training in history or the social sciences which he wanted; the eager curiosity of the American graduate student overcame his own shyness, and besides he had reached the age when human relationships could be fitted most easily into the framework of father and son. What they thought of him can be seen in the moving words with which one who stood close to him thanked him not only for help with his thesis but for 'the knowledge, wisdom and grace of guiding' to which he owed 'the better part of my education'.[41]

Harvard gave him scope to build not only a department of Arabic and Islamic studies but an inter-departmental 'center' for Middle Eastern studies as a framework within which orientalists and the new 'amphibians' could work together. The Center fulfilled some of his hopes. As long as he was there he attracted loyal colleagues and good students, and the endowments which would make it possible to advance further. But he did not have time, before illness struck him, to give it the firm foundations he had hoped for. The permanent institutions of an American university are the departments which are responsible for the various disciplines; a body which cuts across the frontiers of several departments can only flourish if its members have firm roots in them. Gibb was not very successful in achieving this. Sound as his judgement was on matters of scholarship, it could be unsure and even odd where human beings were concerned. His administrative arrangements did not always have the results he intended, and those who observed him at work were never quite sure whether he had failed to understand the Harvard system or understood it rather too well. Faced with difficulties in a department he would go to a higher authority or just go his own way, and his construction had the essential fragility of a network of patron–client relations.

But even if his Harvard colleagues might find that he acted with unusual independence, they never had any doubt that his presence there was one of the glories of the University. He was better known there than he had been at Oxford, and it was fitting that, at the last Commencement he attended, he should have been given an honour rare for a serving member of the Faculty, an honorary Doctorate of Letters. He for his part very much enjoyed belonging to one of the great scholarly communities of the world, and his personal relations with many of his colleagues had an ease and warmth which had been difficult for him before. (He belonged to a generation of men who rarely or never used Christian names outside the family. To colleagues and friends he had always been 'Gibb' or 'Professor Gibb', and when he became a knight few knew what name he would use. At Harvard many of his friends called him 'Hamilton', and he adopted the same mode of address. I still remember the point, after twenty years of personal acquaintance, when he first called me 'Albert'. After a decent interval I reciprocated, but with a sense of *lèse-majesté*.)

Contacts and friendships extended easily across the frontiers of subjects. Besides being Jewett Professor he was made a 'University Professor'. Holders of this title are defined by the regulations of the university as being men 'working on the frontiers of knowledge, and in such a way as to cross the conventional boundaries of the specialities'. He did indeed cross many of them: he was closely connected with the School of Divinity and the Department of History as well as that of Near Eastern Languages, and read widely in the social sciences, particularly social anthropology.

(After his first years at Harvard he handed over the teaching of Islamic institutions not to an orientalist but to a sociologist).

His own work now had to be done in the intervals of teaching, administration, and acting as elder statesman of his subject. He prepared a new edition of his early book on Arabic literature; this, together with an earlier article on the same subject written for the second edition of the *Encyclopaedia of Islam*,[42] summed up his views on certain subjects which he had thought about and taught all his life. Much more was said than in the first edition about the relations of literature with social and political life; a favourite theme of his later work, the survival of the Persian bureaucratic tradition and its relations with the newer traditions of Arabic philology and Islamic learning, was used to illuminate the nature of certain kinds of writing. The first section, on the poetry of the 'Heroic Age', was largely rewritten under the influence of recent work on the composition of oral poetry. He took up again another subject he had studied early in life, and began to prepare a complete annotated translation of Ibn Battuta's travels: it would be of value to scholars across 'the boundaries of the specialities', and besides it was something he could do in his spare time. (Every morning he would translate a few pages in his study in Widener Library before going to his office at the Center; the change from the solitary scholar working at home, teaching in an attic in St John's College, and writing his letters by hand, to the scholar-administrator surrounded by secretaries in an office, was a striking one). He also prepared a finished but still unpublished version of his lectures on Islamic history from the beginnings to the rise of the 'Abbasid dynasty: a sober and masterly review, taking into account recently published material, giving the results of half a century of thought, but lacking, in its written form, the excitement he could communicate in the lecture-room, and not yet fertilised by the new kind of book he was reading at this time.

He had planned to retire as professor at the end of the academic year 1963–4 but to continue for a time as Director of the Center. He had already begun to make careful and orderly preparations: he bought a house on Cumnor Hill outside Oxford; St Antony's College offered him a special fellowship; his library was sold to Harvard to be placed in a special room on the top floor of Widener. A few months before these plans could be carried out, in the spring of 1964, he had his stroke. It was a massive one, gravely affecting his power of speech, leaving his right arm paralysed, and restricting his ability to move. He recovered partly, but not wholly: by June he was strong enough to be moved to the new house near Oxford, and there he lived until the spring of 1971, when he moved to a cottage in the village of Cherington, lying just off the road from Oxford to Stratford-upon-Avon.

I shall always remember him as he was in these last years of infirmity, because it was then I came to know him best—I might say, in a sense, to know him at all. It was as if, under the stress of illness, the essential features of his character had broken through the restraints imposed on them by a lifetime of self-control. A new warmth came into his personal relations, just at the moment when he could not easily express it. In a calm, patient, uncomplaining way he adjusted himself to his new way of life; he could scarcely leave the house, but friends came to see him, from Oxford, London, Paris and his specially beloved Harvard. Through them, and by wide reading, he kept in touch with what was happening in the world of scholarship. His speech returned, but only in part; those who were there will not forget the small gathering of colleagues and students to present him with a *Festschrift* to mark his seventieth birthday, and at which he was able, with effort, to say some graceful words. He taught himself to write with his left hand (but he could no longer write Arabic). In time he was even able to take up his work again, and to complete what he had begun although not to begin anything new. He finished the notes to the third volume of Ibn Battuta, and used his articles on Saladin as the basis of a short book; his notes for books he would not write were given to others—notes on poetry to one, on history to another, for the last volume of Ibn Battuta to a third.

As the infirmities and sorrows of age closed in on him he met them with the strength of his forbears. A leg had to be amputated. In the summer of 1969 Ella fell ill and died. A courageous spirit in a frail body, she had borne his illness with calm cheerfulness, but in the end it wore her out. She left with all who had known her the memory of a truly angelic character, and after she had gone the world became for him a shadowy place, although the outward rhythm of his life continued as before: a devoted housekeeper to look after him, days of reading, writing, and receiving friends, watching his roses and apple-tree grow, seeing children and grandchildren when they could make the journey from their homes. Confined to one house, then to one room, then to one chair, he could still look out in calm acceptance on the whole human world, and see behind it 'the vision of the great overriding movement of the Eternal Reason'.[43]

7 Toynbee's Vision of History

With the publication in October 1954 of the last four volumes of *A Study of History*, Toynbee's great work is complete. Twenty years separate these volumes from the first three, published in 1934, and fifteen years from the second group of three, which appeared in 1939. To have had to wait so long has been in one way a gain. So big a book, so full of facts and with so complex a theme, needed to be thoroughly digested. In the last fifteen years there has been time to digest the first six volumes, to discover what Toynbee was trying to do, to formulate the questions which these volumes posed and left unanswered, and to think about the form which the answers might take when they appeared.

It was clear from the start that, considered in the most superficial way, as a storehouse of facts, the book was remarkable. It gathered together a variety of strange and interesting facts about the human world, and even the most casual reader, looking at a page here or there in bed or on a journey, would go away with his store of knowledge increased, and his sense of the strangeness of human life deepened. If some of the details were inaccurate, we could say of them what Toynbee himself said of Wells's *Outline of History*: that such mistakes were inevitable, and could easily be pardoned, in a book which attempted to re-live 'the entire life of Mankind as a single imaginative experience'.[1] Moreover, they were described vividly, and put together in suggestive ways which revealed whole vistas of history; sometimes they were collected into monographs which, breaking the sequence of the narrative or placed as annexes to it, could be read as separate works and for themselves alone. Such are the monographs on *lingue franche* in Volume V, that on pilgrimages in Volume IX, and that on headgear in Volume X.

II

The book, of course, is far more than a collection of facts, to be judged by the same standards as those which would be appropriate to Pliny's *Natural History* or a medieval bestiary. Its explicit purpose is to try by the empirical method to formulate certain principles which would be valid for human history as a whole. It must therefore be judged (partly at least) by whether or not it succeeds in this purpose.

It will be profitable to begin by some indications of the origin and main outlines of the theory of history elaborated in the first six volumes. Two forces seem to have moulded the theory. On the one hand, Toynbee's training was that of an ancient historian. His early travels took him to the lands lying around the Aegean where Greek civilisation grew and decayed; and in later years he was to study and to observe the decline and fall of the Ottoman Empire. In this mind which broods on all civilisations, it is above all the life and death of the Eastern Mediterranean societies and their interactions which hold the centre of the stage. Again and again, in considering the genesis of some idea of his, we can see him giving it shape with Near Eastern history in mind, and then applying it to other worlds.

On the other hand, his theory springs from a strong conviction about the Western mind. Western historians, he believes, have gone wrong because they are egocentric, in diverse ways: because they deal only with Western history, or because they consider other histories only in so far as they are relevant to Western history, or because they look at other histories through categories applicable only to Western history, or because they think of themselves as standing outside history and so able to judge it, as if history had somehow come to an end in their own Western world.[2] (If this is scarcely true of Western thinkers now, perhaps it was partly true in the 1920s, when the book was taking shape, and even more true in the years before 1914 when its author's mind was formed).

There is a particular form of self-worship which blurs the vision of Western historians when they write about the West, and that is the worship of the nation-state. They tend either to deal with its history in isolation, as if it were an intelligible field of study in itself, or to treat of all history as it affected the interests or impinged on the mind of one nation. But the nation-state, for

Toynbee, is 'the social prison-house in which our Western souls are incarcerated';[3] and it is the attempt to escape from this prison which determines the starting-point of his study. The nation-state, he says, is demonstrably not an intelligible field of historical study; we cannot understand the history of any one such state until we enlarge our vision to include a whole network of them bound together not only by intimate political ties but by a common culture and a long tradition of things done and suffered in common. Such a network constitutes a 'civilisation'. Let us start from the assumption that 'civilisations' are intelligible units of historical study, and see what we can say about them: in particular, let us see whether we can say anything which is true of the whole class of 'civilisations'. Thus modestly and experimentally, and without too high a claim, the search is launched. It throws up, in the first place, twenty-one identical specimens of the class; and in the second, a whole theory about how they are born, grow, decline, give birth to others and interact with others.

At the root of this theory lies a distinction between two human states, symbolised for Toynbee by the Chinese terms *Yin* and *Yang*: the state of quiescence, of passive maintenance of an achieved uniformity, and that of creative advance into the unknown, a turning-away from the customs of the ancestors into a new, still uncharted, unformalised way of life. This is the final dichotomy in human life, and the first principle of historical thought. The processes of history spring from the transition of a human group from *Yin* to *Yang*. All that historical thought can do is to trace the circumstances in which the change takes place, and the results it produces; why it happens in those circumstances is a mystery, hidden in the freedom of the human response. (We may note in passing that this dichotomy of *Yin* and *Yang*, which expresses itself in numerous forms, is only one example of Toynbee's fondness for duality).

It is by one such transition that civilisations grow. Growth means a transference of the scale of action and challenge from external challenge to internal: a progress towards self-determination, a tendency for the personality of a civilisation to become its own field of action. It occurs when a civilisation is presented with a challenge to which it makes a successful response, and in so doing not only absorbs into itself that element which, precisely by being unabsorbed, presented the challenge, but also generates in itself the energy to meet a further challenge. But how is it that one civilisation responds to the challenge while another does not? The answer is to be found in the existence, in the successful civilisation, of a creative minority—an individual, a few men or a whole group—which, taking upon itself the burden of the challenge in the solitude of withdrawal, returns into the heart of the community with the problem solved, and draws after it the whole uncreative mass by the force of imitation or 'mimesis'.

But this force of mimesis, which makes possible the transmission of new ideas or skills from the minority to the majority, and so gives its strength to a growing society, is also the weakness of all civilisations. The uncreative majority can only be dislodged from its state of *Yin* by the force of charm; but once the charm no longer works its magic the symbiosis is dissolved. 'All action that proceeds from mimesis is essentially precarious because it is not self-determined'; and this is especially so in a dynamic society, where the bond of charm is no longer reinforced by that of custom. Sooner or later a 'breakdown' may occur: that is to say, there is a loss of harmony in one form or another—between the old institutions of a society and its new ideas, for example, or between majority and minority. The latter may either withdraw from responsibility for society into 'esotericism', or else, on the contrary, it may impose its will too heavily and so distort the whole of society. If it follows either of these paths, it may cease to be capable of responding creatively to new challenges; indeed, its very success in facing one challenge may make it incapable of dealing with the next.

If this should happen (and we say 'if', because there is nowhere a hint that the whole process *must* happen, on the contrary, there is every insistence that man can always, if he wills, break the chains which seem to bind him), then the civilisation may pass from 'breakdown' to 'disintegration'. The same challenge, never successfully faced and so repeating itself again and again in 'merciless uniformity', turns the lack of harmony into a schism, a gulf slowly widening within the body of the community. The gulf may appear between the different 'parochial' communities into which the civilisation is divided (for example, the national communities which make up Western civilisation); or it may be a gulf between the different 'elements' or 'classes' which form the civilisation. The civilisation will fall apart into three 'classes'. The former creative minority, since it no longer responds creatively to challenges, becomes a dominant minority, thinking of its position of leadership as a position of privilege, and clinging to it in ways which do not help the civilisation to overcome its problems. Over against it there emerges an internal proletariat, a mass which, no longer being bound to the minority by mimesis, has made an act of secession and does not regard itself as belonging to the civilisation; and an external proletariat, formed of elements drawn to the frontier of the civilisation in its days of growth by its attractive force, but no longer willing to accept the role for which the civilisation had intended them.

As the disintegration proceeds (and again we must add, 'if'), the relations between these elements turn from those of harmony to those of force; the minority tries ever more desperately to retain its position, and the proletariat reacts by violence. But this is not the whole story: for at the moment when the three classes by the violence of their conflict are destroying both themselves and the civilisation as a whole, all three of them explode in acts of creation which light up the dying world. The dominant minority at its last gasp may produce a universal state, the internal proletariat a universal church, while the external proletariat gives birth to barbarian states and war-gods, heroism and epic poetry.

Of these, only the universal church is 'forward-looking', the chrysalis of a new civilisation, and also the path by which men may save themselves from the death of the old. For the church is created by a new minority which appears in the ranks of the proletariat, and it is a minority of a new sort. The experience of life in a decaying society poses a challenge to the individual soul. The schism in society gives rise to schism in the soul, and there may emerge a new type of leader who will show how to cure it: the saviour who leads those who will follow him out of the doomed society. But those who will not follow are caught in the rhythm of disintegration, which typically takes the form: rout-rally-collapse. The collapsing society pulls itself together on the edge of defeat, seems to restore its strength, but then once more hears the merciless insistence of the returning challenge. Of these efforts to cheat death, the strongest is that which gives birth to the universal state; and when the universal state collapses, the civilisation dies, either through absorption into some other, or else by dissolving into chaos, from which, in the fullness of time, a new civilisation *may* arise.

This is the briefest sketch of a theory which has been formulated with nuances and with respect for the complexity of human history, and in some measure tested by being applied in detail to many historic situations. It contains ideas and suggestions which have helped to fertilise historical studies in the last twenty years. The idea that a civilisation should not be treated as something unique, but as a representative of a species; the idea of the internal and external proletariat; the detailed analysis of the ways in which social schism casts its shadow in the individual soul; the description of the great acts which illuminate the death of a society, and the idea that a heroic age is not a primitive age, but the product of a civilisation in decline—such thoughts can open a new vista on many a field of studies, and if some of them seem commonplace now, it is partly because Toynbee has made them so. Yet although few of those who have read him, and even of his critics, have failed to profit from one or other element in his thought, fewer still have been ready to accept his theory as a whole, and this not always because of prejudice against the idea of law in history as such, but often because of valid objections which can be made to the basic concepts of Toynbee's thought and to the use he makes of them.

It could be pointed out, for example, that the prime categories of his thought are irremediably vague. It is difficult to find in his work a clear definition of what he means by a 'civilisation'; and this lack of definition accounts for something arbitrary in his list of civilisations. Of the twenty-one civilisations, why should no less than eight be found in the Near and Middle East? Why should Japanese civilisation be distinguished from the main body of Far Eastern, while English civilisation is not distinguished, as with almost equal reason it could be, from the main body of the West? Why should the apparently unified civilisation of the Islamic world be split up, as it were arbitrarily, into three civilisations (revived Syriac, Arabic, Iranic)? Why should the Ottoman Empire be regarded as an 'abortive civilisation', while other empires are treated as manifestations of some civilisation which extends beyond them in time? Again, when 'the Nomads' are introduced as another 'abortive civilisation', surely the term 'civilisation' is being used in a different sense, not to denote a particular society but to indicate a whole type of societies?

Nor is the use which is made of the concepts above criticism. In spite of all attempts to be flexible, the schematism is too rigid. A proposition is formulated, then in some or all of the twenty-one civilisations some phenomenon is discovered, after more or less search, which seems to exemplify it; often, however, to single out this phenomenon and give it the importance which the theory postulates is to give a picture of a civilisation which would not be accepted by those with detailed knowledge of it. Russian civilisation for example is said to have broken down in the twelfth century or thereabouts. The theory demands this; but would any Russian historian accept its implication, which is that the movement of Russian society after this moment was fundamentally different from what it had been before—that whereas before it had been moving in a harmony of classes towards self-determination, afterwards it moved through increasing alienation of classes toward dissolution? It is at this point that we feel the effect of the author's special concern with the eastern Mediterranean. Ultimately his theory has been built up to explain the development of Greek civilisation since the Homeric age; it is only with difficulty that other historical movements can be fitted into the mould.

Even if some of the propositions are true, it has not been *proved* that they are true. For all Toynbee's insistence on the 'empirical method of proof', he does not give rigid proofs of his theories. Sometimes he is content simply to assert them; sometimes he supports them with a single example; sometimes he proceeds by simple enumeration of instances, although simple enumeration is no method of proof, unless it is complete enumeration of all the instances of a species, or of all the relevantly different species of a genus.

Even supposing this were not so, and it had been shown that certain uniformities exist in history, there would still be certain questions to ask about them. After it had been proved that civilisations were the final entities of human history, that all of them were subject to the same forces, and that all until now had suffered the same fate, it would still be right to ask what the status of these 'laws' was, and why they existed. Is it just an accident that civilisations arise, or is there something in the nature of man which leads to the emergence of units of this type and size, to the separation between them, to the growth and breakdown through which each passes, and to the death which so far has befallen them? To be firmly established, a theory of history must be grounded in a theory of man and of the universe. In the first six volumes the theory is not so grounded, although there are hints of the way in which it might be. Thus there appears throughout a clear belief in human freedom: the process of growth, breakdown, disintegration and dissolution can be interrupted at any point. But there is no clear explanation of why, in spite of freedom, certain recurrences can be found in history; and if one asks for an explanation of that rhythm of *Yin* and *Yang* to which all these recurrences can be reduced, one is given not an explanation but a poetic description of the 'Promethean *élan*' which, as in Plato, can be hinted at in myths but not elucidated by discursive reason.

III

If such criticisms have been made of Toynbee's work, and if many of those who have made or who accept them have drawn the conclusion that the work is of no theoretical value, he is himself partly to blame. To judge by the evidence of the whole book, no less than by the fascinating autobiography with which, in Volume X, he ends it, his mind was formed early and (apart from Jung and Bergson) has known no profound influences since 1914. Like all his generation he was impressed by the prestige of the natural sciences, and his thought about history seems unquestioningly to have taken the form which would have been appropriate to physics or biology. That is to say, he believes that the right thing to do with the objects which form the material of his study is to group them together and try to discover uniformities in their structure or their way of behaving; and that the right way of establishing such uniformities is the 'empirical method'. He cannot complain if his critics, taking him at his word, should point out that his 'laws' are not universally true and his proofs of them not convincing.

Yet it is possible to see the book in another light, as an imaginative vision of history, having the same relation to fact as has poetry, gaining its value and validity not from its literal accuracy but from its originality, its internal consistency, the method of its expression and the help it gives us in understanding the historical process.

What are we to say of the nature and quality of this vision of history? It is the product of a strange, haunted and powerful imagination. It can hear the echoes resounding from one world to another, and knows how the echo distorts the original voice; among the most interesting sections of the book are those dealing with renaissances, with the evocation in one world of another's ghost. It is haunted by memories of ruins; in quoting Volney on the Levant, Gibbon on the fragments of Imperial Rome, Toynbee is acknowledging a spiritual affinity. It was the sight of Mistra, seen on a walking-tour in Greece when he was twenty-one, which was the starting point of the whole long meditation from which this book has sprung: 'Mistra had continued ... to reign for ... 600 years as the queen of the broad landscape that could be surveyed from her topmost battlements; and then, one April morning, out of the blue, the avalanche of wild highlanders ... had overwhelmed her ... and her ruins had been left desolate from that day to this'.[4] This was the first of many lessons in the fragility of all civilisations, our own among them. The sight of a baroque villa, built in Crete under the Venetian occupation and soon abandoned to the Turks, was 'a *memento mori* for an England that was then still alive';[5] later he was to see the unclouded afternoon of the English middle class end in the First World War, and to observe and write one of the best of his books about the destruction, in a single year, of three millenia of Greek civilisation in Asia Minor.[6]

Behind the echoes and ruins there lies a moral vision of history. All Toynbee's concepts in the end are moral ones. Casual moral judgements are strewn loosely over his pages. Acts are 'unpardonable', motives are 'cynical', historic figures are accused of 'intellectual stupidity' and 'moral aberration'. It is not an accident that such words appear. They are necessary implications of Toynbee's whole view of history. The categories in terms of which he sees the historical process are ethical. 'Harmony' and 'self-determination' are normative concepts. They are something one can aim at but never wholly achieve; they are, moreover, something which, in Toynbee's view, a civilisation ought to aim at, and it is for this reason that he calls progress towards them 'growth', and regress from them 'breakdown'. Further, they are ends which can only be achieved by the practice of virtue. Virtue is both the essence and the cause of breakdown, and again and again throughout the book there recurs a line from Meredith, 'We are betrayed by what is false within'.

Put in the simplest and most general terms, Toynbee's view of history consists of one statement of value and two of fact. Civilisations ought to aim at harmony and self-determination; in their earlier stages they approach this goal; in their later stages they have all so far abandoned it, and in so doing have killed themselves.

More specifically, what the book is about is *hubris*, the self-destroying pride which tempts men at the moment of triumph and power. Creative minorities and the institutions they have made easily fall into self-worship, and in so doing they perish. If they can resist the temptation, or if having fallen into it they can come to themselves and repent, they may avoid dissolution. That is the message of the book: but it raises the most urgent question of all. Even if a civilisation avoids the path of decay, what other path can it follow? Once having achieved harmony and self-determination, to what purpose, if any, can it use them? Can it have any purpose beyond itself, or, in the end, is there no more to be said of it than that it was born, grew, and died or avoided death? Such questions lie only just below the surface of these first six volumes, and there are hints of an answer to them: or rather of two answers, each very different from the other.

On the one hand, 'civilisation' is seen as something ultimate. Each civilisation has its norm within it, just as each has its timescale within it; it is possible to judge each phase of it by how near it approaches the norm, just as it is possible to date each event in it by how near it is to its death or birth. But civilisations as a whole are 'philosophically' identical just as they are 'philosophically' contemporaneous. It is pointless to talk of one civilisation as coming before or after another in time, and pointless also to compare them or judge between them. Here once more we can see the author's eagerness to escape from Western 'egocentrism', the tendency to judge one civilisation by the standards of another, and here too we can see the influence of concepts drawn from the natural sciences. The biologist, for example, is concerned with growth; that one man is taller than another is for him of importance not in itself, but only in that study of the reasons for it may throw light on the process of growth in general. When this idea is uppermost in Toynbee's mind, he applies his relativism not only to the political and social aspects of a civilisation, those elements which by their very nature are ephemeral, but also to its thoughts and its beliefs. Religion is seen only as the end-product of a civilisation, important because it is the one successful way of responding to a certain stage in the decline of a civilisation, and because of the part it may play in bringing a new civilisation to birth. It is a 'response to the challenge presented by the disintegration of civilisations'.[7]

There is now and then, however, a hint that human history as a whole has a meaning; man as such has a purpose, and therefore civilisations can be judged by whether they bring him nearer to it, and even the relation of before-and-after between them will have a meaning. A hint of this first emerges in Volume I, where the author, reviving an almost forgotten theory of Bernard Shaw, sees the purpose of life as 'the transformation of Sub-Man through Man into Super-Man'.[8] But the idea of the superman is soon absorbed in another. Not to transcend mankind but to perfect it is seen as the goal, and all growth in civilisation is equated with progress towards sainthood.

The meaning of sainthood, however, is not yet clearly defined, and here again we can find a contradiction of emphases. If sometimes it seems that Toynbee identifies sainthood with all human success, and regards the emergence of any creative minority as a step towards it, at other times he uses the word in a sense much nearer to that which is traditional. There is a Christian note running through his volumes, and it becomes louder when the decay and death of civilisations are discussed. The only true response to the experience of living in a disintegrating society is 'transfiguration'—to see the Kingdom of God lying behind the facts of human history, and to enrol oneself in it—and only a Christian can take this path, for only he knows the truth of God's love. The 'stone which both Zeno and Gautama have so obstinately rejected is become the head of the corner of the temple of the New Testament'.[9] When tested all saviours fail us except one: 'a single figure rises from the flood and straightway fills the whole horizon'.[10]

IV

From these brief notes it is possible to discover what questions were still unanswered when the sixth volume ended. There was a question about man: is he free in history and, insofar as history obeys laws, what is the human basis of those laws? There was a question about the universe: what, if any, is the purpose of human history as a whole? There were two more questions, however, implied but not yet made explicit, and of a more immediate relevance.

First, what can we expect of our own Western civilisation? Whereabouts in the life-cycle of a civilisation can we place the present phase of our own society? Is there any hope that we may escape from the fate which has fallen upon all societies previous to

ours? If so, what must we do to be saved? There is a hint, in
Volume VI, that the West has reached that point which follows
breakdown and precedes the establishment of a universal state;[11]
and there is an analysis of that factor in which the author finds the
challenge which confronts the West today—the combination of
democracy and industrialism with the parochial state, giving rise
to nationalism and war.[12] But at the end of the sixth volume the
question still remains open.

Secondly, what of Toynbee himself? A book of this sort is bound
to be in some sense a work of self-revelation, and this is more so
than most. Toynbee forgets nothing, and for him nothing is
without significance. Sooner or later, everything he has seen,
heard, read or otherwise learned emerges. Indeed, it would not be
too much to say that the book *is* his education: not only enriched
by, but built up out of, the experience of an Englishman of the
middle class, brought up in the last years before 1914 and nurtured
in the classical tradition of a public school. It is impossible for him
to write a single sentence which does not carry with it echoes, in
its rhythm and phrases, of the Bible in its Anglican version and
the classical authors whom he studied at Winchester. Indeed, the
very elements of which his theory are built are the commonplaces
of an English classical education. The concept of a 'civilisation'
which holds together different political units with a profound even
if unembodied bond; the idea of the withdrawal and return of the
creative minority (so similar to Plato's myth of the return of the
philosophers into the Cave); the ideal of harmony and the danger
of *hubris*—these are lessons which English schoolmasters draw
from the study of the history and literature of ancient Greece.
Would it even be fanciful to hear in the idea of rout and rally an
echo of the Winchester playing-fields, with the school team going
down valiantly against overwhelming odds, in the fading light of
a winter's afternoon, but snatching from defeat the crown of an
unyielding heroism?

Although the book in a sense is typical of a certain age and
class—even in a sense conventional for all its air of originality—in
a more profound way it is deeply personal. It is impossible not to
hear, in the voice of Toynbee brooding on civilisation, the anguish
of a man brooding on himself. *A Study of History* is a spiritual
autobiography, but one of a peculiar sort. Something (perhaps that
reserve which makes him express his feelings, when he must
express them, not in his own language but in Greek) makes him

incapable of writing about himself in the first person. Whenever he has occasion to refer to himself, it is always in the third person,and always one tense backwards in the past, so that instead of saying 'I was', he will write 'the author had been ... '. In this and other ways the personal note is muted, but it is still there. It is not difficult to hear the cry of a human soul in anguish, searching amidst the ruins of history for an abiding city; nor is it difficult to see in what direction, when Volume VI ended, his search was taking him. For all his knowledge of the Bible he seems to have little systematic knowledge of the traditional science of theology; what makes these first six volumes most moving is their revelation of a powerful and earnest mind painfully stumbling back to the Church its ancestors had known.

V

Those who admired Toynbee's work, and had come near enough to the radiation of his charm, kindness and nobility to care that he should find what he was seeking, had fifteen years to think of these questions before the last four volumes appeared and gave them answers which, although foreshadowed to some extent by minor writings in the last few years, were nevertheless not quite what anyone had expected, and were far from what many might have hoped.

It is clear that in the last few years Toynbee's view of history and of the universe has changed radically. Such a change does not matter perhaps in itself, and was indeed only to be expected in a book which had been thirty years in the making; but here it is important both because of its extent and because in spite of all its claims the book is by no means empirical in its method. Its main outlines were sketched thirty-five years ago, in the course of a journey from London to Constantinople by the Orient Express. 'Before I went to sleep that night', the author tells us, 'I found that I had put down on half a sheet of notepaper a list of topics which, in its contents and in their order, was substantially identical with the plan of this book'.[13] Thus the framework of the book has not been changed, but new ideas have now been inserted in it, and these ideas, were all their implications worked out, might demand a book of a very different shape. It is possibly this new disharmony between what the author is trying to say and the form in which he is saying it which acounts for a certain loss of literary mastery in the last four volumes. No longer is the main theme expressed precisely, briefly and often elegantly, and broken by digressions which can be read for themselves. Now the theories are elaborated at length, with endless repetition and a new note of dogmatism; the sentences have lost their structure and their unity, and have become shapeless jungles, in which subordinate clauses writhe in tortuous embraces, the paths are cluttered with parentheses and the ground rocky with technical terms.

Such a change in style must surely be a sign of a change in thought, and so it proves. The book is still a study of civilisations, but the concept of 'civilisation' now shows itself unable to carry the burden of the thought. The disintegration of a civilisation, we are told, cannot be explained in terms of itself alone; its relations with others of the species, in space and time, are of the essence of the story.[14] But in saying this, are we not repeating the argument by which it was proved, in Volume I, that the nation-state is not an intelligible field of study; and if this argument is valid too of civilisations, does not the whole basis of the theory disappear? Toynbee might reply that this phenomenon of interaction appears only in the phases of decline, and indeed is implied in the very definition of disintegration, which is loss of self-determination. But surely one would find a similar phenomenon even in the phase of growth? Growth, by Toynbee's definition, is progress towards self-determination. This implies that self-determination has not yet been achieved, and that in its progress towards it the civilisation is struggling with something other than itself which it is trying to bring within its own control. Here too the movement of a civilisation cannot be understood without reference to something other than itself, and the basic assumption of the study—that civilisations are separate entities which can be understood in abstraction—falls to the ground.

At the same time as the theory is losing its basis, it is undergoing a vast extension which, if all its implications were worked out, might leave nothing of it standing. In these last volumes the author at last considers the question of the status of his laws, and gives us a doctrine of man to underpin his doctrine of civilisation. In doing so, the author reveals that his mind has undergone in mid-course one of those sudden and violent impacts which are the more dangerous and intense the later in life they come. There is a moving passage in Volume X in which he talks of his loneliness in 'an adverse Western mental environment in which I did not find any outstanding contemporary good example to follow ... before Jung's star at last rose above my horizon'.[15]

The influence of Jung's *Psychological Types* indeed has been overwhelming (although behind it, unobtrusive but scarcely less important, one can see another influence, that of Bergson's *Two Sources of Morality and Religion*). It is from the standpoint of Jung that the author now approaches the question of why there is or seems to be a rhythm in history. The forces which impose or seem to impose this rhythm are now to be found within the soul. Beneath the surface of individual will and reason there lies the psyche, which includes in its depths the subconscious as well as the conscious, the collective as well as the individual. It is from this dark realm that there emerge those 'psychic principalities and powers', those 'non-personal emanations' which express themselves in the tendency of human groups to act in habitual ways, and to which we give such abstract names as law and fortune, archaism and futurism, democracy and industrialism.[16] But although the subconscious is important in human affairs, it is not all-important. Every now and then there arises a challenge to which the system of habitual actions which has served mankind until now can offer no response. Then the only way of safety lies through a change of soul;[17] and this is only possible through an act of conscious thought, by which man shakes himself free from the shackles of the subconscious, and calls on the help of conscious will and conscious reason to make the response which the new challenge demands. Such a free, conscious and novel exercise of human faculties means a step forward in human development.

Thus the alternation of *Yin* and *Yang*, which from the beginning has been the author's final interpretation of historical movement, now acquires a new meaning. Two rhythms of social and individual life appear, analogous to Bergson's two systems of morality. On the one hand is the subconscious, the realm of law and uniformity in history, the basis of the closed habitual life; on the other is consciousness, the realm of freedom, the basis of free and open response to new challenges. But this new distinction contains within it implications which shake the whole basis of Toynbee's thought. We have moved from an alternation of good and evil to an alternation of conscious and subconscious; and this change may underline that thesis about *hubris* which lies at the heart of the whole book. The first volumes taught us that civilisations break down from within, by self-worship and the escape into falsity; but they can avoid the breakdown by avoiding the sin, and if they can, they should. But if, as we are now told, civilisations break down because the subconscious asserts its power, then two questions arise. First, how can we possibly avoid this fate? According to Toynbee the subconscious is not only something which lies within each of us, it is something which extends beyond each of us, and is indeed 'the matrix of personalities'; in what sense then can we control it?[18] Secondly, even if we could avoid this fate, why *should* we avoid it? It is self-evident that we should seek virtue and eschew vice; but it is not self-evident that when faced with a challenge we should abandon the rhythm of habit and make an act of freedom. It may be right for us to do so, but we must be shown why it is right; and this can be done only by showing us what is the meaning of those challenges which can be met only by reason, and what is the purpose of our responses.

VI

Who sends the challenge, and to what end? To this, the final question of his work, Toynbee gives a clear answer. It is God who gives us the challenge, and His purpose in so doing is to evoke a free response which will actualise potentialities in the human soul, and so draw men nearer to their own perfection and to Himself. History is the process by which God's creation moves 'from God its source towards God its goal'.[19] In thus giving us his new version of a theme which passed from Neo-Platonism through Erigena into Christian thought, Toynbee is—as he himself is aware—making a radical change in his whole system of thought. Religion can no longer be regarded as a human response to a social challenge. Its main purpose can no longer be to console the death or help in the birth of civilisations. It plays this role by exception, not universally, and even when it plays it, does so only incidentally. Religion cannot be explained in terms of civilisations; on the contrary, civilisations themselves exist only in order to produce religions. It is through the struggle with the challenges which societies must face that men become more perfect and more themselves; and it is in the suffering caused by the death of civilisations that men's hearts turn to God.

The implications of this are far-reaching, and destroy the

principle from which Toynbee started: that civilisations can be treated as representatives of the same species, each of them 'philosophically' equivalent to all the rest, and that what is important about them is the generic character which they possess. Now there has emerged something in history more important than the civilisations themselves, something of which civilisations are only the handmaids, and in terms of which they can be classified and judged. They must now be separated into sub-species, and some of them will be in some sense 'higher' or even 'better' than others. More than that, since a potentiality which has once been actualised cannot return to its former state without leaving some traces behind it, civilisations which come late in time start with some capital left to them from their predecessors, and have at least the chance to rise higher than they. Thus the value-scale and the time-scale of civilisations are connected with one another: a civilisation which is later is likely also to be 'more advanced' than one which went before, and history as a whole is moving to some end.

It is possible therefore to discover different classes of civilisation, distinguished from one another by their relations to religion and by their temporal relation with one another. First come the primary civilisations, which spring directly from primitive societies. They may produce, by way of their internal proletariats, rudimentary higher religions, like the worship of Osiris and Isis in Egypt; but their main function in the divine economy is to produce secondary civilisations in one way or another. The essential purpose of secondary civilisations is to give birth, at their moment of dissolution, to higher religions; but they may also produce tertiary civilisations, emerging from the 'chrysalis' of the universal church. Of such tertiary civilisations our Western civilisation is one; but egocentrism should not make us forget that tertiary civilisations are irrelevant to the purpose of history. For not only a particular civilisation, but civilisation as a whole, has fulfilled its purpose once the higher religions have emerged; from the moment of their birth it is these which carry the burden of history, and they may even constitute or give rise to a new species of human society as different from civilisations as civilisations are from primitive societies. If we understand rightly a distinction which is not clearly made, primitive societies are those where habit and the subconscious rule supreme; in civilisations, reason struggles against the unconscious, and having freed itself in the minority imposes

itself by mimesis upon the majority, in whom however the acts
dictated by reason, not being themselves understood, turn into a
new rhythm of habit where the subconscious reasserts its reign; in
the higher societies all will freely and lovingly apprehend the truth
and live in its light. In this new doctrine another basic principle of
Toynbee's thought, implicit in the whole work from the beginning,
becomes explicit: the belief that the Kingdom of God can, and
therefore should, and some day will be built on earth.

VII

Can the process of classification and judgement be carried a stage
further? Of the higher religions which have emerged in the
historical process, four stand out: Christianity, Islam, Hinduism
and Mahayana Buddhism. In that they conflict, or seem to conflict,
with each other, is it possible to say which of them represents the
highest point man has reached in his return to God, and which, if
any of them, is likely to command the future allegiance of
mankind?

To this question Toynbee replies by emphasising the elements
common to all four. All believe in man's fellowship with the one
true God, in the spiritual meaning of history, in the overcoming of
discord, in an effective ideal of conduct, and in the transformation
of mimesis from imitation of a creative minority to imitation of
God.[20] In that they are different, it is a difference of expression, of
custom, of 'ways'. Toynbee quotes with approval the words of a
Mongol Khan: 'Even as God has given several fingers to the hand,
so He has given Man several ways.'[21] Each way, moreover,
corresponds to one of the basic 'psychological types', and provides
for those who belong to that type an adequate path for their
approach to God.

Now if this is true, it is clear that any of the four religions
which claims to have the whole and exclusive truth is in error and
indeed in sin: by so claiming, it will be limiting not only the ways
by which man comes to God but those by which God comes to
man, and it may easily lead those who believe its claim into acting
intolerantly towards those who do not. For Toynbee, to make such
a claim is 'sacrilegious . . . chauvinism'.[22] It is clear, too, that those
who are most likely to fall into this error are the Christians. While
Muslims can believe in the essential truth of Christianity as being

one with the essential truth of Islam, and while to Hindus and Buddhists differences of human belief need not be of great importance, Christians are bound by the very nature of their faith to be in some sense exclusive. Since they believe that only Christ was God, and that only He redeemed the world, they cannot admit that religions which deny the Incarnation and the Redemption are the truth in the sense in which Christianity is the truth. Thus the main brunt of Toynbee's denunciation of the sin of false exclusiveness is directed against Christianity: and although he still uses mainly Christian terminology, quotes incessantly from the Bible and thinks of himself as being *in some sense* a Christian, there is in these last volumes much emphasis on what he believes to be the error of traditional Christianity.

Two lines of attack converge upon Christianity, the first issuing from what to some will appear an excessive duality in his thought, and the second from an excessive unity. On the one hand, the truths of Christianity have embodied themselves in institutions, but like all institutions the Church has tended to worship itself and to persecute those who do not accept its authority. The 'vanity of the lust for power'[23] has turned the Catholic Church into a 'civilisation', and like all civilisations it has fallen victim to its own pride. Now if this were only an attack upon the abuses which have been committed by authorities of the Church at certain times nobody would object to Toynbee's recounting them, and many would agree with him. But he puts his thesis forward as a necessary proposition: institutions *as such* worship themselves, and to embody a truth is to pervert it. Can we not find here another of those final dichotomies which are scattered all through Toynbee's work: heart and head, gentleness and violence, and now idea and institution?

This, however, is not his real difficulty with Christianity. His real stumbling-block is something different and less easy to remove. In an imaginary monologue he makes his *advocatus diaboli* say: 'How can the presence of a hypothetically infinite and eternal God be supposed to make itself felt more palpably in Palestine than in Alberta?'[24] And Toynbee himself adds: 'The words that we have put into his mouth were true to fact, and the facts were surprising, because it was also true that this parochialism, of which the higher religions stood convicted in practice, was the antithesis of the revelation which was their common essence.'[25] To say that God revealed Himself in one time and place seems to Toynbee so obviously absurd that he who says it must be moved by that 'sacrilegious chauvinism' which is the worst of sins.

This is not the place to argue whether Toynbee's doctrine of the Incarnation is the correct one, but one implication of his argument must be pointed out. The assertion that God was incarnate in Palestine in the first century in a sense in which He is not incarnate in Alberta in the twentieth may seem to him to be an expression of pride and to lead necessarily to intolerance; but assuredly it is not only or mainly pride which prompts Christians to make it, but rather the logic of their faith. It can mean nothing to say that God became Man, if we do not mean that He became one particular man; and particular men live only in one place in the world, and only at one time in history. If we find it impossible to believe that the Incarnation took place at one point in space and time, then logically we should find it impossible to accept the Incarnation at all; and if we reject the Incarnation, we reject the whole of Christianity. The whole Christian doctrine of God and man and time and history has the Incarnation implicit in it; if we reject the Incarnation we will still be able to have *a certain* doctrine of God and man and time and history, but it will not be the Christian doctrine.

Unless God was present in Palestine in a way in which He is not present in Alberta the whole of Christianity is false; yet clearly Toynbee in some sense believes that it is true. How can this be? Here we stumble upon the greatest difficulty of Toynbee's theory, and one in regard to which he elaborates the most startling of his views. The argument he brings against the exclusive claims of Christianity could be brought against any proposition which claims to be true; and it is truth as traditionally conceived, not just Christianity as traditionally conceived, which is his stumbling-block. If I affirm anything I am necessarily excluding something else; this seems obvious, yet Toynbee cannot accept it. He so longs for peace and harmony, he is so filled with the vision of men as brothers, that he wishes for a truth which excludes nothing. He cannot have it unless he radically changes our conception of truth, and this is what he proceeds to do. Talking specifically of 'the conflict between Science and Religion', but in terms more widely relevant, he revives the ancient theory of the 'two truths'. There are, he suggests, two essential faculties of human reason, two 'modes of experience', two ways of apprehending truth, and, by implication, two uses of language. Discursive reason gives us scientific truth, and intuition, issuing from the depths of the psyche, gives us the truths of revelation. 'The Subconscious, not the Intellect, is the organ through which Man lives his spiritual life for good or evil. It is the fount of poetry, Music and the Visual Arts, and the channel through which the Soul is in communion with God when it does not steel itself against God's influence.'[26] Both these faculties give us truth. There is indeed one fundamental truth in which both truths are founded, but so far man's spiritual vision has not been able to attain it, and so far, therefore, the division between intuitive and rational truth remains final. Hence the conflict of science and religion; religion has tried to formulate its truths in terms suitable for formulating truths of reason, and the conflict could only be ended if religion gave up much of its traditional theology and recognised the light cast on it by the new science of psychology. Hence, too, the apparent conflict between different religions; when they try to formulate their doctrines in too rationalist a way they come into conflict not only with science but with one another.

Here again we shall not raise the question whether Toynbee is wrong, but simply try to make clear what he is saying and what its implications are. He is not merely saying that there are some truths which poets understand more easily than scientists, nor that it is easier to evoke some truths through the rhythm and music of poetry than to express them in plain scientific language; neither of these statements need imply that there is more than one truth. Nor is he simply saying that there is some ineffable experience of God which cannot be put into words at all; for this again would not be to deny that all that can be thought and put into words forms a single system. What he is saying is that there are two systems of thought, both of which can be formulated in words and both accepted by the same mind, but which nevertheless contradict one another.

The belief that the conscious human mind is effectively governed by laws of thought is, Toynbee tells us, a 'mental illusion'.[27] If this is so, all rational discourse is at an end. In speaking or writing, I am merely the mouthpiece for whatever happens to come up from the 'intuitive and emotional depths of the Psyche'. Can I be certain—is there even any sense in asking—whether the God to whom the psyche leads me is other than the psyche itself? The whole long journey of *A Study of History* leads us back to ourselves alone.

VIII

How does Western civilisation appear to Toynbee's new eyes? The image from which he starts is still the same, although the years have made it more vivid. It is an image of sin, sharpened by the horrors of Nazism in the years since the first volumes were published. The Germans could not have committed their crimes if the same criminality had not been festering below the surface of life in the West:

> In chastened Western eyes, from which the scales had now fallen, the first vision of Reality was a recognition of the Western civilisation's mortality; but the tardy dawning of enlightenment through suffering did not stop here; and the second vision was a conviction of sin which was a still more shattering spiritual experience than the recognition of mortality.[28]

These last volumes contain, however, a more detailed analysis of the Western problem than did the first six, and an analysis which leads, as we shall see, to a new conclusion. For Toynbee the most important feature of modern Western civilisation, and the origin of its specific problems, is the development of technology. The new techniques of production and communication make some sort of political unity inevitable; in a disunited world, where the parochial state is the final object of loyalty and even of worship, the alliance of nationalism with modern techniques can produce a terrifying explosive force. Again, modern techniques by their very nature demand regulation and discipline, and have given rise to a world-wide system of 'classes'—a dominant 'white minority', an internal proletariat of Western workers, and an 'external proletariat' in Asia and Africa which is gradually being absorbed into the Western world as it expands; but the human spirit craves freedom, and the revolt against the social system may lead to a conflict of classes which could be no less destructive than that of states. Beneath the tensions of society lies a tension in the individual soul. The new techniques presuppose new 'habits' of thought, but the adoption of these habits is resisted by the psyche, which still clings to old familiar habits like those to which we give the names of 'nationalism' and 'industrialism'.

It is inevitable, according to Toynbee, that some sort of political unity will come about; the only question is how it will come about, peacefully or as a result of war in which one Great Power imposes its domination over the world. There are factors in the modern world making for war, and others working on the opposite side. The polarisation of world-power between Russia and America, the existence of a shifting and uncertain frontier between them, the growth of nationalism and militarism in countries outside Europe, the transfer of power to the inexperienced hands of Western workers and Asian nationalists—all these factors strengthen the tendency towards war. But on the other side are the decline of militarism in Europe, and that conception of peace as a positive good which the modern West has derived from its Christian past. The best hope lies in a 'pacific partition of the Oekumene' between the two Great Powers for an indefinite time. Patience is the virtue most needed, for the subconscious must be given time to make the changes in human habits demanded by the new techniques.

So with the tension of classes too: the question is not whether it will be resolved, but how. Here again Western society is faced with two conflicting systems and with the choice between the victory of one of them and some compromise between them. Between the American ideal of 'opportunity for all' and the Russian ideal of 'the classless society' there lies the middle path of British and Scandinavian social democracy, and once more it is the middle path which best meets the needs of the modern age.

If peace between nations should come, if peace between classes should come, technology will be left free to produce its natural results: the abolition of poverty, and the extension of leisure. Psychic energy will be transferred from work to enjoyment, and so a new problem will arise: how should leisure be profitably used? For Toynbee, the only satisfactory use of leisure is religion; and perhaps it throws some light on his view of religion, and of the relation between thought and life, that he should regard religion as an occupation for leisured hours.

There are two fundamental kinds of religion, worship of God and worship of man, and of these the second is the ultimate source of *hubris*, and therefore of all the ills which befall mankind. But of the different modes of worship of God, which should Western civilisation in its next phase adopt? Here, Toynbee resumes his attack upon Christian orthodoxy. It would, he tells us, be

'intellectually and morally wrong' for Western man to turn back
to traditional Christianity, and he explains why:

> Archaistic religious movements are intellectually indefensible
> because the antecedent Rationalism that has driven a traditional
> religious faith off the field does not in reality just come and go
> ... a higher religion, after its descent from Heaven, picks up
> and carries along with it on its territorial journey a fog of alien
> matter . . . The onset of Rationalism is a process . . . of
> enlightenment . . . Souls that have once had the experience of
> intellectual enlightenment can never therefore find spiritual
> salvation by committing intellectual suicide.[29]

It would be morally wrong to return to the Christianity of the past
because of the 'moral scandal through which the Western Church
had forfeited Western man's esteem . . . a schism that it had
allowed to rankle into the savage Western Wars of Religion'.[30]

The future path which Toynbee sketches for us would lead the
Church through suffering to purge itself of errors, to free itself
from 'the worship of Yahweh'[31] and in the process to drop a great
part of its traditional theology. It would lead the adherents of each
of the four higher religions to try to reconcile the differences
between them, and science and religion into the 'Common
Endeavour' of 'drawing nearer to God by jointly seeking to
comprehend God's protean creature of the Psyche in its subconscious depths as well as on its conscious surface.[32] It would leave
each human soul free to choose the path which suited it best, not
bound to follow the path its ancestors had chosen.

IX

The vision of a world where all are reconciled is for Toynbee a
vision of the Kingdom of God on earth, but to other eyes it may
seem no more than a vision of the kingdom of man. His criticism
of traditional Christianity makes it clear that for him there is
something which stands above religions, just as religions stand
above Christianity. For when he says that a religion cannot return
to what it was before the attacks of rationalism broke upon it, he
treats this as a universally true proposition, without raising the
obvious question whether the attacks of rationalism were justified

or not. That there might be a false rationalism of which the attacks need not trouble religion is nowhere hinted. In his view, either the attacks of rationalism upon religion are always justified, or else a later movement of thought is always 'truer' than an earlier. Again, when he says that the Church has 'forfeited Western man's esteem', is he not assuming that Western man, or man in general, has a right to judge Christianity?

In short, is all this more than the religion of man which arose in the nineteenth century, restated in new terms? There is about all these last volumes a strange, exalted, excited note, more fitting to prophecy than to science. The image of the historian as a natural scientist has been replaced by that of the historian as mystic and as prophet. The task of the historian is to rise through knowledge of the past to knowledge of God's work in history:

> When the feeling for poetry in the facts of History is thus commuted into awe at the epiphany of God in History, the historian's inspiration is preparing him for an experience that has been described as 'the Beatific Vision' by souls to whom it has been vouchsafed.[33]

In his own work the historian may sometimes have a quasi-mystical experience of communion with the past which will raise him out of the bonds of time and start him on his way to the 'Beatific Vision'. Toynbee claims to have had such a direct experience of the past six times, and once to have had an experience rarer still: in Buckingham Palace Road, he

> had found himself in communion, not just with this or that episode in History, but with all that had been, and was, and was to come. In that instant he was directly aware of the passage of History gently flowing through him in a mighty current, and of his own life welling like a wave in the flow of this vast tide.[34]

In this passage we can see clearly how strange are the paths down which Toynbee's adventure has led him.

But is the adventure ended? Must our last sight of Toynbee be that of a mystic claiming to be in communion, not only with all that has been, but also with all that is to come? When he has been so brave in throwing down his challenge and so frank in working out all its implications no matter where the logos will lead him, the only fitting response we can make is to tell him what we think of it. Speaking for myself, but perhaps not for myself alone, I do not believe that Toynbee has found the port he was seeking in his long voyage across the seas of history. The last pages still reveal the same strangled anguish as the first. The needs of a profound and passionate spirit have not been satisfied—and surely could not be—by the syncretist prayer with which the whole work ends, nor by those six experiences of 'communion with the past' which turn out to be six vivid dreams of having been present at certain episodes of war and violence. That there is still some unsatisfied longing in him is shown by the tenacity with which he still holds to Christian phrases, and by his description of a dream he once had:

In the summer of AD 1936, in a time of physical sickness and spiritual travail, he dreamed, during a spell of sleep in a wakeful night, that he was clasping the foot of the crucifix hanging over the high altar of the Abbey of Ampleforth, and was hearing a voice saying to him: *Amplexus expecta* ('Cling and wait').[35]

8 The Present State of Islamic and Middle Eastern Historiography

This paper is the result of an inquiry into the present state of Middle Eastern studies set on foot by the Middle East Studies Association of North America. It is based partly on answers to a questionnaire sent out to a number of historians, partly on my own reading. The limits of that reading will be clear to the reader; in particular, he will find few references to the work of younger German historians, and almost none to those of Russian and Iranian scholars. This would be a serious defect if I had attempted to make a complete survey of the whole field; perhaps it is not so serious in an essay intended to raise certain problems and to give some examples to illustrate them.

The essay was completed in 1974; I have added one or two references in the footnotes, in an attempt to bring it up to date. It was written before the publication of M. G. S. Hodgson's **The Venture of Islam,** *3 vols. (Chicago: University of Chicago, 1974). Some of my judgements would have been different, or would have been expressed in a different way, if I had been able to read this important work before writing my essay.*

I am particularly grateful to those with whom I discussed the first draft, among them I. Lapidus, E. Burke, O. Grabar and H. Inalcik.

The civilisation of which Islam was the dominant religion, and which expressed itself mainly in Arabic, Persian, and Turkish, was always aware of its own past, and produced a succession of historians, whose aim was not only to commemorate the deeds of the rulers who were their patrons, but also to record all that was known about the times and places in which, according to the belief of Muslims, the word of God had been revealed to the Prophet

161

Muhammad, and about the chain of witnesses by whom the deeds and sayings of the Prophet had been passed on to later generations, and the scholars who had articulated and transmitted the systems of law and thought derived from prophecy and tradition. This historical tradition has not quite died out. In the early years of the nineteenth century, a full-scale chronicle on the same level of importance as the great medieval ones, the *'Aja'ib al-athar* of al-Jabarti,[1] was produced in Egypt; later in the century there appeared works lying halfway between medieval and modern styles of historiography, like Mubarak's *Khitat*,[2] Cevdet's *Tarih*,[3] al-Nasiri's *Kitab al-istiqsa*,[4] and also the last great biographical dictionaries recording the lives of scholars and saints, al-Bitar's *Hilyat al-bashar*[5] in Syria, al-Kattani's *Salwat al-anfas*[6] in Morocco. By the end of the nineteenth century, however, traditional historiography could no longer provide a framework within which Muslims of modern education could see their own past, or Western scholars could understand the development of Islamic society and civilisation.

In Europe and North America, the professional study of Islamic history by historians scarcely goes back two generations. For a long time Islamic history was part of 'Islamic studies', and Islamic studies were themselves a byproduct of studies more central to the great concerns of the nineteenth century mind: comparative philology, Biblical criticism, and the 'science of religion'.[7] It was only with the generation of I. Goldziher (1850–1921) and C. Snouck Hurgronje (1857–1936) that the study of Islam became an independent discipline demanding a scholar's whole attention, and a generation later, with C. H. Becker (1876–1933) and W. Barthold (1869–1930), that some of those who studied Islam began to think of themselves as primarily historians, concerned with bringing the highest standards of historical scholarship and interpretation to bear on Islamic history; it is only in the present generation that, in some universities, some of those who think of themselves as historians have been able to devote all or most of their time to teaching Islamic history.

Thus the study of Islamic history lies at least 100 years behind that of European history, and there has been no time yet to lay the necessary foundations or create cumulative traditions of craftsmanship. Even in the present age, the study of Islamic history has not attracted enough scholars for all the urgent tasks. It has not moved the imagination of European and American scholars as China and

Japan are doing. At a rough estimate, the serious teaching of Islamic history, above the level of an elementary survey course, takes place at perhaps 20 universities in North America, 20 in Western Europe, and 20 in the Middle East and North Africa. In North America, there are perhaps between 30 and 50 university teachers who can give their main attention to Islamic history; in each of Great Britain, France, and Germany, perhaps 15 to 20; similar numbers in Egypt, Turkey, and Israel; and fewer in other Middle Eastern countries. Altogether, therefore, there may be 200–300 scholars who can be regarded primarily as Islamic historians. In Western Europe and North America some hundreds of university students are exposed each year to elementary courses on Islamic history, and in the Middle East and North Africa some thousands; but only a small proportion of them are studying for a first degree of which Islamic history forms a major part, and only a few dozen go on to higher study. In some parts of the field, those who emerge as fully trained historians are scarcely numerous enough to fill vacant teaching posts.

The simple fact that there are so few teachers and research workers has certain results. Few of them can specialise; most of them have to teach over too wide a range. However hard they work as scholars and writers, they cannot fill all the gaps. To take some obvious examples, few collections of documents have been properly catalogued; not all the basic chronicles have been published; there are few general surveys of periods or regions incorporating recent research; there are few monographs, even on periods or personalities of major importance; and there are almost no satisfactory biographies, even in the modern period. (We shall return to some of these points in other contexts).

Even those workers who exist live for the most part in isolation: physical isolation first of all, scattered as they are by ones and twos in many universities, but also intellectual isolation. Each studies his own subject—there is a kind of tacit agreement that scholars do not impinge on each other's field, and there is a lack of those scholarly controversies which provide a stimulus to further research and thought. Students of English history, for example, are familiar with such great and fruitful arguments as those about the gentry in the seventeenth century or the structure of politics in the eighteenth. In the Islamic field there are few equivalents to them: recent discussions among French and North African historians about the invasions of Beni Hilal,[8] and the arguments about

Jamal al-Din al-Afghani to which Kedourie and Keddie have contributed,[9] but not many others, although Islamic history is full of problems in regard to which the discussion of different explanations may offer the best way of advance.

The obstacles posed by the shortage of European and American historians in this field are all the greater because of the relatively backward state of indigenous scholarship. Any Western scholar working on Chinese or Japanese history knows how much he owes, in the way of solid foundations, stimulus, and fruitful collaboration, to Chinese and Japanese scholars. In the Middle East, however, although narrative histories and biographical dictionaries of an old-fashioned kind continued to be written in this century (those of al-Rafi'i in Egypt,[10] al Ghazzi,[11] al Tabbakh,[12] and Kurd 'Ali in Syria,[13] and 'Azzawi[14] in Iraq), the emergence of modern historiography in the full sense was slow, and hindered by obstacles such as the slow development of higher education, the absence of an environment conducive to research, and the existence of political limitations upon free inquiry and publication.

In some countries this situation has changed. In Egypt there is now a genuine historical tradition which shows itself in the publication of Arabic texts and documents and the production of some good work on local history. In Israel the methods and standards of European scholarship were brought in by immigrant scholars and have taken root. The development of Turkish historiography is perhaps the most interesting because it took place in the same kind of circumstances as those of Europe in the nineteenth century: the growth of national consciousness and the emergence of the nation-state. In Turkey as in Europe this stimulated the desire to understand one's own past and provided a guiding concept, that of the nation, which, however much it has been criticised by thinkers, is a satisfactory focus for some kinds of historical work. The Kemalist revolution tried to explain and justify itself in explicitly historical terms, to remake the historical self-consciousness of a nation. This impulse, working on ideas derived from the French sociologists of the nineteenth century, produced the seminal work of Fuad Köprülü as scholar and teacher, and his students, doing research in the Ottoman archives, have formed a considerable historical school.

In other countries, however, progress has been slower and there are fewer historians; in Lebanon, for example, the long tradition of local history is virtually carried on by one scholar. This is harmful in more ways than one. Self-interpretation is an important element in historiography, and there is something lacking in the history of a society written mainly from outside. Moreover, there are some things which indigenous scholars can do better than others, such as the collection of local documents and the editing of texts. In North Africa, a number of striking interpretative essays have appeared in recent years (for example, Laroui's *Histoire du Maghreb*[15]), but they still await the painstaking research that will make it possible to test or modify the ideas in them.

In such circumstances, progress in historical inquiry is bound to be slow, but nevertheless it has been made, and there is now a separate academic discipline of Islamic history. Like all historical disciplines it consists of two closely related activities: the discovery, collection, and editing of sources, and the interpretation of them. For purposes of exposition we must separate them, and it is perhaps truer to the nature of historical thought, which is oriented toward the particular, to begin with the sources.

The Islamic historians of the classical tradition built upon each other's work: each chronicle contained, in some form, the substance of earlier chronicles. In a sense the earlier European historians of Islam followed the same procedure. Their basic sources were the chronicles, and to find and edit them was an important task of scholarship. A large number of the essential chronicles are now available in printed form, but some are lost in whole or in part, some are still unpublished, and some have been published only in old and uncritical editions, for example the Arabic works published in Cairo in the nineteenth century, and the Ottoman histories published in Istanbul. Only a few new and more satisfactory editions have appeared, for example, the new Cairo edition of al-Tabari.[16]

The use of the literary sources will always remain an important part of the Islamic historian's work. For some periods, in particular the early centuries of Islam, few other kinds of source exist. Even when they do, significant results can still be obtained by a traditional method: the careful study of written sources, whether they are chronicles, biographies, or works of quite a different kind (for example, legal texts), by scholars who combine a full philological training with the historian's craft of asking questions that will uncover their latent meaning and implications. The literature of Islamic studies provides some classic examples:

Goldziher's use of the *hadith* literature to illuminate the political and theological controversies of the early centuries,[17] and Lammens' use of the *Kitab al-aghani* to throw light on pre-Islamic and early Islamic society.[18] More recent works show how effective such a method can be; for example, Udovitch's study of legal texts to explain the organisation of medieval commerce,[19] and Shaban's careful examination of the precise meaning of the relevant chronicles in order to explain the nature of the 'Abbasid revolution.[20]

Nevertheless attention has moved in the last years, here as in other fields of historical study, from the use of literary sources to the collection and use of documents; that is, texts written for an immediate practical purpose such as trade or administration, but which can be used by the historian for other purposes. It is sometimes said that Islamic history, at least before the Ottoman period, can never be as firmly based as is that of medieval Europe because of the lack of solid documentary evidence. It is true that no complete and organised archives of medieval governments appear to have survived, similar to the papal archives or those of the kings of England and France. But there are usually more sources than one thinks, and the discovery of them waits for the scholars with the curiosity to ask new questions and the enterprise and luck to find new materials to provide the answers. A more systematic and successful attempt is now being made to collect and study chancery and diplomatic documents. They have been found in many places: in monasteries and synagogues, in European archives, in libraries of Istanbul to which documents from many countries occupied by the Ottoman armies found their way, or incorporated in manuals and chronicles. Works such as the two volumes edited by S. M. Stern (*Fatimid Decrees* and *Documents from Islamic Chanceries*)[21] show how much can be learned from them. Medieval *waqfiyyas* also exist, and some of those for the great Mamluk foundations in Cairo are now being used. For one country, Egypt, the mass of documents is particularly great because of the dry climate and the continuity of administrative life in spite of political changes. They include papyri, containing administrative and financial material, which are important because they are so detailed and can be used together with similar material from pre-Islamic times; they have in fact been little used, and since Grohmann there have been few Arabic papyrologists. There are also the commercial and legal documents preserved, together with religious and literary works, in the Geniza of the Fustat synagogue; many of them have now been published and studied, and they form the basis of a major work now being written, Goitein's *A Mediterranean Society*.[22] It seems unlikely that any other hoard of this size will come to light, but Richards has published a smaller collection of documents from the Karaite synagogue in Cario,[23] and D. and J. Sourdel have found (significantly, in Istanbul) a collection of documents from Damascus in the tenth century.[24]

For the early modern period, that of the great empires, there are above all the inexhaustible riches of the Ottoman archives, which throw light not only on the central institutions of the empire but on all the provinces it ruled, including the North African regions where its hold was light, and on all the countries with which the Ottoman sultan had dealings, eastern and central Europe, Russia, the Caucasus, and Iran. They contain information not only about the period of Ottoman rule, but about earlier periods as well.

The archives of Ottoman provincial governments have been to a great extent destroyed or scattered, but they still exist in some cities which had considerable autonomy or a developed bureaucracy, for example, Sofia, Cairo, and Tunis. Recently an Egyptian historian, 'Abd al-Rahim, has found and used documentary sources for Egyptian local history in the eighteenth century.[25] For the history of the provinces, however, there is another rich source, the archives of the religious courts which contain not only records of judicial cases, but a variety of other documents both public and private (for example wills) which were registered in them; Raymond has recently used those of the Cairo court to investigate the structure of property and wealth in eighteenth century Egypt.[26] In Syria and other countries they are now being collected and made available for study.

Of the other states of the same period, archives exist in Morocco but have scarcely yet been studied. There are no surviving organised archives for Safavid Iran, but some attempts have recently been made to collect documents, and a work by Busse shows how much can be gathered even from a small number of documents.[27] For the eastern part of the Muslim world there is a source of vast potential importance, the Chinese archives of the Ming and Ch'ing dynasties.

For the Middle East in the nineteenth and twentieth centuries, much of what has been written is based on British and French diplomatic and consular papers. They will continue to be used for many different purposes, but so far as the internal history of the Ottoman, Qajar, and 'Alawi states is concerned, they are too well-known to make it likely that the study of them will generate exciting new ideas. The introduction of the 'thirty years' rule' in the British Public Record Office has made it possible, however, to study the period of British ascendancy in depth, and so illuminate the colonial relationship from one side at least. The archives of other European states, in particular the Austro-Hungarian Empire and Russia, have not been used so fully, and each will add something of its own: in the last phase of Ottoman history each consulate and embassy had its own group of clients and derived from them its own picture of Ottoman politics and society. But there is more to be learned from indigenous archives, which exist in abundance and have scarcely been used. Apart from Ottoman sources, the Egyptian state archives are particularly rich; organised for the use of scholars in the reign of King Fuad, they were used at that time by some historians for the history both of Egypt and of Syria under Muhammad 'Ali (A. Rustum published a large calendar of those dealing with Syria under Muhammad 'Ali,[28] and Deny a catalogue of the Turkish documents[29]). More recently, A. Schölch has made them the basis of a new study of the 'Urabi period,[30] which now for the first time can be seen through Egyptian rather than British eyes. Of other archives, perhaps the most unexpected discovery was that by Holt of the records of the Mahdist government in the Sudan,[31] a proof that all governments, however remote they seem from the ideal of bureaucratic order, rest upon paper, and paper is more often forgotten than destroyed. The Israeli state archives are also very complete and well-organised. In almost all Middle Eastern and North African countries a determined effort is now being made by local historians, with help from their governments, to discover and collect the documents for their national history.

Also for the modern period, the papers of banks and companies have scarcely been looked at, except in such pioneer works as Landes's *Bankers and Pashas*.[32] There are also more family and personal papers than might be expected. The private papers of British diplomats, officials and businessmen are being collected at Durham (for the Sudan) and Oxford (for other countries); there is no similar plan for collecting the papers of French officials in North Africa and Syria. Middle Eastern politicians keep more papers than they admit: in Egypt those of Nubar Pasha have been used by at least one historian, and those of Zaghlul Pasha also exist; for general Arab politics there is a large collection of Shakib Arslan's papers; for the development of the Jewish National Home, the Central Zionist Archives and the Weizmann Archives are of basic importance.

Rural records are the most difficult to find and use in any country where a traditional social order exists, but even they are coming to light. There are a large number of agricultural contracts among the papers of the Khazin family in the Lebanese Museum, and similar materials are now being used for work in progress in Morocco and Jordan. The writings of some French officials in North Africa contain a mass of precise and detailed observations of rural processes which have almost the value of documentary evidence: special mention can be made of Berque's *Structures sociales du Haut Atlas.*[33]

Archives and documents once discovered must be well looked after, and here all scholars are conscious of difficulties. The great archives of western European states are open, well arranged, and easy to use; the Russian Foreign Ministry papers are closed to most foreigners, although other Russian archives arc open; those of the Middle East tend to lie somewhere between these two points—sometimes open, sometimes not, access given to some scholars and not to others. Political strains, the desire of officials to use their authority, and of scholars to preserve their cultural capital all play a part. Even when open the archives are not always easy to use: they may be badly arranged, badly indexed, and catalogued badly if at all; there may be few trained archivists to look after them, and few or no facilities for photocopying. In Turkey, a commission has been studying the reorganisation of the archives and there is a plan to train archivists, but here and elsewhere there is a long way to go.

There are two types of document which, in Bernard Lewis's words, have survived 'because they are written on metal and on stone': coins and inscriptions. The study of coins can of course help to elucidate not only the history of dynasties but economic and financial history and, within limits, the transmission of artistic forms. Much work has been done to collect and study them, largely under the inspiration of G. C. Miles, and collections exist for many of the Muslim dynasties. Inscriptions are more valuable still. As Sauvaget has said (following van Berchem),[35] most Islamic inscriptions illustrate one or the other of two great themes, divine power and political authority, and there are fewer administrative inscriptions than in classical antiquity; but those that record endowments can be used to date buildings and identify patrons, and so trace the lines of trade or conquest and the accumulation of wealth. Medieval Arabic inscriptions have been collected on a large scale in the *Corpus Inscriptionum Arabicarum*[36] and the *Répertoire chronologique d'épigraphie arabe*,[37] but little has been done to collect Persian inscriptions, or Arabic ones in Iran.

Buildings and the sites or ruins of them could also be more fully used as sources of historical information. There have been surprisingly few serious excavations of Islamic sites since Hamilton excavated at Khirbat al-Mafjar[38] and Schlumberger at Qasr al-Hayr al-Gharbi and Lashkari Bazar. Only a handful of recent or current excavations exist: those of Scanlon at Fustat, Whitehouse at Siraf, Grabar at Qasr al-Hayr al-Sharqi, a few done by the Iraqi Department of Antiquities, and a few in Iran. The reasons are obvious, shortage of trained personnel and money: it is natural that whatever funds are available should go mainly to excavations of ancient sites of periods for which no written sources exist. But lack of funds can only partly explain the long delay before definitive reports are published.

Rather more has been done to study buildings which still stand. Sauvaget's classical studies of Muslim cities in Syria,[39] Creswell's of Cairo,[40] and those of G. and W. Marçais in North Africa[41] have provided solid foundations on which a few scholars are building: Kessler in Cairo,[42] Sourdel-Thomine in Syria and Iran,[43] Pugachenkova in Central Asia,[44] and Ayverdi[45] and Kuran[46] in Turkey. Very recently, however, it has been possible for a reviewer to describe Golombek's study of the shrine at Gazur Gah as 'the only major study of any Timurid monument in a Western language'.[47] There are still major cities and buildings for which no adequate study exists, and the need is the more urgent because many of the monuments are in a bad state of repair; at least work is now starting on a French survey of medieval buildings in Cairo and a British one in Jerusalem.

When cities have still to be studied, it is too much to expect that much work should have been done on the archaeology of the countryside. Adams' *Land Behind Baghdad*[48] is a good example of the way in which archaeological and other techniques can be combined in order to study the changing pattern of land use in a single district. In regions like the inner plain of Syria and the Sahel of Tunisia, where land use has shifted throughout history, the excavation of abandoned villages might help us to understand the interaction of settled and pastoral life.

A historical method now used profitably in other parts of the world, but scarcely at all in the Middle East, is that of recording 'oral history'. This expression covers two very different kinds of activity. The first is the recording of the memoirs of people who have played a part in public life; the only systematic attempts being made are those at the Hebrew University of Jerusalem and the American University of Beirut, but Seale's *The Struggle for Syria*[49] shows how a book can be built upon hundreds of interviews with politicians, whose replies to skilful questions have been subtly analysed. By oral history we can also mean, however, the recording of the collective memory of a community, particularly of a small-scale, self-enclosed, illiterate community. This method has been much used in sub-Saharan Africa to supplement the limited written sources, and its use is one of the reasons for the rapid advance made in African history in the present generation. For the Middle East there are only a few works (done more by anthropologists than historians) in which personal observation and interviews are used together with documentary sources: good examples are Evans-Pritchard's *The Sanusi of Cyrenaica*[50] and Berque's *Histoire sociale d'un village égyptien au XXème siècle.*[51]

If the sources are to be properly used there is a need for various 'tools', not all of which exist. In some ways indeed the worker in Islamic history is well favoured. As bibliographical aids he has Sauvaget's *Introduction to the History of the Muslim East*,[52] revised by Cahen and translated into English with further revisions; the older biobibliographical work for Arabic literature by Brockelmann,[53] a more recent one by Kahhala,[54] and the latest by Sezgin;[55] a similar work by Graf for Christian Arabic literature;[56] and for Persian that by Storey (of which the revised version only exists in Russian).[57] But catalogues or even simple lists of many archives and important collections of documents and manuscripts are defective. Published selections of documents with annotations, which can serve as manuals of diplomatic, are not entirely absent; apart from those by Stern and Busse already mentioned, different kinds of Ottoman document have been published in English by

B. Lewis[58] and Heyd,[59] in French by Sauvaget and Mantran,[60] and in Turkish by Barkan[61] and others.

For articles in European languages, the *Index Islamicus* is an excellent working tool: there is an *Index Iranicus* for Persian articles and a similar work for Turkish articles; an *Index Arabicus* is in an advanced state of preparation in England; and an *Index Hebraicus* is being compiled, also in England.[62] We need cumulative lists of books newly published in Middle Eastern countries where the practice of reviewing books is not widespread, and abstracts of books and articles in languages not widely known among scholars (in particular, Russian, but in future, Japanese as well), to supplement those which appear in *Abstract Islamica* and *Orientalistische Literaturzeitung*.

Of handbooks which offer a wide range of basic information, the *Encyclopaedia of Islam*,[63] in both the first and second editions, is a magnificent product of sustained international cooperation; it should be supplemented by the Turkish *Islam-Ansiklopedisi*.[64] The *Handbuch der Orientalistik*[65] and the 'index documentaire' in D. and J. Sourdel's *La Civilisation de l'Islam classique*[66] are useful for quick and reliable reference. For genealogies there is Zambaur's *Manuel*[67] and Bosworth's *The Islamic Dynasties*,[68] and for chronology, Freeman-Grenville's *The Muslim and Christian Calendars*.[69]

Other kinds of tools are more defective, however. A need felt by historians of all periods is for better maps and plans. Roolvink's *Historical Atlas of the Muslim Peoples*[70] is excellent for introductory teaching purposes, but not detailed enough for research. Of modern maps showing towns and routes as well as physical features, those produced by the French administrations in Syria and Lebanon and in North Africa are admirable, but for some other regions there seems to be nothing more reliable and full than the maps produced by European General Staffs before the First World War. Of city plans, those for Cairo compiled by Bonaparte's savants and published in the *Description de l'Egypte*[71] are unique; for most other cities there can be nothing so full, but Sauvaget's plans of the growth and development of Aleppo and Damascus[72] provide a model to follow.

A need which historians share with others working in Islamic studies is for more adequate dictionaries. For Ottoman Turkish, a reprint of Redhouse's *Lexicon*[73] appeared recently, but for Arabic and Persian there is a need for dictionaries on historical principles.

The task of compiling them, however, is probably too great—the prototype of them, the Oxford English Dictionary, took half a century to complete in more spacious days. Failing this, what is perhaps most urgently needed is an Arabic dictionary which gives special attention to the middle period of Arabic, when the specialised vocabulary for every sphere of knowledge had been more or less fixed in the form it retained until the nineteenth century. Dozy's *Supplement*[74] is still the best guide to it, but it needs to be expanded and brought up to date.

It would be helpful, too, to have more dictionaries for Arabic dialects, and detailed studies of the development and meaning of technical terms, which are living beings undergoing continuous change. Massignon's study of the growth of the technical language of Sufism provides a model,[75] and some suggestive essays by B. Lewis have traced the evolution of political terms.[76] The language of poetry is of particular importance for all researchers, as almost every work contains a wealth of allusions to Arabic and Persian poetry, which lie at the heart of secular culture; the Hebrew University of Jerusalem has built up on index cards a valuable concordance of early Arabic poetry, and something like it is needed for Persian.

Adequate facilities for publication are also needed. The editing of texts goes on all the time, but important works too numerous to mention still lie in manuscript, and many of those printed long ago need to be republished in critical editions, and some of them with subject indexes. Of editions of Arabic histories, among those for which many scholars feel the need are the *Kamil* of Ibn al-Athir, the *Masalik al-absar* of al-'Umari, the *Muqaddima* of Ibn Khaldun, and al-Jabarti's *'Aja'ib al-athar*. The vast bulk of the Ottoman chronicles also needs re-editing.

It has become increasingly difficult to publish academic theses and monographs in the traditional form, even with a subsidy. Most American theses can be obtained on microfilm, but this is not satisfactory for general use. A combination of offset printing with direct distribution, through exchange between universities and advertisement in periodicals, would seem to be the most promising approach. This has already been tried in Germany with the series *Islamkundliche Untersuchungen*.

The general opinion seems to be that there are enough learned periodicals. Apart from general historical periodicals of a kind which are open to articles dealing with non-Western history, like

Annales or *Comparative Studies in Society and History*, there are now almost too many general 'orientalist' and 'Islamic' periodicals. It would be useful if some of them could become more specialised in their interests; *The International Journal of Middle East Studies, Middle Eastern Studies,* and *The Journal of the Economic and Social History of the Orient* show how valuable it is to have periodicals focused, through the personal concern of an editor, on a certain type of problem. Apart from learned journals in the strict sense, there is a need for regular 'newsletters', which give news of recent publications, conferences, and work in progress, and publish bibliographical or other 'notes and queries', and also for yearbooks or special issues of periodicals which could include works of, say, 100 pages, too long for an article in a journal, but too short for a book.

In a discipline practised by so few, and where most of the few are scattered and isolated, it is essential to have some kind of framework within which ideas can be exchanged. There is a place, although it tends to be a marginal one, for Islamic historians in general congresses of historians or orientalists, but perhaps the most fruitful exchanges now take place among small groups of scholars discussing a limited and carefully defined problem: to give two examples, a series held in London (*Historians of the Middle East,*[77] *Political and Social Change in Modern Egypt,*[78] *Studies in the Economic History of the Middle East*[79]) and a series held in Oxford (*The Islamic City,*[80] *Islam and the Trade of Asia,*[81] *Islamic Civilisation 950–1150*[82]).

With so few specialists, it is probably too much to expect that there should be permanent organisations of Islamic historians in most countries, but mention should be made of the historical associations in Turkey which both express and have helped to direct that effort to rethink the Turkish past, which was one of the essential parts of the Kemalist revolution: the Turkish Historical Society, the Institute for the Study of Turkish Culture, and the Institute for Seljuk History and Civilisation.

It might be useful at this point to take stock of the progress made by our few dozen specialists, working for two generations or so with such sources and tools as we have described. It would be long and tedious to make a detailed survey of the field, period by period and country by country, but it may be possible to make some broad general statements.

First of all, there is a marked difference between the work done on different kinds of history. Most work has been done on explicitly political history, the narrative of wars and conquests, rulers, and governments. After that comes 'intellectual history': movements of thought, legal schools, and the scholars and writers who have carried on the inner process of Islamic history. Less has been written on social history, even if that term is used in the loosest possible way, and still less on economic history, even for the modern period where statistical material exists. (But there has been a change, as we shall see, in the last few years). Some kinds of history are just beginning to be written, for example, those of technology and population.

Secondly, there is a marked difference also between the extent to which different regions of the Muslim world have been studied. Most attention has been given to the lands lying around the eastern end of the Mediterranean, Asia Minor, Syria in the broader sense, and Egypt. The reasons for this are obvious: the close connection between these countries and the rest of the Mediterranean World, the richness of the historical sources, and the relative strength of the indigenous tradition of historiography, both medieval and modern. For similar reasons, much attention has been paid to the history of Muslim Spain and its interaction with Europe. But less work has been done on the North African coast, the Sudan and the Arabian Peninsula, and Iraq after the first few centuries, and least of all on Iran and the lands beyond the Oxus.

Thirdly, some periods have been more thoroughly studied than others, although none of them is near being exhausted. In spite of the paucity of literary sources, the study of Umayyad history has been renewed by archaeological methods and by meticulous examination of the sources, and has probably reached a point where a new synthesis could be made to supplement that of Wellhausen.[83] But the same cannot be said of the 'Abbasids; the revolution by which they took power has recently been studied by Shaban, and there is some work on some of the institutions of their rule, notably Sourdel on the Vizirate,[84] but later 'Abbasid history has been little studied except in patches (for example, Makdisi's work on eleventh century Baghdad[85]). Various chapters in the fifth volume of the *Cambridge History of Iran*[86] provide at least a chronological and institutional framework for the history of the Seljuks; in an early work, *La Syrie du nord à l'époque des croisades*,[87] Cahen studied Syria during the Seljuk period, and in a later one, *Pre-Ottoman Turkey*,[88] the expansion of the Turks and Islam into Asia Minor. There is very little about the Fatimids or about early Maghribi history, although there is more for the later Middle Ages—Brunschvig's *La Berbérie orientale sous les Hafsids*[89] deserves special mention. About Spain, there is above all the work of Lévi-Provençal.[90] For the Ayyubids, Gibb has written some penetrating essays;[91] for the Mamluks of Egypt even the basic institution, the military society, has not yet been thoroughly studied, although Ayalon has laid very solid foundations[92] and Darrag has studied one reign in depth.[93]

For Iran in the same period, the work of Spuler is important.[94] For the Safavid period, there are a number of monographs, mainly by German scholars, and there has been a certain concentration on the origins of the dynasty;[95] Minorsky's annotated translation of *Tadhkirat al-muluk*[96] elucidates the administrative system, and Aubin's studies[97] throw light on the way in which the regime inserted itself into Iranian society.

In general, however, much less work has been done on Safavids than on the Ottomans, and it is easy to see why: the immense range of Ottoman rule or influence, and the existence of the archives. Already twenty years ago, before the archives had been explored, Gibb and Bowen[98] tried to provide a framework within which later Ottoman history at least could be understood. This has stood for a generation, but has probably now served its purpose of stimulating thought. Detailed research in the archives and other manuscript sources has made it possible to form a clearer, fuller, and in some ways different view of the nature and working of the central government and the system of taxation. Much of this work has been done by Turkish scholars, notably by Uzunçarşili[99] and Inalcik, whose recent book, *The Ottoman Empire: the Classical Age 1300–1600*,[100] offers a clear summary of the present state of research.

The strength of such work lies in its grasp of the working of the central government. Less has been done on other aspects of Ottoman society. For the legal system, some articles by Heyd and his posthumous book on Ottoman criminal law[101] go beyond the textbooks to the ways in which law was actually interpreted and administered. The organisation of industry and trade has also attracted some attention; in particular the international trade, for which European sources can be used in conjunction with Ottoman, as they have been by Inalcik in his study of the silk trade.[102]

It is inevitable that more attention should have been paid to the central government and the capital than the provinces, and right that it should be so; any attempt to write the history of the provinces, even of remote ones which appear to have been virtually independent, must take full account of Ottoman policies and methods if the picture is not to be distorted. A considerable amount of work on administration, taxation and land has been done in the Balkans, where a number of Ottomanists in the successor-states have worked effectively on local records, in Hungary, Bulgaria, Albania, Rumania, and above all in Yugoslavia. Apart from them, a great advance has been made in the study of the province of Egypt. Until a few years ago most of what was written was still based on three sources, Jabarti's chronicle, the *Description de l'Egypte,* and Volney's *Voyage.* But in the last few years three historians asking different questions have changed our understanding. Shaw, basing himself on fiscal records, has explained in great detail the administrative structure,[103] Holt, using a wide range of chronicles, has analysed the nature and history of the Mamluk beys;[104] and Raymond has studied, among much else, the delicate balance between government control and political activity in Cairo.[105] For other provinces less work has been done. In Anatolia there are some local histories of varying quality; in Syria, two or three works on the cities and—something very rare—Salibi's investigations of the rural nobility of Mount Lebanon.[106] For Ottoman North Africa (and for Morocco in the same period) there is least work of all; but articles by Hess[107] and by Mantran[108] remind us that here also the Ottoman presence was a reality.

For modern history much the same can be said; considerable work has been done or is in progress, but it is not evenly spread over the field. The greater part of it deals with two kinds of subject. The older books dealt mainly with the European powers' relations with each other and with the Ottoman Empire, Iran, Egypt, or Morocco; these states appeared only as the passive body over which the powers argued and negotiated, or as the scene of disturbances which led to a readjustment of their relations with each other. Langer's *The Diplomacy of Imperialism*[109] is a classic example of the meticulous research produced within such a framework, and Anderson's *The Eastern Question*[110] a useful summary of the results of such work. The opening of the British

archives to the end of the Second World War has made possible a
large amount of new work, in particular on the relations between
the powers and the nationalist movements of the Middle East
during the First World War.[111] But only a few articles, for
example, those of Naff[112] and Cunningham,[113] try to see the local
governments as active parties.

More recent work has somewhat shifted the point of view, and
deals mainly with the attempts of central governments to 'reform'
or 'modernise' their countries in the light of ideas derived from
Europe. In this perspective the local governments are seen as
active, but only with an activity derived from Western models, and
the societies they ruled appear as passive masses. Much work of
this kind has been done by Turkish as well as Western scholars,
and two important works of synthesis, Lewis's *The Emergence of
Modern Turkey*[114] and Davison's *Reform in the Ottoman Empire
1856–1876*,[115] represent this tradition at its best. On the similar
movement in Egypt there is old work by French, Italian, and
Egyptian scholars, but little up-to-date critical work. There is a
rapidly increasing amount of work on 'reforming' policies carried
out by European imperial governments; the older books tend to
accept uncritically the imperial rulers' own explanation of their
motives and assessment of their success but more recent works,
based on archives and private papers, try to relate reforming
policies more realistically to imperial interests, and to set them in
the context of a relationship between peoples rather than dealing
with them in a vacuum. Here again most work has been done on
Egypt (books by Tignor[116] and Lutfi al-Sayyid[117] come to mind),
and less on French than on British dependencies, apart from a few
works like Ageron's important analysis of French policy in
Algeria.[118]

By a logical extension, the ideas or ideologies in terms of which
'reform' or modernisation could be justified or criticised have
attracted much attention. On movements of Islamic reform, there
are important works by Adams[119] and Jomier,[120] and a deep
critique by Gibb;[121] on Pan-Islam as a political movement, Keddie's
life of Jamal al-Din al-Afghani[122] summarises recent research and
answers some but not all questions; S. Mardin's *The Genesis of
Young Ottoman Thought*[123] investigates the origins of one kind of
nationalism; for Arab nationalism, works by Zeine,[124] Dawn,[125]
Haim,[126] and Kedourie[127] query an older interpretation derived
from Antonius' *The Arab Awakening*.[128] On the changes of social

structure that underlie political change or are moulded by it, not much was written until a few historians began to look at the Middle East from a new angle.

If we were concerned with quantity alone, the picture which has just been sketched would be one of a field in which not much work was done in the past, but more is now being done (at least in parts of it), and still more will be done in future. But no one working in the field or looking at it closely would feel quite so confident about the progress being made. In the discussions out of which this study arose, considerable disquiet was expressed about the quality of the work being produced. It was generally felt that the standard of work being done on Islamic history was not only far lower than that on European or American history, which have had a 100 years' start, but also lower than that being done on Chinese and Japanese history. When we talk of lower standards, we may mean something which can be perceived but is difficult to define: standards of 'craftsmanship' shown in the use of sources, the arrangement of materials, and the mastery of argument, for example. But we mean here something more specific: the extent to which attention is paid to the kind of problems that absorb historians today, and to ideas derived from the general historical culture of the age.

When we speak of a historian's 'ideas', we do not mean that he need work in the same way as a social scientist, by framing a hypothesis and looking for materials by which it can be tested. In the mind of every historian the particular has a certain primacy; there is something, which perhaps he cannot put into words, that moves his imagination toward some country, some age, some person, or some aspect of the human scene. Of course he must have a principle of selection and emphasis when he works on it, but he can derive it from more than one source. He may have an explicit theory, a hypothesis about causal or logical connections, or an 'organising concept', an 'ideal type' which particulars imperfectly embody; or ideas may come to him hidden and implicit in a moral norm, in some other work of history which has excited his mind, or diffused throughout his general culture. From these principles and ideas there flows in turn a certain definition of the subject matter: what is meant by 'Islamic' or 'Middle Eastern' history, and how it should be divided into periods or into regions of the 'Islamic world'.

To many of those who took part in the discussions from which this study sprang, it seemed that the structure of ideas around which historical writing on Islamic history has been built is inadequate, in the sense that it does not enable the historians to explain many of the features of Islamic history, or to answer the questions or satisfy the demands of historians working in other fields. In other words, too little work in Islamic history has been written by those whom other historians would recognise as genuine historians sharing in their historical culture. In spite of changes in the past generation, most work has been done by 'general orientalists'. At one time it was inevitable that this should be so. As the only scholars genuinely interested in the Muslim world, and the only ones who possessed the essential key to unlock its secrets, the knowledge of its languages, the orientalists of an older generation were called upon to do many things without being fully prepared to do all of them: to teach languages, appreciate literature, study history, explain religious and legal systems, even to advise governments and enlighten public opinion on political matters. The greatest of them wrote and taught well over an amazingly wide field, and showed a breadth of knowledge and understanding to which few modern scholars can aspire, but they did so at a price. In some parts of their vast field they had to be content with a lower standard of craftsmanship than perhaps they would themselves have liked; most of them were at home in philology and religious studies, less so in pure literature, less still in history, and least of all in the social sciences. When writing history, they tended either to transpose into the field of historical study concepts drawn from fields in which they were more at home, for example that of religious studies, or else to take over the commonplaces of the general culture and information of their age—the political ideas of the day, or the historical or sociological ideas of yesterday—and to work within a framework already being discarded or refined by historians contemporary with them.

Very roughly, we can distinguish two main types of writing about Islamic history which sprang from these sources: the 'cultural–religious' and the 'political–institutional'. Of course these are ideal types and not mutually exclusive, and most writers on Islamic history belong to some extent to both, but as preliminary descriptions of leading ideas they may be useful.

For those who adopted the 'cultural–religious' approach, the organising principle was that of a 'culture', which could be defined in either of two main ways: first, in terms of a particular religious experience which, so far as the Islamic culture was concerned, was that of a prophet preaching a message which was later embodied in a tradition, that is to say, in systems of practices, beliefs and laws. From this leading idea sprang a historiography of which the characteristic problems were those of the way in which the prophetic message gave rise to the tradition, and the way in which the tradition moulded the lives of those who accepted the message, so that even the most 'secular' aspects of life could be seen as specifically 'Islamic', and it was possible, for example, to speak of an Islamic city, an Islamic countryside, and Islamic governments or armies. Secondly, the unifying factor in the culture could be seen in terms of a human 'world view', transmitted from one culture to another and modified by the transmission: the Islamic world view was created by the transmission of that of classical antiquity and its modification (to a greater or lesser extent) by Islam, and its characteristic problems were those of the ways in which the Muslim world adopted classical culture, and the ways in which it preserved, developed, or distorted it before handing it on to Western Europe. With all the necessary reservations, we might regard Goldziher,[129] Arnold,[130] and Gibb[131] as falling within the first group, and Becker,[132] von Grunebaum,[133] and Sauvaget[134] within the second.

The political–institutional approach also starts from a general concept, that of an organised system of government. Insofar as books in this category went beyond narrative—of the ways in which power was seized, used, and lost—to interpretation, they too tended to fall into two groups: those concerned with the analysis of institutions, for example, fiscal institutions; and those concerned with politics as the expression of a certain 'spirit', defined in Islamic or in 'national' terms. The typical problems of this kind of history were problems about how power was obtained, organised, justified, used, and lost; there was an underlying assumption that society was moulded by political power. This kind of writing can be traced back to von Hammer[135] and Wellhausen,[136] and forward through Barthold[137] and Gibb again. For those like Gibb, who combined the political with the cultural approach, there was a special concern with the kind of culture which rulers patronised and from which they derived their moral or political concepts.

Both these schools of historians had a concept of Islamic history as something distinct and to be understood in its own terms. Of course even the firmest believer in Islamic history would have agreed that the Islamic world was contiguous with other worlds in time and space, but awareness of this was more fully present in intellectual than in political or social history. Schacht, following Goldziher, could show that elements from Roman, Byzantine, Talmudic and Sassanian law had infiltrated into the nascent religious law of Islam,[138] but historians tended to look at the Islamic state as something produced by internal processes. Thus most books on Islamic history began with a chapter on pre-Islamic Arabia but said almost nothing about Byzantium and the Sassanians. In the same way, the 'social system of Islam' was explained from within. What happened in the regions where Islam was the dominant religion was explained in terms of the nature of Islamic tradition, and a knowledge of Islam was regarded as the main key to an understanding of this tradition.

As a result, what Muslim countries and peoples had in common tended to be seen as more important than the differences between them; this meant in practice that, given the disproportionate amounts of work done in different parts of the field, a stereotype taken from the 'Turco–Arab' parts of the Near East was applied to other parts of the Muslim world. In the same way, there was a tendency to view Islamic history in terms of 'rise' and 'decline': Muhammad plants a seed, which grows to its full height under the early 'Abbasids, in terms both of political power and cultural 'renaissance'; after that, political fragmentation and cultural stagnation lead to a long decline from which the Muslim world does not begin to awaken until the nineteenth century, with the impact of Western civilisation and the stirrings of 'national spirit'.

It is only in this generation that historical work on the Middle East has begun to be fertilised by a new concept: that of 'social history', of which the principle is that of a 'social system', a whole system of human relationships in which a change in any part reacts on every other part. This idea can of course be developed and used in more than one way. There is an empirical English and American tradition, which springs less from an elaborate theory than from a shift of sentiment and interest away from rulers and governments to 'how ordinary people lived'. But three types of systematic thought about society and its past have also had an influence on historians of the Middle East: that of Max Weber, that of Marx and that of the *Annales* school of French historians, with their care for quantitative precision and their willingness to learn from other disciplines and to subject Islamic, like other, history to questions drawn from the general scientific activity of the age. In particular, the work of Braudel has had a profound influence, because of its underlying concepts and its methods, and also because of its obvious relevance to the history of the Middle East and North Africa.

For those who would call themselves social historians in one sense or another, 'Islamic history' means something different and must be subdivided in different ways. Few historians would wish to abandon the concept of Islamic history completely. Most would find it valid and useful within limits, and are aware of the danger of looking at the world in which Islam was the dominant religion as having no reality of its own, and having to be explained in terms of something other than itself: in its medieval phase as being simply a stage in the transmission of classical culture to Europe, a 'Middle East' in time as well as space, and in the modern phase a passive body on which Europe imposed itself.

But it is necessary to try to make sharper definitions and distinctions than earlier historians would have done. First of all we should separate two different groups of characteristics which seem to be common to most countries where Islam is the dominant religion. There are those which can be explained in terms of a common acceptance of Islam as a system of beliefs and worship: systems of law, certain kinds of social institutions moulded by law, common intellectual concerns, a certain relationship with the non-Muslim world, and a certain tradition of political discourse. On the other hand, there are similarities connected with the fact that, at least west of the Indian subcontinent, Islam has spread and taken root mainly in regions with a certain geographical and therefore socioeconomic structure: regions where land and water resources are most effectively used by a combination of sedentary cultivation and transhumant pasturage, a combination unstable and shifting by its nature; where long-distance trade routes have made possible the growth of large urban conglomerations in fertile areas; and where the combination of these two factors has produced a certain kind of symbiosis between cities and their rural hinterlands. It is important not to misinterpret the relationship between these two types of similarity. It is tempting and dangerous to suggest that Islam spread in areas of a certain kind because it was specially suited to them, but it is safer to look at the relationship as a sociologist would, as one between two separate elements interacting within a single system, Islam 'embodying' itself in different forms in different ecological areas but also modifying the ways in which people live in them.

Secondly, it is important to distinguish different periods, in each of which terms like 'Islamic history' must be understood in different senses, and also where necessary to divide different kinds of history in different ways. So far as political history is concerned, a rough division would be this: an early period in which a Muslim élite ruled a society still largely non-Muslim in culture and norms, and did so within a single political structure; a second or medieval period marked by the dissolution of the unified structure and the establishment of a new kind of relationship between a ruling élite, mainly Turkish, and a society which had become predominantly Muslim by conversion and the extension of Islamic law; a third period, that of the five great integrative states, 'Alawi, Ottoman, Safavid, Uzbek and Mogul; and the modern period of the dissolution of all except one of these states, the domination of Europe, and the emergence of 'nation-states'. In this last period the concept of Islamic history loses some but not all of its value as a principle of explanation, and that of Middle Eastern history, itself a creation of British imperial policy, does not adequately replace it. (This explains why the term 'Islamic history', rather than 'Middle Eastern history', has been used throughout this paper). But it should not be assumed without further thought that economic or intellectual history would fall into the same periods.

Thirdly, we must make certain geographical distinctions. All Iranian historians are aware, as we have said, that the categories in terms of which we tend to see Islamic history are mainly derived from a study of the western or 'Turco-Arab' part of the Muslim world. The eastern or 'Turco-Iranian' part needs to be interpreted in other terms: because of the different forms that Islamic belief and culture took there, different ecologies, and geographical links with India and Inner Asia. So too does the Maghrib, which can be regarded as a separate unit culturally and ecologically; in a striking article, Burke has shown that the framework into which Gibb and Bowen fitted Ottoman history in the eighteenth century cannot be used for that of Morocco.[139] These broad divisions of course can in their turn be subdivided.

It is clear, then, that words like 'Islamic history' do not mean the same things in different contexts, and that in no context are they enough by themselves to explain all that exists. In other words, 'Islam' and the terms derived from it are 'ideal types', to be used subtly, with infinite reservations and adjustments of meaning, and in conjunction with other ideal types, if they are to serve as principles of historical explanation. The extent to which they can be used varies according to the type of history we are writing. They are least relevant to economic history; as Rodinson has shown in *Islam et capitalisme*,[140] the economic life of societies where Islam is dominant cannot be explained primarily in terms of religious beliefs or laws. In spite of the influence of Islamic law on commercial forms, other kinds of explanation are more relevant: as Cahen[141] and others have suggested, concepts such as 'Near Eastern', 'Mediterranean', 'medieval', 'preindustrial' society are more useful than that of Islamic. For sociopolitical history, Islam can furnish some elements of explanation but by no means all that are needed. The institutions and policies of even the most fervently 'Islamic' states cannot be explained without taking into account geographical position, economic needs, and the interests of dynasties and rulers. Even the history of those institutions that seem to be based upon Islamic law cannot be wholly explained in these terms: a concept like 'Islamic slavery' dissolves if one looks at it closely; as Milliot's examination of the *'amal* literature of Morocco suggests,[142] there were always ways in which local customs were incorporated into Islamic law as it was actually practised. Only some kinds of intellectual history, at least before the modern period, can be explained in mainly Islamic terms, as a process by which ideas from outside were blended with those generated from within Islam itself to form a self-maintaining and self-developing system; even the *falasifa* must now be seen, not as Greek philosophers in Arab clothes, but as Muslims using the concepts and methods of Greek philosophy to give their own explanation of the Islamic faith.[143]

New concepts of 'social history' lead also to a different emphasis in the choice of subjects, in particular, to a new preference for economic subjects, for the study of those gradual and long-term changes in production and trade which can modify the basic social and even ecological structure of a society. A little work is now being done in medieval economic history; to older works on Iraq by Duri[144] and al-'Ali[145] can now be added newer ones on Egypt by Rabie[146] and Goitein[147] and a joint article by Lopez, Miskimin, and Udovitch,[148] which places Islamic trade in a wider context of the Mediterranean world. For the early modern period sources become more reliable, in the form of the Ottoman archives and the papers of European trading companies; works by Inalcik[149] based on the former and by Davis,[150] Valensi,[151] and Svoronos[152] on the latter show how effectively the methods of economic history can now be applied to these sources. For the nineteenth and twentieth centuries quantitative materials become fuller and more reliable, but surprisingly little use has been made of them, apart from the works of O'Brien,[153] Owen,[154] and Chevallier,[155] dealing with basic problems of development, and some suggestive essays by Issawi.[156] A newer kind of history, that of population and all the factors which affect it, has scarcely begun to be written for the Muslim world, but once more there are exceptions: writings on Ottoman population by Barkan,[157] Issawi,[158] Todorov,[159] and Cook;[160] some remarks about disease and epidemics in North Africa by Valensi;[161] and a completed but unpublished work by Musallam on Muslim attitudes to birth control,[162] as shown in the legal, medical, pharmacological, and erotic literature.

But something else is beginning as well; it is an attempt to rethink old subjects by placing them in a new framework, that of society considered as a whole. Thus a new kind of political history can be written, in which governments are seen not as bodies acting freely upon a passive mass of subjects, but as one element in a system all parts of which are active in some sense. In political history conceived in this way, all kinds of questions arise in addition to the traditional one of the way in which control over the machine of government is seized and used. What are the ways in which those who control the government, whether rulers, soldiers, or officials, are themselves rooted in the society they rule and moulded by it? By what mixture of obedience, resistance, or acquiescence do different social groups react to the attempts of governments to control them? What are the different ways in which governments try to achieve their aims, by pressure and manipulation as well as bureaucratic control? What are the ways in which those who stand outside the machine of government in fact secure a share of political power or influence? How do those inside the government machine try to secure a certain freedom of action through access to the ruler or control of part of the bureaucracy, or through wealth and social power within the society they rule?

In the same way, while there will always be a type of intellectual history which considers the development of systems of ideas and their relationships with each other in abstraction, there are other ways of studying it as well, as a constituent part of a social process. To reduce ideas simply to 'expressions' of some social reality is probably not useful, but they can be studied validly from the point of view of the influence they have on life as it is lived in different social contexts, and the process of 'selection' by which some ideas take root and spread and others do not; what is still more important, thinkers can be seen not just as thinkers but as products of a social milieu and as performing certain social roles. Thus the *'ulama* are not just the preservers and transmitters of a certain intellectual tradition, but hold certain offices, enjoy certain privileges, have links with various social groups, and the fact that they are *'ulama* is not enough by itself to explain their roles; a recent book edited by N. Keddie shows this clearly.[163] In the same way, there can be a social history of the arts, architecture, and science; but so far little has been done to open up such subjects.

So many different historical themes can be seen in these new perspectives, that it is possible only to make a personal choice among them. Here, then, are four different kinds of theme which have excited at least one mind. First, urban history: since so much of the source material deals primarily with cities and their inhabitants, it is natural that social historians should find a particularly rich field here. There is a relatively long tradition of Islamic urban studies, but the older works were concerned mainly with the city as an artifact, that is, the ways in which streets and buildings were made and arranged, and were modified and changed in course of time. In this tradition can be placed the important studies of Hautecoeur and Wiet,[164] Sauvaget,[165] Marçais,[166] and by extension, more modern works concerned with the growth of cities in space, their division into quarters, and other problems of this kind, such as Abu Lughod on Cairo[167] and Ayverdi on Istanbul.[168] In later work, however, the main interest has shifted to the city as a social organism, the way in which the different parts interact so as to maintain a certain equilibrium, the lines along which their strength is mobilised, the bargains they can strike with the government, and the relations of economic change and political dependence between the constituent groups—'*ulama*, merchants, and skilled artisans; Christians and Jews; proletarians and temporary dwellers in the towns. This is a subject mainly exploited by French historians: Cahen on 'Movements populaires et autonomisme urbain',[169] Le Tourneau on Fez,[170] Mantran on Istanbul,[171] and Raymond in a number of articles and a comprehensive book on Cairo;[172] to these we should add Lapidus' *Muslim Cities in the Later Middle Ages*,[173] which, beyond its explicit subject, defines an ideal type of wider relevance.

Closely connected with this, but extending far beyond the city, is the study of the systems of patronage around which society was organised for political purposes: those pyramids of relations of protection and dependence which ran all through society, linking the most remote and 'closed' communities with a broader society and ultimately with the great cities and their governments, providing a certain protection for the powerless, and a machinery for political mobilisation for the 'notables' at the top, and a means of 'manipulation' for governments to extend their influence even beyond the range of bureaucratic control. By their nature they were unstable, because they were always tending to move in both directions, those above trying to strengthen their control over those under them, and those below trying to extend their power of independent action: governments trying to turn 'notables' into bureaucrats, and bureaucrats trying to become 'notables'. Only a study of such systems can enable us to understand the dynamics of sociopolitical action in a 'traditional' society (but also, to some extent, in a 'modernising' society as well). Lapidus' book again provides an 'ideal type' of such systems in an urban environment; for the countryside and steppe, Lambton's *Landlord and Peasant in Persia*[174] analyses in depth the three-cornered relationship of government, landowner and cultivator as it shifts according to the relative strength of the first two; an article by G. Baer[175] describes the ambivalent position of those who occupy intermediate positions in the pyramid, the village '*umdas*, at the same time agents of the government and leaders of the local community.

Thirdly, the study of what appear to be recurrent 'tribal' or nomadic movements in Islamic history needs to be carried further. With many variations, the normal type of Middle Eastern rural community is a mixed society of sedentary cultivation and transhumant pasturage. That being so, it is no longer possible to fall back on an old interpretation of Islamic history in terms of an inherent antagonism between 'the desert and the sown'. Pastors and cultivators may be the same people, or belong to the same community, or live in some kind of symbiosis with each other. The real problems are of two kinds. First, how can we explain the long-term shifts of the balance between cultivation and pasturage? It would be unsafe to assume that they are what they may seem to be, movements of population, with one group pressing against another; they may be so, but they may also be changes within an existing community, from one type of land use to another, and this may be caused by changes of climate, technology, or commercial demand. Secondly, how can we explain those great political movements which lead to changes of ruler and appear to have a nomadic basis? There seems to be a contradiction here between what historians tell us about the rise of great tribes and federations that overrun countries, capture cities, and found empires, and what seems to be the inability of pastoral people to generate from within themselves groupings larger than those necessary for economic life—the units of herding or migration. The beginnings of an answer can be found by carefully distinguishing names from things. Old tribal names may continue to be used although the reality within them has changed, like those of Qays and Yemen in eighteenth century Lebanon or nineteenth century Palestine; the use of those names may mean that the language of kinship is being used to denote not a real kinship group but a 'political' construction, a grouping of different elements, not all of them kin and not all of them nomadic, around a leading man or family. This grouping may be brought about by a leader who himself comes from within a nomadic community, but is more likely to be brought about from outside, by one who controls fixed resources and means of political action in the city.[176]

Fourthly, a special importance attaches to small-scale studies of limited regions and communities within a broader framework, as it is only through them that we can understand what really happened in history. States act differently in different parts of their domains; beliefs mean something different to different communities; the symbiosis between citizens, villagers, and tent dwellers varies for geographical, economic and political reasons. This is true of all periods of history, but let us take the earliest period as an example. The 'Islamic conquest' can be understood further only by regional studies of the process of conquest, the process of Islamisation, and the way in which the new rulers adopted and changed the legal and administrative systems they found. So there is a need—where sources permit—for the study of individual cities or quarters of them, of districts and villages, and of particular social groups and religious communities. Here again, some work is now being done: Goitein's investigations of the Jewish community of medieval Cairo,[177] Salibi's minute inquiries, already mentioned, into the origin of Lebanese families,[178] Chevallier's study of the way in which the small-scale economy of the Lebanese villages was affected by the industrial revolution in Europe and the political results of this,[179] and K. Brown's work on a seaport in Morocco.[180]

The social historian must of course look beyond history to the social sciences for some of the concepts and methods he uses. This is most obvious in economic history: a comparison of Davis's book with older work by Masson and Wood on the Levant trade[181] will show how much more a trained economic historian can extract from the sources. In the same way, Owen's book on *Cotton and the Egyptian Economy*[182] is clearly a product of recent discussions about economic development, and sets Egypt in the nineteenth century in a perspective derived from studies of India and Japan in the same period.

From sociology historians seem to have derived little. Some, for example Lapidus, have been influenced by the ideas of Max Weber, but sociology does not seem to have generated a method which can be validly applied to the past, and to preindustrial societies. Human geography, in the sense in which French scholars understand it, has had a greater influence. More than American scholars, French historians seem almost all to have a vivid sense of ecology, of the relationship between the land and the people.

Few historians would claim to have learned much from political science, and this perhaps is an example of the time lag which exists between changes in the ideas and methods of a subject and the spread of an awareness of them to those practising other disciplines. An old kind of political science, which was concerned with the analysis of formal political institutions, was clearly not relevant to ages and societies which had no such institutions. The theories of political development or modernisation, which were current a few years ago, seemed to most historians too general to help much in studying particular societies, particularly those of previous ages. In the last few years, however, there has developed a new kind of analysis of non-institutional modes of politics, of the different ways in which social groups become political forces oriented toward the acquisition of power. So far, only one or two attempts have been made to apply these concepts to the past: notably by Harik in *Politics and Change in a Traditional Society*,[183] an attempt to see eighteenth and early nineteenth century Lebanon in the framework of a certain theory of politics.

The social science from which many historians claim to have profited most is social anthropology, and it is easy to see why. It deals with societies as a whole; it has developed through the study of small, closed, pre-industrial communities. As such it has concentrated on creating tools for the understanding of societies which work by habit and convention rather than formal rules and institutions; its methods are therefore particularly well adapted to the understanding of such aspects of Islamic society as the nature of patron–client relations, the distribution of power in a segmentary society, the role of kinship as a language to express and give depth to social relations, the integrative function of religious leaders and orders, and the relations of urban entrepreneurs and rural communities. Moreover, it has provided some important studies of Muslim societies; for example, those of Robertson Smith[184] and Evans-Pritchard.[185] For all these reasons social historians of 'Islamic' countries look to anthropology. This is profitable, but it may be a little dangerous: in the absence of historical sources about small rural communities, we may assume that they have never changed, and that what anthropologists have observed in the present or immediate past has always been true. Historians can use the findings of social scientists with safety only if they do not forget that they are historians.

Social history seems likely to be the dominant mode of history writing for the present generation, but as it gathers force its own limitations become clearer. Unless it is practised in the most sensitive way, the individual may disappear, and consciousness may disappear. Thus an even more complex type of history may be needed. Just as for the social historian politics must be seen within an entire social system, so it may be necessary to see the social system within a larger whole: in other words, to see it not only in itself but as it and its changes are mirrored in minds moulded by a particular culture, and not only mirrored but themselves changed by the way in which those minds see them.

There would be two main ways of writing such a history. It could be done in terms of a kind of collective mind: that of a whole age, a social group or a nation. For medieval history, events and changes as reflected in the minds of the urban literate class, the *'ulama,* could well be studied; it would be difficult to do this for any other group. For the modern age, Berque's *L'Egypte, impérialisme et revolution*[186] provides a remarkable example of social and political changes seen simultaneously in two perspectives, as events which lead both to a loss of collective national consciousness through the loss of symbols and to its recovery. It might however be difficult to carry out the same kind of study in countries where a unified national consciousness, moulded by geography and history, and preserved and developed by forces radiating from a single great city, does not exist. As an alternative, it might be possible to study an age as reflected in the mind of a single man. P. Brown's life of St Augustine[187] shows how this might be done, but so far it has not been done for the Muslim world, apart from brief sketches, such as a study by Berque of a Moroccan writer of the seventeenth century.[188]

The ideas which guide us in writing Islamic history will also guide us in forming the historians of a new generation. Clearly Islamic history, as it is now coming to be conceived, cannot be taught in a vacuum, as the only element in a higher education, but what is the larger framework into which it should be fitted? Should those who are primarily interested in Islamic history, and who are the teachers and research workers of the future, be taught within departments of history, or within departments of 'oriental studies'?

In the Middle East itself, the study of the history of the area forms the core of the curriculum of history departments. But in most universities in Europe and some in North America, Islamic history is mainly taught within departments of oriental studies. Most Islamic historians appear to be uneasy about the present situation. They feel that departments of oriental studies are for the most part dominated by the interests of those who teach languages and literature, and are without a full understanding of the nature and needs of historical study, and that history departments are hostile or indifferent to Middle Eastern history, because they do not want to spread limited resources too thinly, or because of a limitation of interests or imagination—or perhaps because Islamic historians have failed to make their subject a part of the general historical culture.

Perhaps the formal problem is not so fundamental as it may appear to be. The real problem is that in most universities there are too few Islamic historians for their views about the special needs of their subject to carry much weight, no matter which department they belong to. Islamic history will flourish as an academic discipline only if there are in some places enough teachers interested in it to be able to put into practice their ideas about how the historians of the future should be trained.

But how *should* they be trained? This is a question to which there could be many different answers, and it is possible only to put forward some personal ideas, which seem, however, to command much support. First, there is no doubt that those who wish to practise Islamic history seriously should sooner or later make a thorough study of Islamic civilisation in a broad sense, and of the languages in which it expressed itself. But it may be best for this study in depth to come after, not before, they have acquired a good general historical background. In Western Europe in particular, where specialised study may begin at the age of sixteen or so, the first degree can give a student's mind a basic formation it will never lose, and it is best that this formation should be in the fullest sense a historical one. (There would of course not be universal agreement on this, and that is not harmful; there are irreducible differences of temperament and approach, and disputes about how to teach history can themselves stimulate historical inquiry).

Secondly, what we call 'historical culture' should include from the beginning elements drawn from elsewhere than Islamic history alone, which cannot generate entirely from inside itself the stimulus to its own advance. What those elements should be will depend on the interests of teacher and student: certainly some European history, and perhaps some training in one or other of the social sciences.

Thirdly, within the teaching of Islamic history itself, it is not easy to attain a proper balance between 'medieval' and 'modern'. Probably most teachers would feel that a thorough knowledge of classical Islamic history and civilisation is important even for those who wish ultimately to study the modern world. It can provide a rich education by making the student familiar with great historical events and original ideas; it demands techniques so difficult, and a grasp of a way of thought so different from ours, that it can be acquired only by transmission from teachers. Besides, its legacy survives in the modern world. On the other side, however, there are dangers in approaching the modern world with a mind formed in the study of medieval history. He who wishes to understand modern history must have a deep knowledge of the great worldwide changes in thought, sentiment, and society that have occurred in recent times. A classical Islamist who looks at the modern Middle East may fall into a kind of 'reductionism', and minimise the extent to which even 'traditional' ideas and institutions have changed.

Just as some tools of research are defective or lacking, so are some teaching instruments. There are few introductory books that can be put into the hands of a beginner, at least in English-reading countries. Most students still begin, as they have done for the last twenty years, with Gibb's *Mohammedanism*[189] and Lewis's *The Arabs in History,*[190] but it is not easy to find books to read after them.

There are perhaps four kinds of books needed for teaching. First come works of *vulgarisation* or tentative synthesis (it can be no more than that in the present state of research). It is too early to hope for such a synthesis of the whole of Islamic history; the new *The Cambridge History of Islam,*[191] in spite of some excellent chapters, lacks a conceptual framework, a shared understanding of Islamic history. But the time has come when it should be possible to synthesise recent research on the first few centuries of Islamic history; French readers are better served here than English, by D. and J. Sourdel's *La civilisation de l'islam classique*[192] and Cahen's *L'islam des origines au début de l'empire ottoman.*[193] Something similar might be done for Ayyubid and Mamluk Egypt. For the first centuries of the Ottoman empire we now have Inalcik's book,[194] and for North Africa Julien's history in a revised edition,[195] and Abun-Nasr's more recent book,[196] but for Iran there is virtually nothing of an introductory kind except for a suggestive sketch by Bausani.[197] More generally, there is no comprehensive work on the development of Shi'i Muslim society. In spite of all the interest shown in modern history, there are no good surveys that go much beyond a narrative of political events on the eastern Mediterranean seacoast.

Secondly, teachers need books of a different kind, oriented toward problems rather than periods, surveying the present state of a problem and suggesting directions for future research. A good example of what is needed is provided by L. Valensi's *Le Maghreb avant la prise d'Alger*[198] in the series *Questions d'histoire,* a summing up, on the basis of current research, of the problem of whether or not the coming of French colonialism was a reaction to the socioeconomic stagnation of the Maghreb.

Thirdly, some teachers feel the need for source books, translated and annotated extracts from Islamic writings and other primary sources, which can be used to supplement the introductory surveys. Some good ones do exist: Lewis's *Islam,*[199] Sauvaget's *Historiens arabes,*[200] Williams's *Themes of Islamic Civilization,*[201] Gabrieli's *Arab Historians of the Crusades,*[202] and Issawi's volumes on economic history in the nineteenth century,[203] but more are needed. (Some teachers, however, prefer to make their own selection of sources, appropriate to the content and direction of their own teaching).

Fourthly, there is a general demand for translations into English or French of some at least of the chronicles and other sources, so that students may have some kind of contact with the original sources and the men who wrote them, even before they are able to read them in the original languages. Here once more the French student is better served than the English, thanks to the institution (now abolished) of the *thèse complementaire,* for which an edition or translation of a text was acceptable.

All through this study, it has been clear that scholarly work of every kind is needed. But this makes some kind of understanding about priorities more, rather than less, urgent, since research workers and resources are so scarce.

The scholar's imagination moves as it will, and it would be quite impossible to make decisions about priorities as between different countries or periods of history. But it might be possible to form a general opinion about the kind of work which should be encouraged and funded. There would probably be wide agreement about the urgency of such tasks as the following:

1. So far as *sources are concerned*, there seems an equal need for (a) the critical edition or re-edition of important chronicles in Arabic, Turkish and Persian and (b) the collection of documents of governments, law courts, religious communities, business concerns, and families, their proper classification, cataloguing, and

maintenance, and, as a necessary complement to this, the training of archivists.

2. So far as *tools* of research and teaching are concerned, a particular urgency seems to attach to (*a*) the publication of large-scale dictionaries of Arabic and Persian, dealing in particular with the language of the fully developed Islamic society and culture and (*b*) the publication of large-scale historical maps and atlases.

3. So far as the *organisation* of teaching and research is concerned, there seems a need for (*a*) the creation of groups of Islamic historians in at least a few universities and (*b*) the maintenance of close relations between historians through the organisation of specialised meetings and visits.

4. So far as the *content* of research is concerned, as we have said, in the last analysis every scholar must go his own way, but bodies that organise or finance research might pay special attention to projects concerned with (*a*) economic history, and more generally any work that tries to go beyond impressions and lay down firm quantitative bases; (*b*) detailed work on a small scale, such as the precise study of regions, cities, villages, families, religious communities or administrative institutions; and (*c*) work that tries to insert political and religious history into the total history of a society, in other words, by tracing the interaction between political institutions and movements, movements of thought and ideology, and the societies in which they exist, to form a more accurate and comprehensive, sensitive and living picture of 'Islamic history'.

Notes

Notes to Introduction

1. London etc., 1962.
2. J. Daniélou, *Le mystère du salut des nations* (Paris, 1948).
3. C. Journet, *L'église du verbe incarné*, 2 vols. (Paris, 1951, 1955); English trs., *The Church of the Word Incarnate*, vol. 1 (London, 1955).
4. R. W. Southern, *Western Views of Islam in the Middle Ages* (Cambridge, Mass., 1962); N. Daniel, *Islam and the West: the Making of an Image* (Edinburgh, 1960) and *Islam, Europe and Empire* (Edinburgh, 1966); J. D. J. Waardenburg, *L'islam dans le miroir de l'occident* (The Hague, 1961).
5. J. M. Keynes, *Essays in Biography* (London, 1933).
6. R. W. Chapman, *The Portrait of a Scholar, and other Essays* . . . (Oxford, etc., 1920).
7. E. H. Gombrich, *Aby Warburg, an Intellectual Biography* (London, 1970). See also the review of it by F. Gilbert, 'From art history to the history of civilization: Gombrich's biography of Aby Warburg', *Journal of Modern History,* vol. 44 (1972) p. 381.

Notes to Chapter 1

1. C. G. Montefiore, *Lectures on the Origin and Growth of Religion, as illustrated in The Religion of the ancient Hebrews* (London, 1892).
2. *Ibid.*, p. 548.
3. L. Goldziher, *Muhammedanische Studien*, vol. 2 (Halle, 1889–1890), English trs. S. M. Stern (ed.), *Muslim Studies*, vol. 2 (London, 1971); J. Wellhausen, *Das arabische Reich und sein Sturz* (Berlin, 1902), English trs. *The Arab Kingdom and its Fall* (Calcutta, 1927).
4. Montefiore, *op. cit.*, pp. 551–2.
5. Goldziher, *op. cit.*, p. 346f.
6. L. Gardet, *L'islam, religion et communauté* (Paris, 1967) p. 391f.
7. al-Ghazālī, *al-Radd al-jamīl li-ilāhīyāt 'Isa bi-sarīh al-injīl*, ed. and French trs. by R. Chidiac (Paris, 1939).
8. Rahmattallah al-Dihlawī, *Izhār al-haqq* (Istanbul A. H. 1284 [1867]). I must thank Miss A. Powell for drawing my attention to this book. See her article, 'Mawlānā Rahmat Allāh Kairāwanī and Muslim-Christian controversy in India in the mid-19th century', *Journal of the Royal Asiatic Society* (1976) i, p. 42f.

9. J. Jomier, 'L'Evangile selon Barnabe' in Institut Dominicain d'Etudes Orientales, *Mélanges 6* (Cairo 1959-61) p. 137f.

10. M. K. Husayn, *Garya zālima* (Cairo, 1958), English trs. by K. Cragg, M. K. Hussein, *City of Wrong: a Friday in Jerusalem* (Amsterdam, 1959).

11. *Ibid.*, English trs., p. 222.

12. M. T. d'Alverny, 'Deux traductions latines du Coran au moyen age', *Archives d'histoire doctrinale et littéraire du Moyen Age,* vol. 16 (1948) p. 69f.; R. W. Southern, *Western Views of Islam in the Middle Ages* (Cambridge, Mass., 1962); N. Daniel, *Islam and the West: the Making of an Image* (Edinburgh, 1960).

13. St John of Damascus, *De Haeresibus* in J. P. Migne, *Patrologia Graeca* 94, p. 764f., English trs. in D. J. Sahas, *John of Damascus on Islam* (Leiden, 1972) p. 51f.

14. St John of Damascus, *Disputatio Saraceni et Christiani,* Migne 96, p. 1336f., English trs. in Sahas, *op. cit.,* p. 99f.

15. St Thomas Aquinas, *Summa Theologica*, Part 2 ii, Question 10, 'Of Unbelief, in general'.

16. M. Luther in A. Malvezzi, *L'islamismo e la cultura europea* (Florence, 1956) p. 235.

17. W. Rainolds, *Calvino-Turcismus* (Antwerp, 1597) preface: quoted in Malvezzi, p. 247.

18. See N. Daniel, *Islam, Europe and Empire* (Edinburgh, 1966) p. 9.

19. See P. M. Holt, 'The treatment of Arab history by Prideaux, Ockley and Sale' in B. Lewis and P. M. Holt (ed.), *Historians of the Middle East* (London, 1962) p. 290f.

20. In J. A. Voltaire, *OEuvres complètes,* vol. 4 (Paris, 1877).

21. E. Renan, *L'islamisme et la science* (Paris, 1883) pp. 2-3.

22. E. Renan, *L'avenir de la science* (Paris, 1890) p. 50.

23. Lord Cromer, *Modern Egypt,* vol. 2 (London, 1908) pp. 123f., 569f.

24. See A. Hourani, 'Islam and the philosophers of history', chapter 2 of this volume.

25. E. Renan, *Histoire générale et système comparé des langues sémitiques,* pt. 1. 5th ed. (Paris, 1878) p. 409f.

26. See A. Hourani and S. M. Stern (eds.), *The Islamic City* (Oxford, 1970).

27. M. Rodinson, *Islam et capitalisme* (Paris, 1966), English trs. *Islam and Capitalism* (London, 1974).

28. C. Geertz, *Islam Observed; religious development in Morocco and Indonesia* (New Haven, 1968).

29. W. Cantwell Smith, 'Is the Qur'an the Word of God', *Questions of Religious Truth* (London, 1967) p. 39f.

30. H. Kraemer, *Religion and the Christian Faith* (London, 1956) p. 144.

31. C. Journet, *L'Eglise du Verbe incarné,* English trs. *The Church of the Incarnate* (London, 1955) p. 35f.

32. *Concile oecumenique Vatican II: documents conciliaires* (Paris, 1965) p. 215.

33. R. C. Zaehner, *At Sundry Times* (London, 1958) p. 27.

34. *Ibid.,* p. 195f.

35. L. Massignon, 'Les trois prières d'Abraham', *Opera Minora,* vol. 3

(Beirut, 1963) p. 804f. See J. D. J. Waardenburg, *L'islam dans le miroir de l'occident* (The Hague, 1961).

Notes to Chapter 2

1. L. Massignon, 'Situation de l'Islam', *Opera Minora*, vol. 1 (Beirut, 1963) p. 12.
2. R. W. Southern, *Western Views of Islam in the Middle Ages* (Cambridge, Mass., 1962).
3. *Ibid.*, p. 1.
4. *Ibid.*, p. 29.
5. *Ibid.*, p. 67.
6. *Ibid.*, p. 34.
7. N. Daniel, *Islam and the West: the Making of an Image* (Edinburgh, 1960).
8. *Ibid.*, p. 246.
9. *Ibid.*, p. 5
10. *Ibid.*, p. 272.
11. Malvezzi, *L'islamismo e la cultura europea* (Florence, 1956) p. 235.
12. *Ibid.*, p. 239.
13. *Ibid.*, pp. 261–2.
14. *Ibid.*, p. 241.
15. W. Rainolds, *Calvino-Turcismus* (Antwerp, 1597) preface: quoted in Malvezzi, *ibid.*, p. 247.
16. L. Brunschvicg (ed.), B. Pascal, *Oeuvres*, vol. 14 (Paris, 1921) pp. 37–8.
17. *Ibid.*, p. 38.
18. *Ibid.*, pp. 34, 36.
19 (London, 1697); cf. P. M. Holt, 'The treatment of Arab history by Prideaux, Ockley and Sale' in B. Lewis and P. M. Holt (eds.), *Historians of the Middle East* (London, 1962) p. 290f.; reprinted in P. M. Holt, *Studies in the History of the Near East* (London, 1973) p. 50f.
20. Holt, *ibid.*, p. 292.
21. J. M. A. Voltaire, *Essai sur les Moeurs*, chapter 7.
22. In J. M. A. Voltaire, *Oeuvres Complètes*, vol. 4 (Paris, 1877) p. 115.
23. *Ibid.*, p. 162.
24. D. Diderot and J. le R. d'Alembert, *Encyclopédie*, vol. 9 (Neufchatel, 1765) p. 864.
25. G. W. von Leibnitz, *Essai de Theodicée*, in C. J. Gerhardt (ed.), *Philosophischen Schriften*, vol. 6 (Berlin, 1885) p. 27; English trs. by E. M. Huggerd (London, 1952) p. 51.
26. J. J. Rousseau, 'Du Contrat Social' in B. Gagnebin and M. Raymond (eds.), *Oeuvres Complètes* (Paris, 1964) Book 4, chapter 8, pp. 462–3.
27. Marquis de Condorcet, 'Esquisse d'un Tableau historique des Progrès de l'Esprit humain' in A. Condorcet O'Connor and M. F. Arago (eds.), *Oeuvres*, vol. 6 (Paris, 1847) p. 1202; English trs. by J. Barraclough (London, 1953) pp. 86–7.

28. Comte de Boulainvilliers, *La Vie de Mahomed* (London, 1730) p. 247. (The spelling is that of the first edition.)
29. *Ibid.,* p. 3.
30. Cf. R. Simon, *Henry de Boulainviller* (Paris, n.d. [1941]).
31. M. Dunan (ed.), Comte de las Casas, *Le Memorial de Sainte-Hélène* (Paris, 1951) vol. 1, pp. 528-9; cf. C. Cherfils, *Bonaparte et l'Islam* (Paris, 1914).
32. J. B. Bury (ed.) E. Gibbon, *The History of the Decline and Fall of the Roman Empire,* vol. 5 (London, 1911) p. 361.
33. *Ibid.,* pp. 400-1.
34. *Ibid.,* pp. 419-21.
35. C. W. F. von Schlegel, *Philosophie der Geschichte,* vol. 2 (Vienna, 1829) pp. 70-107; English trs. by J. B. Robertson (London, 1846) pp. 317-42.
36. [J. H. Newman], *Lectures on the History of the Turks in its Relation to Christianity* (Dublin, 1854) p. 105.
37. *Ibid.,* p. 248.
38. *Ibid.,* p. 277.
39. *Ibid.,* p. 106.
40. *Ibid.,* p. 128.
41. Sir W. Muir, *The Caliphate, its Rise, Decline and Fall* (Edinburgh, 1924) p. 601.
42. Sir W. Muir, *The Life of Mohammed* (Edinburgh, 1912) p. 522.
43. H. Lammens, 'Mohamet fut-il sincère?', *Recherches de sciences réligieuses,* vol. 2 (1911) p. 48.
44. Cf. K. S. Salibi, 'Islam and Syria in the writings of Henri Lammens' in Lewis and Holt, *op. cit.,* pp. 330-42.
45. C. Forster, *Mohametanism Unveiled,* vol. 1 (London, 1829) p. 62; for Forster, see a work by his grandson, E. M. Forster, *Marianne Thornton* (London, 1956), in particular p. 145 and 163 ('his books . . . are worthless').
46. *Ibid.,* vol. 1, pp. 68-9.
47. *Ibid.,* vol. 1, p. 107.
48. *Ibid.,* vol. 2, p. 378.
49. Cf. J. Daniélou, *Le mystère du salut des nations* (Paris, 1948).
50. Cf. J. D. J. Waardenburg, pp. 136f., 257f., 283f.
51. L. Massignon, 'La Palestine et la paix dans la justice', *Opera Minora,* vol. 3 (Beirut, 1963) p. 461.
52. L. Massignon, 'Les trois prières d'Abraham', *Opera Minora,* vol. 3, pp. 811-12.
53. L. Massignon, 'Situation de l'Islam', *Opera Minora,* vol. 1, p. 14.
54. L. Massignon, *La passion d'al-Hosayn-ibn Mansour Hallaj,* vol. 2 (Paris, 1922) p. 463.
55. L. Massignon, 'L'homme parfait en Islam et son originalité eschatologique' in *Opera Minora,* vol. 1, p. 107f.
56. N. Daniel, 'Some recent developments in the attitude of Christians towards Islam' in A. H. Armstrong and E. J. B. Fry (eds.), *Rediscovering Eastern Christendom* (London, 1963) p. 165.
57. Y. Moubarac, *Abraham dans le Coran* (Paris, 1958) pp. 100, 107, 143.
58. M. Hayek, *Le Christ de l'islam* (Paris, 1959) pp. 10-16.

59. J. M. Abdel-Jalil, *Marie et l'Islam* (Paris, 1950).
60. Cf. D. Masson, *Le Coran et la révélation judeo-chrétienne*, 2 vols. (Paris, 1959); for a careful and responsible criticism by a Christian theologian, cf. G. C. Anawati, 'Vers un dialogue islamo-chrétien', *Revue Thomiste* (1964) 2 and 4.
61. L. Gardet, *La cité musulmane* (Paris, 1954); *Connaitre l'Islam* (Paris, 1958); 'Recherches de l'Absolu', *Les Mardis de Dar el-Salam 1951* (Cairo n.d.); L. Gardet and M. M. Anawati, *Introduction à la théologie musulmane* (Paris, 1948); G. C. Anawati and L. Gardet, *La mystique musulmane* (Paris, 1961).
62. J. Jomier, *Bible et Coran* (Paris, 1959) pp. 117-8.
63. *Concile OEcuménique Vatican II: Documents conciliaires* (Paris, 1965) p. 215.
64. K. Cragg, *Sandals at the Mosque* (London, 1959) p. 103f.
65. H. Kraemer, *Religion and the Christian Faith* (London, 1956) p. 144.
66. *Ibid.*, p. 85.
67. *Ibid.*, p. 334.
68. *Ibid.*
69. H. Kraemer, *World Cultures and World Religions: the Coming Dialogue* (London, 1960) p. 24.
70. *Ibid.*, p. 20f.
71. H. Kraemer, *The Christian Message in a Non-Christian World* (London, 1938) p. 215f.
72. I. Kant, 'Die Religion innerhalb der Grenzen der blossen Vernunft', *Werke*, vol. 6 (Berlin, 1907) p. 107; English trs. by T. M. Green and H. H. Hudson (Chicago, 1934) p. 98.
73. *Ibid.*, p. 103; English trs. p. 95.
74. *Ibid.*, pp. 111, 184n; English trs. pp. 102, 172n.
75. A. Quinton, 'Thought' in S. Nowell Smith (ed.), *Edwardian England, 1901-1914* (London, 1964) p. 277.
76. J. Strachan, 'Criticism (Old Test.)' in J. Hastings (ed.), *Encyclopedia of Religion and Ethics*, vol. 4 (Edinburgh, 1911) p. 314.
77. *Ibid.*, p. 317.
78. E. Renan, *Vie de Jésus* (Paris, 1879) pp. 158, 169.
79. D. F. Strauss, *Das Leben Jesu*, 2 vols. (Tübingen, 1840); English trs. by George Eliot, 3 vols. (London, 1846).
80. Cf. A. Schweitzer, *Von Reimarus zu Wrede* (Tübingen, 1906) pp. 137-59; English trs. by W. Montgomery, *The Quest of the Historical Jesus* (London, 1910) pp. 137-60.
81. A. von Harnack, *Mission and Ausbreitung der Christentums*, vol. 1 (Leipzig, 1915) p. 58; English trs. by J. Moffatt, vol. 1 (London, 1908) p. 56.
82. *Ibid.*, p. 44f; English trs. p. 42f.
83. C. H. Becker, 'Christentum und Islam', *Islamstudien*, vol. 1 (Leipzig, 1924) p. 386f; English trs. *Christianity and Islam* (London, 1909) p. 2f.
84. J. Wellhausen, *Prolegomena zur Geschichte Israels* (Berlin, 1883) p. 448; English trs. by J. S. Black and A. Menzies (Edinburgh, 1885) p. 422.
85. *Ibid.*, p. 422; English trs. p. 398.
86. *Ibid.*, p. 434; English trs. p. 409.

87. Cf. J. Wellhausen, *Das arabische Reich und sein Sturz* (Berlin, 1902); English trs. *The Arab Kingdom and its Fall* (Calcutta, 1927).

88. Cf. S. Dubnow, *Weltgeschichte des jüdischen Volkes*, vol. 9 (Berlin, 1929) p. 385f.

89. (Leipzig, 1876); English trs. by R. Martineau, *Mythology among the Hebrews* (London, 1877).

90. I. Goldziher, 'Muruwwa und Din', *Muhammedanische Studien*, vol. 1 (Halle, 1889) p. 1f; English trs. S. M. Stern (ed.), *Muslim Studies*, vol. 1 (London, 1967) p. 11f.

91. I. Goldziher, *Muhammedanische Studien*, vol. 2 (Halle, 1889–1890); English trs. S. M. Stern (ed.), *Muslim Studies*, vol. 2 (London, 1971); *Le Dogme et la loi de l'islam* (Paris, 1920); *Die Zâhiriten. Ihr Lehrsystem und ihre Geschichte* (Leipzig, 1884); cf. J. D. J. Waardenburg, pp. 11f, 111f, 125f, 239f, 265f.

92. H. A. R. Gibb, *Modern Trends in Islam* (Chicago, 1947) p. xi.

93. W. Cantwell Smith, *The Faith of Other Men* (New York, 1965) p. 17.

94. *Ibid.*, p. 20.

95. *Ibid.*, p. 16.

96. *Ibid.*, p. 59.

97. W. Cantwell Smith, *The Meaning and End of Religion* (New York, 1964).

98. G. W. F. Hegel, 'Vorlesungen über die Philosophie der Geschichte' in *Werke*, vol. 9 (Berlin, 1848) p. 431f; English trs. by J. Sibree (London, 1857) p. 369f.

99. A. Comte, *Système de Politique Positive*, vol. 3 (Paris, 1853) pp. 490–1: vol. 4 (Paris, 1854) p. 505f.

100. *Ibid.*, vol. 3, pp. xlvii–xlix.

101. *Ibid.*, vol. 4, pp. 508–9.

102. *Ibid.*, p. 145.

103. A. Von Kremer, *Culturgeschichte des Orients unter den Chalifen*, 2 vols. (Vienna, 1875–7); A. Sprenger, *Das Leben und die Lehre des Mohammed*, 3 vols. (Berlin, 1861–5); cf. J. W. Fück, 'Islam in European historiography', in Lewis and Holt (eds.), *op. cit.*, pp. 305–6.

104. L. Caetani, 'La funzione dell' Islam nell' evoluzione della civiltà' in *Scientia*, vol. 11 (Bologna, 1912) p. 397f.

105. C. H. Becker, *Islamstudien*, vol. 1, p. 16.

106. C. H. Becker, 'Christentum und Islam', p. 401; English trs. p. 39.

107. C. H. Becker, 'Der Islam als Problem', 'Der Islam im Rahmen einer allgemeinen Kulturgeschichte', 'Die Ausbreitung der Araber im Mittelmeergebiet', all in *Islamstudien*, vol. 1; cf. J. D. J. Waardenburg, pp. 50f, 88f, 121f, 249f.

108. G. Levi Della Vida, *Aneddoti e svaghi arabi e non arabi* (Milan and Naples, 1959) pp. 8–9.

109. E. Renan, *L'Islamisme et la Science* (Paris, 1883) p. 11.

110. *Ibid.;* cf. E. Renan, *Averroès et l'Averroïsme* (Paris, 1852) p. iii.

111. Comte de Gobineau, *Essai sur l'Inégalité des Races Humaines*, vol. 1 (Paris, 1884) p. 181f.

112. E. Renan, *Histoire générale et système comparé des langues sémitiques*, Part 1, 5th ed. (Paris, 1878) p. 3.

113. *Ibid.,* p. 6.
114. *Ibid.,* p. 14.
115. *Ibid.,* p. 409f.
116. Jamal al-Din al-Afghani, 'L'Islamisme et la Science', *Journal des Débats,* 18 and 19 May 1883; reproduced in *La Réfutation des Matérialistes,* French trs. by A. M. Goichon (Paris, 1942). For Jamal al-Din's Persian origin, see N. R. Keddie, *Sayyid Jamāl ad-Dīn 'al-Afghānī': a Political Biography* (Berkeley, Cal., 1972) p. 10f.
117. J. Burckhardt, *Historiche Fragmente* (Stuttgart, 1957) pp. 56–7; English trs. by H. Zohn, *Judgements on History and Historians* (London, 1959) p. 61.
118. *Ibid.,* p. 58; English trs. p. 62.
119. *Ibid.,* p. 60; English trs. p. 63.
120. *Ibid.,* p. 64; English trs. p. 66.
121. J. Burckhardt, *Weltgeschichtliche Betrachtungen* (Leipzig, 1935) p. 169; English trs. by M. D. H., *Reflections on History* (London, 1943) p. 87; cf. *Historische Fragmente,* p. 61f, English trs. p. 64f.
122. Cf. K. A. Wittfogel, *Oriental Despotism* (New Haven, 1957) p. 372f.
123. Karl Marx, Friedrich Engels, *Briefwechsel* in D. Rjazanov (ed.), *Marx Engels, Gesamtausgabe,* 3 Abteilung, vol. 1 (Berlin, 1929) pp. 470-81; English trs. K. Marx and F. Engels, *Correspondence 1846-1895: a Selection* (New York, n.d.) pp. 63-8; cf. also Wittfogel, *Oriental Despotism.*
124. T. Carlyle, 'The Hero-Prophet. Mahomet: Islam', *On Heroes, Hero Worship and the Heroic in History* (London, 1841); cf. W. M. Watt, 'Carlyle on Muhammed', *Hibbert Journal,* vol. 53 (1954-5) pp. 247-54.
125. G. Le Bon, *Les lois psychologiques de l'évolution des peuples* (Paris, 1909) p. 145.
126. G. Le Bon, *La civilisation des Arabes* (Paris, 1884) p. 464.
127. *Ibid.,* p. 656f.
128. O. Spengler, *Der Untergang des Abendlandes,* revised ed., vol. 1 (Munich, 1923) p. 228; English trs. by C. F. Atkinson, *The Decline of the West,* vol. 1 (London, 1926) p. 174.
129. *Ibid.,* vol. 2 (Munich, 1922) pp. 49f, 227f, 304f; English trs. vol. 2 (London, 1929) pp. 42f, 189f, 248f.
130. *Ibid.,* vol. 1, p. 276; English trs. vol. 1, p. 212.
131. *Ibid.,* vol. 1, p. 274, vol. 2, p. 304f; English trs. vol. 1, p. 211, vol. 2, p. 248f.
132. *Ibid.,* vol. 2, p. 227f, 296, 311; English trs. vol. 2, p. 189f, 243, 253.
133. A. J. Toynbee, *A Study of History,* vol. 1 (London, 1934) p. 72f; vol. 2 (1934) p. 137; vol. 4 (1939) pp. 67-8.
134. *Ibid.,* vol. 5 (1939) p. 244f.
135. *Ibid.,* vol. 1, pp. 67f, 347, 391f; vol. 4, p. 113.
136. H. H. Gerth and C. Wright Mills (eds.), *From Max Weber: Essays in Sociology* (London, 1947) p. 53.
137. M. Weber, *Wirtschaft und Gesellschaft,* vol. 2 (Tübingen, 1956) pp. 459, 474; English trs. M. Rheinstein (ed.), *Max Weber on Law in Economy and Society* (Cambridge, Mass., 1954) pp. 206, 237.

138.   *Ibid.,* vol. 1, pp. 288-9; English trs. by E. Fischoff, *The Sociology of Religion* (London, 1965) pp. 86-7.

139.   *Ibid.,* vol. 1, p. 375f; English trs. p. 262f.

140.   *Ibid.,* vol. 1, p. 376; English trs. p. 264.

141.   *Ibid.,* vol. 1, p. 311; English trs. p. 132.

142.   *Ibid.,* vol. 1, pp. 370-6; English trs. pp. 251, 266.

143.   J. Berque, 'Perspectives de l'orientalisme contemporain', *Institut des belles lettres arabes* (IBLA), (1957) p. 220; cf. two critiques by Arab scholars: A. L. Tibawi, 'English-speaking Orientalists: a critique of their approach to Islam and Arab nationalism' I and II, *Muslim World,* vol. 53 (1963) p. 285f, 298f; A. Abdel-Malek, 'L'Orientalisme en crise', *Diogène* 44 (1963).

144.   Cf. J. Berque, *Les Arabes d'hier à demain* (Paris, 1960); English trs. *The Arabs, their History and Future* (London, 1960).

145.   G. E. von Grunebaum, *Islam. Essays in the Nature and Growth of a Cultural Tradition* (London, 1955) p. 31.

146.   H. A. R. Gibb, *Studies on the Civilization of Islam* (London, 1962).

147.   W. M. Watt, *Islam and the Integration of Society* (London, 1961).

148.   M. Rodinson, *Islam et capitalisme* (Paris, 1966); English trs. *Islam and Capitalism* (London, 1974).

149.   *Ibid.,* p. 21.

150.   C. Cahen, 'L'histoire économique et sociale de l'orient musulman médiéval', *Studia Islamica* 3 (1955) p. 93f. Reprinted in *Les peuples musulmans dans l'histoire médiévale* (Damascus, 1977) p. 209f.

151.   Cf. in particular, Cahen, 'Mouvements populaires et autonomisme urbain dans l'Asie musulmane du moyen âge', *Arabica* 5 (1958), pp. 225-50, 6 (1959) pp. 25-6, 233-65.

Notes to Chapter 3

1.   Review of K. Cragg, *Sandals at the Mosque* (London, 1959) and M. K. Hussein, *City of Wrong: a Friday in Jerusalem,* trs, K. Cragg (Amsterdam, 1959).

2.   R. C. Zaehner, *At Sundry Times* (London, 1958) pp. 16-20.

3.   *Ibid.,* p. 27.

4.   Cragg, pp. 91-2.

5.   Hussein, p. xii

6.   *Ibid.,* p. 53.

7.   *Ibid.,* p. 209.

8.   *Ibid.,* p. 224.

9.   Cragg, p. 135.

Note to Chapter 4

Bibliographical Note

1. There is a good modern edition of the French text of the *Voyage*, with an introduction and notes by J. Gaulmier (Paris and The Hague, 1959). M. Gaulmier has also written a full biography of Volney, *L'idéologue Volney* (Beirut, 1951), and a shorter life, *Volney, un grand témoin de la Révolution et de l'Empire* (Paris, 1959). The best critical study of Volney as a writer and thinker is still that of Sainte-Beuve in the seventh volume of his *Causeries du Lundi*. G. Chinard, *Volney et l'Amérique* (Baltimore and Paris, 1923) deals with his visit to the United States and his correspondence with Jefferson. N. Daniel, *Islam, Europe and Empire* (Edinburgh, 1966) analyses the ways in which Europeans of Volney's and later generations looked at the Muslim world.

Notes to Chapter 5

1. *The Seven Golden Odes of Pagan Arabia, known also as the Moallakat*, translated from the original Arabic by Lady Anne Blunt. Done into English verse by Wilfrid Scawen Blunt (London, 1903) p. 26.
2. On Ezra Pound the event left a lasting impression, and much later he recorded it with pride in the *Pisan Cantos*:

    > To have, with decency, knocked
    > That a Blunt should open
    > To have gathered from the air a live tradition
    > Or from a fine old eye the unconquered flame
    > This is not vanity.

    For a study of the episode see William T. Going, 'A peacock dinner: the homage of Pound and Yeats to Wilfrid Scawen Blunt', *Journal of Modern Literature* 1 (1971) p. 303.
3. Quoted in Lytton, *Wilfrid Scawen Blunt*, pp. 161-3.
4. Quoted in Lytton, p. 203.

Bibliographical Note

There is a full life of Blunt by Edith Finch, *Wilfrid Scawen Blunt 1840-1922* (London, 1938) and a shorter and more recent one by his grandson the Earl of Lytton, *Wilfrid Scawen Blunt a memoir* (London, 1961). The Blunt papers in the Fitzwilliam Museum at Cambridge are now open in principle, and it is likely that other studies will be made. There is a vivid description of Blunt in old age in D. MacCarthy, *Portraits I* (London, 1931) p. 29, and Lady Emily Lutyens throws a disagreeable light on some sides of his personality in *A Blessed Girl* (London, 1953).

There is a collected edition of his poems, *The Poetical Works of Wilfrid Scawen Blunt*, 2 vols. (London, 1914). Of his writings about the Near East, the following are particularly important: *The Future of Islam* (London, 1882), *The Secret History of the English Occupation of Egypt* (London, 1907), *Gordon at Khartoum* (London, 1911), and *My Diaries 1888-1914* (London, 1919-20). The early travels are described in two books by his wife Lady Anne Blunt, *Bedouin Tribes of the Euphrates*, 2 vols. (London, 1879) and *A Pilgrimage to Nejd*, 2 vols. (London, 1881).

His relations with Muslim reformers can be studied in A. Hourani, *Arabic Thought in the Liberal Age 1798-1939* (London, 1962) p. 110f, 133f, N. R. Keddie, *Sayyid Jāmāl ad-Dīn 'al-Afghani'* (Berkeley etc., 1972) p. 229f, and S. G. Haim, 'Blunt and al-Kawakibi', *Oriente Moderno*, 35 (1955) vol. 1, p. 133. His narrative of the British occupation of Egypt should be read in the light of two recent studies, Alexander Schölch, *Ägypten den Ägyptern: die politische und gesellschaftliche Krise der Jahre 1878-1882 in Ägypten* (Zurich etc. n.d.) and Afaf Lutfi al-Sayyid, *Egypt and Cromer* (London, 1968).

Notes to Chapter 6

Note on Sources

G. Makdisi (ed.), *Arabic and Islamic Studies in Honor of Hamilton A. R. Gibb* (Leiden, 1965) contains a brief biographical note by the editor and a complete bibliography down to 1965 by S. J. Shaw. I am grateful to Sir Hamilton's son, Mr J. A. C. Gibb, and to a number of former pupils, colleagues, and friends, who have provided information and commented on the first draft of this study. It was written for the most part in the Gibb Seminar Room in Widener Library at Harvard; long hours spent sitting among his books and using them helped to create in my mind a clear image of his personality as a scholar.

1. Cf. A. L. Turner, *History of the University of Edinburgh 1883-1933* (Edinburgh, 1933), W. C. A. Ross, *The Royal High School* (Edinburgh, 1934), and G. E. Davie, *The Democratic Intellect: Scotland and her Universities in the Nineteenth Century* (Edinburgh, 1961). I owe these references to Professors C. W. Dunn and H. J. Hanham, both of Harvard University.
2. 'Edward Denison Ross, 1871-1940', *Journal of the Royal Asiatic Society*, (1941) p. 49f.
3. 'Studies in contemporary Arabic literature', *Studies on the Civilization of Islam* (London, 1962) p. 304; dedication of *Modern Trends in Islam* (Chicago, 1947). Referred to as *Studies* and *Modern Trends* respectively.
4. Reprinted later in *Studies*, p. 245f.
5. G. Levi Della Vida, 'Letter of Dedication' in Makdisi, *Arabic and Islamic Studies*, p. xiii.
6. *Modern Trends*, p. 5.
7. 'Literature' in Sir T. Arnold and A. Guillaume (eds.), *The Legacy of Islam* (Oxford, 1931) p. 180f.
8. 'David Samuel Margoliouth, 1858-1940', *Journal of the Royal Asiatic Society* (1940) p. 393.

9. 'Louis Massignon, 1882-1962', *Journal of the Royal Asiatic Society* (1963) p. 119f.

10. Review of F. Rosenthal (trs.), *Ibn Khaldun: the Muqadimmah*, *Speculum* xxxv (1960) p. 139.

11. *Arabic Literature*, 2nd edition (Oxford, 1963) p. 112.

12. Levi Della Vida, 'Letter of Dedication', p. xiii.

13. *Whither Islam?* (London, 1932) p. 40.

14. 'Anglo-Egyptian relations: a revaluation', *International Affairs,* vol. 27 (1951) p. 440f.

15. Chapters 8-10 in *Studies.*

16. 'The Islamic background of Ibn Khaldun's political theory', *Bulletin of the School of Oriental Studies*, vol. 7 (1933) p. 23f; reprinted in *Studies*, p. 174.

17. See his note on Shi'ism in A. J. Toynbee, *A Study of History*, vol. 1 (London, 1934) p. 400f.

18. H. A. R. Gibb and H. Bowen, *Islamic Society and the West*, vol. 1, part i (London, 1950) p. 1.

19. *Ibid.*, p. 30.

20. N. Itzkowitz, 'Eighteenth century Ottoman realities', *Studia Islamica*, xvi (1962) p. 73f. See also review by B. Lewis, *Bulletin of the School of Oriental and African Studies*, vol. 16 (1954) p. 598f.

21. Reprinted *Studies*, p. 3f, 176f.

22. 'Ta'rikh', *Encyclopaedia of Islam, Supplement* (1938) p. 233f; 'Arabiyya', *Encyclopaedia of Islam,* 2nd ed., vol 1 (1960) p. 583f.

23. *Modern Trends*, xii.

24. A. S. Pringle-Pattison, *Studies in the Philosophy of Religion* (Oxford, 1930).

25. D. B Macdonald, *The Development of Muslim Theology, Jurisprudence and Constitutional Theory* (London, 1903) p. 2. See the study of Macdonald in J. D. J. Waardenburg, *L'islam dans le miroir de l'occident* (The Hague, 1961) a book which throws much light on the intellectual genealogies of European students of Islam.

26. Macdonald, *The Religious Attitude and Life in Islam* (Chicago, 1909) p. 215.

27. *Mohammedanism* (London, 1949) p. 31.

28. 'The structure of religious thought in Islam', *Studies*, p. 213.

29. *Mohammedanism*, p. 163.

30. 'Islamic biographical literature' in B. Lewis and P. M. Holt (eds.), *Historians of the Middle East* (London, 1962) p. 54.

31. Note in Toynbee, *Study of History*, vol. 1, p. 402; 'Structure of religious thought', *Studies*, p. 199.

32 K. M. Setton and others, *A History of the Crusades*, vol. 1 (Philadelphia, 1955), chapters 3, 14, 16, and 18, vol. 2 (1962), chapter 20. See also *Studies*, chapters 5 and 6.

33. 'The achievement of Saladin', *Bulletin of the John Rylands Library*, vol 35 (1952), reprinted, *Studies*, p. 91f.

34. 'The influence of Islamic culture on mediaeval Europe', *Bulletin of the John Rylands Library*, vol. 38 (1955) p. 82f.

35. *Modern Trends*, p. 77.

36. 'The community in Islamic history', *Proceedings of the American Philosophical Society*, vol. 107 (1963) p. 176.
37. *Modern Trends*, p. 38.
38. Letter to Professor Bernard Lewis, 2 March 1955. I am most grateful to Professor Lewis for allowing me to quote from it.
39. *Area Studies Reconsidered* (London, 1963) p. 3.
40. *Ibid.*, pp. 14-15.
41. I. M. Lapidus, *Muslim Cities in the Later Middle Ages* (Cambridge, Mass., 1967) p. xi.
42. See note 21.
43. *Modern Trends*, p. 126.

Notes to Chapter 7

1. Vol. I, p. 5.
2. '. . . an unprecedently prosperous and comfortable Western middle-class was taking it as a matter of course that the end of one age of one civilization's history was the end of history itself — at least so far as they and their kind were concerned' (IX, 420). All references are to the first edition: Arnold J. Toynbee, *A Study of History*, vols. 1-3 (London etc., 1934), vols. 4-6 (1939), vols. 7-10 (1954). Two more volumes were published after this essay was written: vol. 11, 'Historical Atlas and Gazetteer' (1959), and vol. 12, 'Reconsiderations' (1961).
3. V, 373.
4. X, 108.
5. IV, 202.
6. *The Western Question in Greece and Turkey* (London, 1922).
7. IV, 222.
8. I, 159.
9. VI, 164.
10. VI, 278.
11. VI, 316.
12. IV, 137 f.
13. VII, 10.
14. VIII, 89.
15. X, 228.
16. X, 230-1.
17. IX, 347.
18. X, 231.
19. VII, 423-5.
20. VII, 506.
21. X, 238 note.
22. VIII, 627.
23. VII, 535.
24. VII, 430-1.
25. VII, 433.
26. VII, 500.
27. IX, 185.

28. IX, 431-3.
29. IX, 631.
30. IX. 635.
31. VII, 441.
32. VII, 500.
33. X, 129.
34. X, 139.
35. IX, 634-5.

Notes to Chapter 8

1. 'A. al-Jabartī, *'Ajā'ib al-āthār*, 4 vols. (Cairo, 1880).
2. 'A. Mubārak, *Al-khitat al-tawfiqīyya*, 20 vols. (Cairo, 1888).
3. A. Cevdet, *Tarih-i Cevdet*, 12 vols., 2nd ed. (Istanbul, 1891).
4. A. al-Nāṣirī, *Kitāb al-istiqṣā*, 4 vols. (Cairo, 1895).
5. 'A. Bītār, *Ḥilyat al-bashar*, 3 vols. (Damascus, 1961-3).
6. M. al-Kattānī, *Salwat al-anfās*, 3 vols. (Fez, 1898-9).
7. For Islamic history and other studies, cf. B. Lewis and P. M. Holt (eds.),
   Historians of the Middle East (London, 1962); J. D. J. Waardenburg,
   L'Islam dans le miroir de l'occident (The Hague, 1961); A. Hourani,
   'Islam and the philosophers of history', chapter 2 in this book.
8. C. Cahen, 'Quelques notes sur les Hilaliens et le nomadisme', *Journal of
   the Economic and Social History of the Orient*, vol. 11 (1968) p. 130f; J.
   Poncet, 'Le mythe de la "catastrophe" hilalienne', *Annales*, vol. 22
   (1967) p. 1099f; H. R. Idris, 'De la realité de la catastrophe hilalienne',
   Annales, vol. 23 (1968) p. 660f; J. Berque, 'Du nouveau sur les Beni
   Hilal', *Studia Islamica*, vol. 36 (1972) p. 99f.
9. E. Kedourie, *Afghani and 'Abduh* (London, 1966); N. R. Keddie, *Sayyid
   Jamāl ad-Dīn 'al-Afghānī': a Political Biography* (Berkeley, Cal., 1972).
10. 'A. al-Rāfi'ī, *Ta'rīkh al-ḥaraka al-qawmiyya*, 3 vols. (Cairo, 1929-30) and
    subsequent works.
11. K. al Ghazzī, *Nahr al-dhahab fī ta'rīkh ḥalab*, 3 vols. (Aleppo, 1923-6).
12. R. al-Ṭabbākh, *A'lām al-nubalā bi-ta'rīkh ḥalab al-shahbā*, 7 vols.
    (Aleppo, 1923-6).
13. M. Kurd 'Alī, *Khiṭat al-shām*, 6 vols. (Damascus, 1925-8).
14. 'A. M. al-'Azzāwī, *Ta'rīkh al-'irāq bayn ihtilālayn* (cover title: *Histoire de
    l'Irâq entre deux occupations*), 8 vols. (Baghdad, 1935-56).
15. A. Laroui, *L'Histoire du Maghreb* (Paris, 1970).
16. M. al-Tabarī, *Ta'rīkh al-rusūl wa al-mulūk*, 10 parts (Cairo, 1960-9).
17. I. Goldziher, *Muhammedanische Studien*, vol. 2 (Halle, 1890). See note
    129.
18. H. Lammens, *Études sur le siècle des Omayyades* (Beirut, 1930) and other
    works.
19. A. L. Udovitch (ed.), *Partnership and Profit in Medieval Islam* (Princeton,
    1970).
20. M. A. Shaban, *The Abbasid Revolution* (Cambridge, 1970).
21. S. M. Stern, *Fātimid Decrees* (London, 1964); S. M. Stern (ed.),
    Documents from Islamic Chanceries (Cambridge, Mass., 1965).

22. S. D. Goitein, *A Mediterranean Society*, 2 vols. (Berkeley, Cal., 1967, 1971).

23. D. S. Richards, 'Arabic documents from the Karaite community in Cairo', *Journal of the Economic and Social History of the Orient*, vol. 15 (1972) p. 105f.

24. J. Sourdel-Thomine and D. Sourdel, 'Nouveaux documents sur l'histoire religieuse et sociale de Damas au Moyen Age', *Revue des études islamiques*, vol. 32 (1964) p. 1f.

25. 'A. 'A. 'Abd al-Rahīm, *al-Rīf al-miṣrī fī al-qarn al-thāmin 'ashar* (Cairo, 1974).

26. A. Raymond, 'Les bains publics au Caire a la fin du XVIIIe siècle', *Annales islamologiques*, vol. 8 (1969) p. 129f; and *Artisans et commerçants au Caire au XVIIIe siècle*, 2 vols. (Damascus, 1973-4).

27. H. Busse, *Untersuchungen zum islamischen Kanzleiwesen* (Cairo, 1958).

28. A. Rustum, *al-Mahfūẓāt al-malikiyya al-miṣriyya*, 4 vols. (Beirut, 1940-3).

29. J. Deny, *Sommaire des archives turques du Caire* (Cairo, 1930).

30. A. Schölch, *Ägypten den Ägyptern* (Zurich, 1973).

31. P. M. Holt, *The Mahdist State in the Sudan 1881-1898* (Oxford, 1958).

32. D. S. Landes, *Bankers and Pashas* (London, 1958).

33. J. Berque, *Structures sociales du Haut Atlas* (Paris, 1955).

34. B. Lewis, 'Sources for the economic history of the Middle East' in M. A. Cook (ed.), *Studies in the Economic History of the Middle East* (London, 1970); reprinted in Lewis, *Islam in History* (New York, 1973).

35. C. Cahen (ed.), J. Sauvaget, *Introduction a l'histoire de l'orient musulman*, 2nd ed. (Paris, 1961) p. 57; English trs. *Introduction to the History of the Muslim East* (Berkeley, Cal., 1965).

36. M. van Berchem and others, *Matériaux pour un Corpus Inscriptionum Arabicarum* (Cairo, 1894-1956).

37. E. Combe, J. Sauvaget and G. Wiet, *Répertoire chronologique d'épigraphie arabe* (Cairo, 1931-   ).

38. R. W. Hamilton, *Khirbat al-Mafjar* (Oxford, 1959).

39. J. Sauvaget, *Alep* (Paris, 1941) and 'Esquisse d'une histoire de la ville de Damas', *Revue des études islamiques*, vol. 8 (1934) p. 421f.

40. K. A. C. Creswell, *The Muslim Architecture of Egypt*, 2 vols. (Oxford, 1952-9) and *Early Muslim Architecture*, 2 vols. (Oxford, 1932-40).

41. G. Marçais, *L'architecture musulmane d'occident* (Paris, 1955).

42. C. Kessler, 'Mecca-oriented architecture and urban growth of Cairo', *Atti del Terzo Congresso di Studi Arabi e Islamici* (Naples, 1967) p. 425f.

43. J. Sourdel-Thomine, 'La mosquée et la madrasa, types monumentaux charactéristiques de l'art islamique médiéval', *Cahiers de civilisation médiévale*, vol. 13 (1970) p. 97f.

44. G. A. Pugachenkova, 'The architecture of Central Asia in the time of the Timurids', *Afghanistan*, 22 (1969-70) p. 15f; 'Les monuments peu connus de l'architecture médiévale de l'Afghanistan', *Afghanistan*, 21 (1968) p. 17f.

45. E. H. Ayverdi, *Osmanli mimârîsinin ilk devri*, 3 vols. (Istanbul, 1966-73).

46. A. Kuran, *The Mosque in Early Ottoman Architecture* (Chicago, 1968).

47. J. M. Rogers, review of L. Golombek, *The Timurid Shrine at Gazur Gah*, *Kunst des Orients*, vol. 7 (1972) p. 175.

48. R. M. Adams, *Land Behind Baghdad* (Chicago, 1965).
49. P. Seale, *The Struggle for Syria* (London and New York, 1965).
50. E. E. Evans-Pritchard, *The Sanusi of Cyrenaica* (Oxford, 1949).
51. J. Berque, *Histoire sociale d'un village égyptien au XXème siècle* (Paris, 1957).
52. See note 35.
53. C. Brockelmann, *Geschichte der arabischen Litteratur*, 5 vols. (Leiden, 1937–49).
54. 'U. R. Kaḥḥāla, *Muʻjam al-muʼallifīn*, 15 parts (Damascus, 1957–61).
55. F. Sezgin, *Geschichte der arabischen Schrifttums*, vols. 1, 3, 4 (Leiden, 1967–71).
56. G. Graf, *Geschichte der christlichen arabischen Literatur*, 5 vols. (Rome, 1944–53).
57. C. A. Storey, *Persian Literature: a bio-bibliographical survey*, 4 parts (London, 1927–71); Russian trs. *Persidskaya Literatura*, 1 (Moscow, 1972).
58. B. Lewis, 'Studies in the Ottoman archives', *Bulletin of the School of Oriental and African Studies*, vol. 16 (1954) p. 469f; and *Notes and Documents from the Turkish Archives* (Jerusalem, 1952).
59. U. Heyd, *Ottoman Documents on Palestine 1552–1615* (Oxford, 1960).
60. R. Mantran and J. Sauvaget, *Règlements fiscaux ottomans* (Beirut, 1951).
61. Ö. L. Barkan, *XV ve XVI inci asirlarda osmanli imperatorluğunda ziraî ekonominin hukukî ve malî esaslari* (Istanbul, 1943).
62. J. D. Pearson, *Index Islamicus* and supplements (first three vols. Cambridge, thereafter London 1958–   ); *Türkiye makaleler bibliografyasi* (Ankara, 1952–   ); I. Afshar, *Index Iranicus*, 2 vols. (Tehran, 1961–70).
63. *Encyclopaedia of Islam*, 1st ed., 4 vols. and supplement (Leiden, 1913–42); 2nd ed., 3 vols. to date (Leiden and London, 1960–   ).
64. *Islâm ansiklopedisi*, 11 vols. published so far (Istanbul, 1940–   ).
65. B. Spuler (ed.), *Handbuch der Orientalistik: I Abteilung, Der Nahe und der Mittlere Osten* (Leiden, 1952).
66. D. and J. Sourdel, *La civilisation de l'islam classique* (Paris, 1968).
67. E. de Zambaur, *Manuel de généalogie et de chronologie pour l'histoire de l'Islam* (Hanover, 1927).
68. C. E. Bosworth, *The Islamic Dynasties* (Edinburgh, 1967).
69. G. S. P. Freeman-Grenville, *The Muslim and Christian Calendars* (London and New York, 1963).
70. R. Roolvink, *Historical Atlas of the Muslim Peoples* (Amsterdam, 1957).
71. *Description de l'Egypte: Etat moderne*, 4 vols. (Paris, 1809–12).
72. See note 39.
73. J. W. Redhouse, *A Turkish and English Lexicon*, 2 vols. (Constantinople, 1890; reprint, Beirut, 1974).
74. R. Dozy, *Supplément aux dictionnaires arabes*, 2 vols. (Leiden, 1881).
75. L. Massignon, *Essai sur les origines de lexique technique de la mystique musulmane* (Paris, 1922).
76. B. Lewis, 'Islamic concepts of revolution' and 'On modern Arabic political terms', *Islam in History*, op. cit.
77. B. Lewis and P. M. Holt (eds.), *Historians of the Middle East*, op. cit.

78. P. M. Holt (ed.), *Political and Social Change in Modern Egypt* (London, 1968).

79. M. A. Cook (ed.), *Studies in the Economic History of the Middle East*.

80. A Hourani and S. M. Stern (eds.), *The Islamic City* (Oxford, 1970).

81. D. S. Richards (ed.), *Islam and the Trade of Asia* (Oxford, 1970).

82. D. S. Richards (ed.), *Islamic Civilization 950–1150* (Oxford, 1973).

83. T. Nagel, *Rechtleitung und Kalifat* (Bonn, 1975); A. Noth, *Quellenkritische Studien zu Themen, Formen und Tendenzen frühislamischer Geschichtsüberlieferung* (Bonn, 1973).

84. D. Sourdel, *Le Vizirat 'abbāside de 749 à 936,* 2 vols. (Damascus, 1959–60); R. N. Frye (ed.), *Cambridge History of Iran*, vol. 4 (Cambridge, 1975). See also note 20.

85. G. Makdisi, 'Autograph diary of an eleventh-century historian of Baghdad', 5 parts, *Bulletin of the School of Oriental and African Studies,* vol. 18 (1956) pp. 9f and 239f; vol. 19 (1957), pp. 13f, 281f and 426f.

86. J. A. Boyle (ed.), *Cambridge History of Iran*, vol. 5 (Cambridge, 1968).

87. C. Cahen, *Pre-Ottoman Turkey* (London, 1968).

89. R. Brunschvig, *La Berbérie orientale sous les Hafsides,* 2 vols. (Paris, 1940–7).

90. E. Lévi-Provençal, *Histoire de l'Espagne musulmane,* 3 vols. (Paris, 1950–7).

91. H. A. R. Gibb, 'The achievement of Saladin', *Studies on the Civilization of Islam* (London, 1962) and *The Life of Saladin* (Oxford, 1973).

92. D. Ayalon, *Gunpowder and Firearms in the Mamluk Kingdom* (London, 1956) and 'Studies on the structure of the Mamluk army', *Bulletin of the School of Oriental and African Studies,* vol. 15 (1953) pp. 203 and 448f; vol. 16 (1954) p. 57f.

93. A. Darrag, *L'Egypte sous le règne de Barsby* (Damascus, 1961).

94. B. Spuler, *Die Mongolen in Iran* (Berlin, 1955).

95. E. Glassen, *Die frühen Safawiden nach Qāzī Ahmad Qumī* (Freiburg, 1970) and M. Mazzaoui, *The Origins of the Safawids* (Wiesbaden, 1972).

96. V. Minorsky, *Tadhkirat al-mulūk* (London, 1943).

97. J. Aubin, 'Etudes safavides I: Shah Isma'il et les notables de l'Iraq persan', *Journal of the Economic and Social History of the Orient,* vol. 2 (1959) p. 37f.

98. H. A. R. Gibb and H. Bowen, *Islamic Society and the West,* vol. 1, 2 parts (London, 1950–7).

99. I. H. Uzunçarşili, *Kapikulu Ocaklari,* 2 vols. (Ankara, 1943–4); *Osmanli devletinin merkez ve bahriye teşkilâti* (Ankara, 1948) and *Osmanli devletinin saray teşkilâti* (Ankara, 1945).

100. H. Inalcik, *The Ottoman Empire: the Classical Age 1300–1600* (London, 1973); see also S. J. Shaw, *History of the Ottoman Empire and Modern Turkey* vol. 1 (Cambridge, 1976).

101. U. Heyd, 'Some aspects of the Ottoman fetva', *Bulletin of the School of Oriental and African Studies,* vol. 32 (1969) p. 35f and *Studies of Old Ottoman Criminal Law* (Oxford, 1973).

102. H. Inalcik, 'Ḥarir', *Encyclopaedia of Islam,* 2nd ed., vol. 3, p. 211f, and

'Bursa and the commerce of the Levant', *Journal of the Economic and Social History of the Orient,* vol. 3 (1960) p. 131f.

103. S. J. Shaw, *The Financial and Administrative Organization of Ottoman Egypt 1517–1798* (Princeton, N.J., 1962).

104. P. M. Holt, 'Studies in Egyptian history', *Studies in the History of the Near East* (London, 1973) p. 151f.

105. A. Raymond, 'Essai de géographie des quartiers de résidence aristocratique au Caire au XVIIIème siècle', *Journal of the Economic and Social History of the Orient,* vol. 6 (1963), p. 58f; 'Quartiers et mouvements populaires au Caire au XVIIIème siècle', in P. M. Holt (ed.), *Political and Social Change in Modern Egypt;* 'Problèmes urbains et urbanisme au Caire aux XVIIème et XVIIIème siècles' in *Colloque internationale sur l'histoire du Caire* (Cairo, n.d.) p. 319f. See also note 26.

106. K. S. Salibi, 'The Maronites of Lebanon under Frankish and Mamluk rule', *Arabica,* vol. 4 (1957) p. 288f; 'The Buhturids of the Garb', *Arabica,* vol. 8 (1961) p. 74f; 'Northern Lebanon under the dominance of Gazir', *Arabica,* vol. 14 (1967) p. 144f; 'The Muqaddams of Bsarri', *Arabica,* vol. 15 (1968) p. 63f; 'The Sayfās and the Eyalat of Tripoli', *Arabica,* vol. 20 (1973) p. 25f.

107. A. C. Hess, 'The forgotten frontier' in E. R. J. Owen and T. Naff (eds.), *The Islamic World in the Eighteenth Century* (Carbondale, Ill., 1977).

108. R. Mantran, 'L'évolution des relations entre la Tunisie et l'Empire Ottoman du XVIe au XIXe siècle', *Cahiers de Tunisie,* vol. 7 (1959) p. 319f.

109. W. L. Langer, *The Diplomacy of Imperialism 1890–1902,* 2nd ed. (New York, 1951).

110. M. S. Anderson, *The Eastern Question 1774–1923* (London, 1966).

111. For a survey of recent work see C. E. Dawn, 'Hashimite aims and policy in the light of recent scholarship on Anglo-Arab relations during World War I', *From Ottomanism to Arabism* (Urbana, Ill., 1973) p. 87f.

112. T. Naff, 'Reform and the conduct of Ottoman diplomacy in the reign of Selim III 1789–1807', *Journal of the American Oriental Society,* vol. 83 (1963) p. 295f.

113. A. Cunningham, 'Stratford Canning and the Tanzimat' in W. R. Polk and R. L. Chambers (eds.), *Beginnings of Modernization in the Middle East* (Chicago, 1968) p. 245f.

114. B. Lewis, *The Emergence of Modern Turkey* (London, 1961).

115. R. H. Davison, *Reform in the Ottoman Empire 1856–1876* (Princeton, N.J., 1963).

116. R. L. Tignor, *Modernization and British Colonial Rule in Egypt 1882–1914* (Princeton, N.J., 1966).

117. A. Lutfi Al-Sayyid, *Egypt and Cromer* (London, 1968).

118. C. R. Ageron, *Les Algériens musulmans et la France,* 2 vols. (Paris, 1968).

119. C. C. Adams, *Islam and Modernism in Egypt* (London, 1933).

120. J. Jomier, *Le Commentaire coranique du Manâr* (Paris, 1954).

121. H. A. R. Gibb, *Modern Trends in Islam* (Chicago, 1947).

122. See note 9.

123. S. Mardin, *The Genesis of Young Ottoman Thought* (Princeton, N.J., 1962).

124. Z. N. Zeine, *The Emergence of Arab Nationalism* (Beirut, 1966).
125. See note 111.
126. S. Haim, *Arab Nationalism* (Berkeley, Cal., 1962).
127. E. Kedourie, *England and the Middle East* (London, 1956).
128. G. Antonius, *The Arab Awakening* (London, 1939).
129. I. Goldziher, *Muhammedanischen Studien*, 2 vols. (Halle, 1889–90); English trs. by S. M. Stern, 2 vols. (London, 1967–71).
130. T. W. Arnold, *The Caliphate* (Oxford, 1924); *The Preaching of Islam*, 2nd ed. (London, 1913).
131. H. A. R. Gibb, *Studies on the Civilization of Islam* (London, 1962).
132. C. H. Becker, *Islamstudien*, 2 vols. (Leipzig, 1924–32).
133. G. E. von Grunebaum, *Medieval Islam* (Chicago, 1946).
134. See note 39 and 'Comment étudier l'histoire du monde arabe' in *Mémorial Jean Sauvaget* (Damascus, 1954) p. 167f.
135. J. von Hammer-Purgstall, *Geschichte des Osmanischen Reiches*, 10 vols. (Pest, 1827–35).
136. J. Wellhausen, *Das arabische Reich und sein Sturz* (Berlin, 1902); English trs. by Margaret Graham Weir, *The Arab Kingdom and its Fall* (Calcutta, 1927).
137. W. Barthold, *Turkestan down to the Mongol Invasion;* English trs. 3rd. ed. (London, 1968).
138. J. Schacht, *The Origins of Muhammedan Jurisprudence* (Oxford, 1950).
139. E. Burke, 'Morocco and the Near East: reflections on some basic differences', *Archives européennes de sociologie*, vol. 10 (1969) p. 70f.
140. M. Rodinson, *Islam et capitalisme* (Paris, 1966); English trs. *Islam and Capitalism* (London, 1974).
141. C. Cahen 'L'histoire économique et sociale de l'Orient musulman médiéval', *Studia Islamica*, vol. 3 (1955) p. 93f.
142. J. Berque, 'Amal', *Encyclopaedia of Islam*, 2nd ed. vol. 1, p. 427f.
143. See R. Walzer, *Greek into Arabic* (Oxford, 1962).
144. A. Duri, *Ta'rīkh al-'iraq al-iqtisādī fī al-qarn al-rābi' al-hijrî* (Baghdad, 1948).
145. S. al-Alī, *al-Tanẓīmāt al-ijtimā'iyya wa al-iqtiṣādiyya fī al-basra fī al-qarn al-awwal al-hijrī* (Baghdad, 1953).
146. H. Rabie, *The Financial System of Egypt A. H. 564–741/1169–1341 A. D.* (London, 1972).
147. See note 22.
148. R. Lopez, H. Miskimin and A. Udovitch, 'England to Egypt 1300–1500: long term trends and long-distance trade' in M. A. Cook (ed.), *Studies in the Economic History of the Middle East*, p. 93f.
149. See note 102.
150. R. Davis, *Aleppo and Devonshire Square* (London, 1967).
151. L. Valensi, *Le Maghreb avant la prise d'Alger* (Paris, 1969).
152. N. G. Svoronos, *Le Commerce de Salonique au XVIIIe siècle* (Paris, 1956).
153. P. K. O'Brien, *The Revolution in Egypt's Economic System* (London, 1966).
154. E. R. J. Owen, *Cotton and the Egyptian Economy 1820–1914* (Oxford, 1969).

155. D. Chevallier, *La Sociéte du Mont Liban à l'époque de la révolution industrielle en Europe* (Paris, 1971).
156. C. Issawi, 'The decline of Middle Eastern trade 1100–1500' in D. S. Richards (ed.), *Islam and the Trade of Asia*; 'Egypt since 1800: a study in lop-sided development', *Journal of Economic History*, vol. 21 (1961).
157. O. L. Barkan, 'Essai sur les données statistiques des registres de récensement dans l'Empire Ottoman au XVe et XVIe siècles', *Journal of the Economic and Social History of the Orient*, vol. 1 (1958) p. 9f.
158. C. Issawi, 'Comment on Professor Barkan's estimate of the population of the Ottoman Empire in 1520–30', *Journal of the Economic and Social History of the Orient*, vol. 1 (1958) p. 329f.
159. N. T. Todorov, *La Ville balkanique aux XVe–XIXe siècles* (in Bulgarian with French summary: Sofia, 1972).
160. M. A. Cook, *Population Pressure in Rural Anatolia 1450–1600* (London and New York, 1972).
161. See note 151.
162. B. Musallam, *Sex and Society in Islam: the Situation and Medieval Techniques of Birth Control*. Unpublished Ph.D dissertation (Harvard, 1973).
163. N. R. Keddie (ed.), *Scholars, Saints and Sufis* (Berkeley, Cal., 1972).
164. L. Hautecoeur and G. Wiet, *Les mosquées du Caire* (Paris, 1932).
165. See note 39.
166. See note 41.
167. J. Abu Lughod, *Cairo, 1001 Years of the City Victorious* (Princeton, N.J., 1971).
168. See note 45.
169. C. Cahen, 'Mouvements populaires et autonomisme urbain', *Arabica*, vol. 5 (1958) p. 225; vol. 6 (1959) pp. 25f and 233f.
170. R. LeTourneau, *Fez avant le protectorat français* (Casablanca, 1949.)
171. R. Mantran, *Istanbul dans la seconde moitié du XVIIe siècle* (Paris, 1962).
172. See notes 26 and 105.
173. I. M. Lapidus, *Muslim Cities in the Later Middle Ages* (Cambridge, Mass., 1967).
174. A. K. S. Lambton, *Landlord and Peasant in Persia* (London, 1953).
175. G. Baer, *Studies in the Social History of Modern Egypt* (Chicago, 1969); in particular 'The village shaykh, 1800–1950', p. 30f.
176. See T. Asad, *The Kababish Arabs* (London, 1970); C. Cahen, 'Nomades et sedentaires dans le monde musulman du milieu du moyen age' in D. S. Richards (ed.), *Islamic Civilization 950–1150*.
177. See note 22.
178. See note 106.
179. See note 155.
180. K. L. Brown, *People of Salé* (Manchester, 1976) and 'An urban view of Moroccan history: Salé 1000 to 1800', *Hesperis-Tamuda*, vol.12 (1971) p. 5f.
181. See note 150; A. C. Wood, *A History of the Levant Company* (London, 1935); P. Masson, *Histoire du commerce française dans le Levant au*

XVIIe siècle (Paris, 1896) and *Histoire . . . au XVIIIe sièle* (Paris, 1911).

182. See note 154.
183. I. Harik, *Politics and Change in a Traditional Society: Lebanon, 1711--1845* (Princeton, N.J., 1968).
184. W. Robertson Smith, *Lectures on the Religion of the Semites* (New York, 1889) and *Kinship and Marriage in Early Arabia* (London, 1903).
185. See note 50.
186. J. Berque, *L'Egypte, imperialisme et révolution* (Paris, 1967); English trs, by Jean Stewart, *Egypt, Imperialism and Revolution* (London, 1972).
187. P. Brown, *Augustine of Hippo* (London, 1967).
188. J. Berque, *Al-Yousi* (Paris, 1958).
189. H. A. R. Gibb, *Mohammedanism* (London, 1949).
190. B. Lewis, *The Arabs in History* (London, 1950).
191. P. M. Holt, A. K. S. Lambton and B. Lewis (eds.), *The Cambridge History of Islam*, 2 vols. (Cambridge, 1970). For an ambitious synthesis, see now M. G. S. Hodgson, *The Venture of Islam*, 3 vols. (Chicago, 1974).
192. See note 66.
193. C. Cahen, *L'Islam des origines au début de l'empire ottoman* (Paris, 1970).
194. See note 100.
195. C. A. Julien, *Histoire de l'Afrique du nord de la conquête arabe à 1830* (Paris, 1951-2).
196. J. M. Abun-Nasr, *A History of the Maghrib* (Cambridge, 1971).
197. A. Bausani, *I Persiani* (Florence, 1962); English trs. by J. B. Donne, *The Persians* (London, 1971).
198. See note 151.
199. B. Lewis (ed. and trs.), *Islam from the Prophet Muhammad to the Capture of Constantinople*, 2 vols. (New York, 1974).
200. J. Sauvaget, *Historiens arabes* (Paris, 1946).
201. J. A. Williams (ed.), *Themes of Islamic Civilization* (Berkeley, Cal., 1971).
202. F. Gabrieli, *Storici arabi delle Crociate* (Turin, 1957), English trs. by E. J. Costello, *Arab Historians of the Crusades* (Berkeley, Cal., 1969).
203. C. Issawi (ed.), *The Economic History of the Middle East 1800-1914* (Chicago, 1966), *The Economic History of Iran 1800-1914* (Chicago, 1971).

Index

'Abbasids, 61, 132, 166, 175, 182
'Abd al-Rahim, 'A. 'A., 167
Abdel-Jalil, Fr J. M., 41
'Abduh, Shaykh Muhammad, xii, 79, 93–5, 98–9, 101
Abraham, 36, 38–41
Abstracta Islamica, 172
Abu Lughod, J., 187
Abun-Nasr, J. M., 194
Academy of the Arabic Language (Egypt), 115
Adams, C. C., 178
Adams, R. M. (*Land Behind Baghdad*), 171
Ageron, C. R., 178
Agricultural contracts, 169
al-'Ali, S., 186
Alawi dynasty, 168, 184
Aldington, Richard, 89
Ali Bey, 84
Aligarh Anglo-Muhammedan College, 108
al-insan al-kamil (the perfect man), 6, 40, 46–7
al-Jabarti, 'A. (*'aja'ib al-athar*), 117, 162, 173
al-Kattani, M. (*salwat al-anfas*), 162
Allenby, 4
American University of Beirut, 171
Anatolia, 92, 177; *see also* Turkey
Anawati, Fr G. C., 41
Anderson, M. S. (*The Eastern Question*), 178
Annales (periodical), 174, 183
Antonius, G. (*The Arab Awakening*), 179
Arabic language and literature, 23–4, 37–8, 40–1, 89, 109–10, 113–14, 132, 161, 173
Arabs: civilisation, 69, 140; early history, 18, 29, 32, 34, 36, 39; Islamic developments, 59–62, 64–9, 92–3; records, 169, 178–9
Archaeology, 170–2, 175
Archivists, 169, 195–6

Arnold, T. W. (*The Caliphate*; *The Preaching of Islam*), 108, 111, 116, 181
al-Ash'ari (Ash'arism), 124
Asquith, H. H., 100
Aubin, J., 176
Austro-Hungarian documents, 168
Averroes, 35
Ayalon, D., 176
Ayverdi, E. H., 170, 187
Ayyubids, 176, 194
al-'Azzawi, 'A. M., 164

Baer, G., 188
Balfour, A. J., 97, 100–3
Balkan states, 20, 177
Barkan, Ö. L., 172, 186
Barthold, W., 162, 181
Bauer, Bruno, 49
Bausani, A., 194
Becker, C. H., 50, 59–60, 162, 181
Beni Hilal, 164
Benda, Julien (*Trahison des clercs*), 126
Bergson, Henri (*Two Sources of Morality and Religion*), 142, 149
Berque, Jacques (*Structures sociales du Haut Atlas*; *Histoire sociale d'un village égyptien au XXème siècle*; *L'Egypte, impérialisme et révolution* ...), 72, 169, 171, 192
Bible: criticism, 1–2, 6, 16–18, 162; philosophers and, 42, 47–8, 52, 64; Toynbee's view, 146–7, 153
Bibliographical aids to research, 171–2, 194–5
Biology, 46, 66, 98, 142, 144
Bismarck, O. von, 4
al-Bitar, 'A. (*Hilyat al-bashar*), 162
Blunt, Lady Anne (*Bedouin Tribes of the Euphrates*; *A Pilgrimage to Nejd*), 90–1

Blunt, Wilfrid Scawen (*The Future of Islam; India under Ripon; The Secret History of the English Occupation of Egypt*; tr. *Mu'allaqât*), 87–103; bibliography, 205–6

Bosworth, C. E. (*The Islamic Dynasties*), 19n, 172

Boulainvilliers, Henri, Comte de, 29–30

Bowen, Harold, 116–18, 176, 185; *see also* Gibb, H. A. R.

Braudel, F., 183

Britain and Egypt, 92, 94–5, 97, 114–15; teaching, 163, 168

Brockelmann, C., 171

Brown, K. L., 190

Brown, P., 192

Brunschvig, R. (*La Berbérie orientale sous les Hafsides*), 176

Buddhism, Mahayana, 74, 152–3

Burckhardt, Jacob, 62–3

Burke, E., 161, 184–5

Busse, H., 167, 172

Bywater, Ingram, xiii

Byzantium, 59, 73, 182

Caetani, L., 59

Cahen, Claude (*La Syrie du nord à l'époque des Croisades; Pre-Ottoman Turkey; L'Islam des origines au début de l'empire ottoman;* 'Mouvements populaires et autonomisme urbain'), 73, 171, 176, 185, 188, 194

Caliphate, 28, 31, 33–4, 67–8, 94, 116–17; 'Abbasid, 61; Umayyad, 8, 24

Calvinism, 11, 16–17, 26, 43–5

Cambridge History of Iran, 176

Cambridge History of Islam, 194

Carlyle, Thomas (*Heroes and Hero-Worship*), 64–5, 69

Catholicism: attitude to Islam, 10–11, 17; Blunt and, 88, 90; historical philosophers, 22, 26, 34, 41–4, 58; Toynbee and, 153–4

Central Zionist Archives, 169

Cevdet, A. (*Tarih*), 162

Chapman, R. W., xiii

Chassebeuf, Constantin-François, *see* Volney

Chevallier, D., 186, 190

China, 20, 111, 137, 162, 164, 168, 179

Christianity: attitude to Islam, 7–18; doctrines, 21–8, 31–8, 41–4, 49, 55–8, 60, 64, 67, 70–1; Muslim viewpoint, 1–7; orthodoxy criticised, 152–4, 157–9; types of religion, 74–8

Chronology, 172, 195–6

Churchill, Lord Randolph, 87, 96, 101

Churchill, Winston, 100

Civilisations, 32–3, 67–9, 72, 123, 137–41, 143–6, 148, 150–1

Cluny monastery, 9, 23

Coins, 169–70

Collingwood, R. G. (*Speculum Mentis*), 122

Comparative Studies in Society and History, 174

Comte, Auguste (*Système de Politique Positive*), xii, 57–9, 93

Condorcet, A.-N., Marquis de, 29, 32, 81

Cook, M. A. (ed. *Studies in the Economic History of the Middle East*), 174, 186

Corpus Inscriptionum Arabicarum (van Berchem and others), 170

Cragg, K., 43, 75–7; quoted, 80

Creswell, K. A. C., 170

Crimean War, 63–4

Cromer, Lord (*Modern Egypt*), 12–13, 98–9

Crusades, 4, 22–3, 35, 111, 126

Cunningham, A., 178

Curzon, Lord, 99

d'Alembert, J. le R., 28; *see also* Diderot, D.

d'Alverny, M. T., 8

Daniel, Norman (*Islam and the West; the Making of an Image*), xiii, 8, 19n, 23–5, 40

Daniélou, J., xii; quoted, 37

Darrag, A., 176
Darwin, Charles (*Origin of Species*),
89–90, 98, 103
Davis, R., 186, 190
Davison, R. H. (*Reform in the
Ottoman Empire 1856–1876*), 178
Dawn, C. E., 178
de Boulainvilliers, Comte Henri, *see*
Boulainvilliers
de Condorcet, Marquis A.-N., *see*
Condorcet
de Gobineau, Comte J.-A., 61
Deism, 11, 27, 30
de Menasce, Jean, xii
Deny, J., 168
Description de l'Egypte, 117, 172
Dictionaries, 117, 125, 173, 196
Diderot, D. (with d'Alembert,
Encyclopédie), 28, 81
Documents, 166–70, 177
Dozy, R. (*Supplément aux
dictionnaires arabes*), 173
Dualism, 63, 67, 137, 153
Duhm, 48
Duri, 'A., 186

Ecology, 186, 190
Edinburgh University, 106
Egypt: Blunt in, 91–2, 94–5, 97–9,
101–3; Gibb's view, 104, 106, 109,
114–15; historiography, 162–70,
172, 176–8; Islamic science, 61;
social history, 186–7, 190; study
material, 194; Toynbee's view, 151;
Volney in, 81, 83–5
Elizabeth I of England, 26
Encyclopaedia of Islam, xiv, 105, 119,
132, 172
Engels, Friedrich, 63–4
Evans-Pritchard, E. E. (*The Sanusi of
Cyrenaica*), 171, 191

Fatimids, 176
Foreign Office Research Department,
114
Forster, C. (*Mahometanism
Unveiled*), 35–7

France: documents, 168–70; Egypt,
94–5; North Africa, 4, 35, 92, 178;
scholarship, 112, 172, 190, 195;
Syria, 115; Turkey, 26
Freeman-Grenville, G. S. P. (*The
Muslim and Christian Calendars*),
172
Freud, S. (*Moses and Monotheism*),
121
Fuad, King of Egypt, 168
Fuad Köprülü, 164–5
Fück, J. W. (*Die arabischen Studien
in Europa*), 19n

Gabrieli, F. (*Arab Historians of the
Crusades*), 195
Gardet, L., 41; quoted, 5
Genealogies, 172
Geography, historical, 108, 111, 184,
190
Geology, 46
Gerth, H. H., 69
Geertz, Clifford, 15
al-Ghazali, 5, 45, 124
al-Ghazzi, K., 164
Gibb, Hamilton A. R., xiii, 19 & n,
53–4, 72, 104–33, 176, 178, 181–2,
185; 'An interpretation of Islamic
history', 119; *Arabic Literature*,
109–10; *Area Studies Reconsidered*,
128–9; career, 104–5, 127–33;
contemporaries, 112–13, 116;
Encyclopaedia of Islam (ed.), 119,
132; influences, 106–7, 120–3;
Islamic Society and the West (with
Bowen), 116–18, 176, 185;
languages and literature, 106–7,
110–11; *Modern Trends in Islam*,
118–21, 126 and quoted, 110, 127,
134, 178; *Mohammedanism: An
Historical Survey*, 119, 194 and
quoted, 123–4; politics, 114–16;
publications, 109—10, 126–7;
research, 123–7; 'The structure of
religious thought in Islam', 118 and
quoted, 124; *Studies on the
civilisation of Islam,* quoted, 108–9,

116, 119, 124–6, 181; style, 113–14;
vocation, 107–9; *Whither Islam*,
109, 114
Gibb, Helen Jessie ('Ella', née Stark),
104, 111, 129, 133
Gibbon, Edward, xiii, 30–1, 84, 142
Gladstone, W. E., 88, 95, 96, 100
Goitein, S. D. (*A Mediterranean
Society*), 167, 186, 190
Goldziher, Ignaz (*Der Mythos bei der
Hebräern und seine geschichtliche
Entwicklung*; 'Muruwwa und
Din'), 3, 5, 14, 51–3, 55, 62, 122,
162, 166, 181, 182
Golombek, L., 170
Gombrich, E. H., xiii
Gospel of Barnabas, 6
Grabar, O., 161, 170
Graf, G., 171
Granville, Lord, 95
Greece, influence of: concepts of
history, 185; Gibb, 123, 136;
philosophy, 26, 37, 56–7, 59–61,
68–9; Toynbee, 141–3, 146
Grey, Lord, 100
Grohmann, A., 167

hadith (tradition), 2–3, 5, 126, 166
Haim, S., 179
al-Hallaj, 6, 40
Hamilton, R. W., 170
Hanbali school of law, 124
Handbooks, 172
Handbuch der Orientalistik, 172
Harik, I. (*Politics and Change in a
Traditional Society*), 191
Harvard, Jewett Professorship, 104,
129–32; Widener Library, 132
Hautecoeur, L., 187
Hayek, Fr M., 41
Hayter Committee, 129
Hebrew University, Jerusalem, 171,
173
Hegel, G. W. F., 13, 47, 56–7, 122
Hess, A. C., 177
Heyd, U., 172, 176
Hinduism, 74, 152
Historians, 13, 129, 161–2, 179–82,
184, 190–4

Historians of the Middle East (ed.
Lewis and Holt), 174
Historical description, 165–70
Historiography, xiii, 46–50, 55–7,
161–96
History: demographic, 175, 184, 186;
departments, 192–3; economic, 175,
184–6; historicist approach, 69,
71–2; institutional, 116; intellectual,
175, 184, 187; political, 175, 184,
186–7, 190–1; regional, 175; social,
175, 182–92, 194; teaching, 162–3;
technological, 175, 184; theory of,
136–45, 149; types, 175–9, 196
Hodgson, M. G. S. (*The Venture of
Islam*), 161
Holt, P. M. (ed. *Political and Social
Change in Modern Egypt*), 168,
174, 177; *see also* Lewis, B.
hubris, 143–4, 146, 149–50, 157
Hurgronje, C. Snouck, 162
Hussein, Dr M. K. Husayn,
Muhammad Kamil (*City of Wrong:
A Friday in Jerusalem*), 7, 76–80

Ibn al-Athir (*Kamil*), 173
Ibn al-Qalanisi, 109, 111
Ibn Battuta, 109, 111, 132–3
Ibn Khaldun (*Muqaddima*), 113, 116,
173
Ibn Rashid, 92–3
Ibrahim Pasha, 97
ijma' (consensus), 127
Inalcik, H. (*The Ottoman Empire: the
Classical Age 1300–1600*), 176–7,
186, 194
Index Islamicus (also *Arabicus/
Hebraicus/Iranicus/
Turcicus*), 172
India, 20, 66, 95, 97, 100–2, 108, 152,
184, 190
Indonesia, 15
Industrialism, 58, 156, 177
Inscriptions, 170–1
Institute for Seljuk History and
Civilisation, 174
Institute for the Study of Turkish
Culture, 174

International Journal of Middle East Studies, 174

Iran (Persia): Blunt's contacts, 91, 93; Gibb on, 116–17, 125, 132; historiography, 167, 170–1, 173, 176, 184, 188, 194; Islamic law, 61; trade routes, 64; *see also* Persia; Shi'ism

Iranic civilisation, 69, 140

Iraq, 38, 58, 64, 91, 93; Department of Antiquities, 170–1; medieval economic history, 186

Ireland, 95–7, 100–3

Islam, xiii; attitudes to Christianity, 2, 4, 6–7, 9; Blunt on, 93–4; Christian attitudes to, 11–12, 14–15, 17–18; doctrine, 20–1, 24–30, 32, 36–43, 53–9, 61–3, 66–8, 70–2; Gibb on, 115–18, 122–6; historiography, 161–3, 165, 167, 180–2, 184–5, 192; religious type, 74–80; Volney on, 85; *see also* Sunnism; Shafi'i school of law; Sufism; Shi'ism

Islam and the Trade of Asia (ed. Richards), 174

Islam-Ansiklopedisi, 172

The Islamic City (ed. Hourani and Stern), 174

Islamic Civilisation 950–1150 (ed. Richards), 174

Islamic history: study and training, 161–3, 180–1, 193–4, 196

Islamkundliche Untersuchungen, 173

Isma'il, Khedive, 92–3, 97

Israel, 22, 36, 163–4, 168–71

Issawi, C., 186, 195

Itzkowitz, N., 118

al-Jabarti, 'A. (*'Aja'ib al-athar*), 117, 162, 173, 177

Jamal al-Din al-Afghani, Sayyid, xii, 62, 87, 93, 97, 164, 178

Japan, 140, 163–4, 172, 179, 190

jihad/mujahid, 4

Jomier, J., 41–2, 178; quoted, 6

Jordan, 169

The Journal of the Economic and Social History of the Orient, 174

Journet, Cardinal, xii, 17

Judaism, 1–3, 17, 36, 38, 45, 50–2, 55–6, 60, 64, 67, 70, 74, 79–80

Julien, C. A., 194

Jung, Carl (*Psychological Types*), 142, 149

Kahhala, 'U. R., 171

Kant, I. (*Religion within the Bounds of Pure Reason*), 15–16, 46–7, 107, 120–1

al-Kattani, M. (*Salwat al-anfas*), 162

Keddie, N. R., 164, 178, 187

Kedourie, E., 164, 179

Kemalist revolution, 164, 174

Kessler, C., 170

Keynes, J. M., xiii

Khazin family (Lebanon), 169

Khedives (Egypt), 92–5, 98

Kitab al-aghani, 166

Kraemer, Hendrik, 16, 43–5

Kuran, A., 170

Kurd 'Ali, M., 164

Lambton, A. K. S. (*Landlord and Peasant in Persia*), 188

Lammens, Henri, 34–5, 166

Landes, D. S. (*Bankers and Pashas*), 168

Langer, W. L. (*The Diplomacy of Imperialism 1890–1902*), 177

Languages, 13, 23, 35, 37, 40, 106–7, 110–11, 161; *see also* Dictionaries

Laoust, H., 124

Lapidus, I. M. (*Muslim Cities in the Later Middle Ages*), 161, 188, 190

Laroui, A. (*L'histoire du Maghreb*), 165

Law systems, 47, 61, 70, 76, 78–80, 123–4, 148, 176, 182, 195–6

Lebanon, 35, 84–6, 165, 190–1

Le Bon, Gustave, 65–6

The Legacy of Islam (ed. Schacht and Bosworth), 19n, 109–10

Leibnitz, G. W. von, 29

Lepanto, Feast of, 58

Le Tourneau, R., 188

Levi Della Vida, G., 60, 109–10, 114

Lévi-Provençal, E., 176

Lewis, Bernard, 169, 172, 173; *The Arabs in History*, 194; *The Emergency of Modern Turkey*, 178; *Historians of the Middle East* (ed. with P. M. Holt), 19n, 174
Literature: *'amal*, 185; *hadith*, 2–3, 5, 126, 166; sources of history, 165–6; tradition, 60, 63
London School of Oriental and African Studies, 104, 107, 109, 128
Lopez, R., 186
Lull, Raymond, 23
Lutfi al-Sayyid, A., 178
Luther, Martin, 10, 26

MacCarthy, Desmond, 100
Macdonald, D. B. (*Development of Muslim Theology, Jurisprudence and Constitutional Theory*; *The Religious Attitude and Life in Islam*), 122–3
Maghrib (Morocco), 176, 184–5, 195
Magian culture, 67
Mahmud II (Sultan), 91
Maimonides, 51
Makdisi, G., 124, 175
Malaysia, 20
Malik, Charles, xii
Malkum Khan, 93
Malvezzi, A. (*L'islamismo e la cultura europea*), 19n; quoted, 26
Mamluk rule (Egypt), 84–5, 176–7, 194
al-Manar (periodical), 6
Manichaean culture, 67
Mantran, R., 172, 177, 188
Maps, atlases, 172, 196
Maracci, 27
Marçais, G. and W., 170, 187
Mardin, S. (*The Genesis of Young Ottoman Thought*), 178
Margoliouth, David Samuel, 112
Marshall, Alfred, xiii
Marx, Karl, 63–4, 73, 183
Massignon, Louis, xiii, 18, 38–41, 43, 107, 112–13, 118, 173; quoted, 20
Masson, P., 190
Middle East Studies Association of North America, 161

Middle Eastern Studies, 174
Midhat Pasha, 92
Miles, G. C., 170
Military challenge of Islam, 19–20, 26, 58, 70–1, 157
Mill, James and John Stewart, 64
Milliot, L., 185
Mills, C. Wright, 69
Mimesis, force of, 138–9, 151–2
Minorsky, V. (tr. *Tadhkirat al-muluk*), 176
Miskimin, H., 186
Moguls, 184
Mongols, 23, 69, 152
Monotheism, 1–3, 6, 12, 15, 21, 24, 40, 52, 57–8, 62
Montefiore, Claud G., 1–4
Montesquieu, 63
Morocco, 4, 15, 35, 167, 169, 176–7, 184–5, 188, 190, 195
Mubarak, 'A. (*al-Khitat al-tawfiqiyya*), 162
Moubarac, Fr Y, 40–1
Muhammad 'Ali, 91, 168
Muir, Sir William, 34–5
Müller, Max, 52
al-Muradi, 117
Musallam, B., 186
Mustafa Kamil, 99
Mysticism, 16, 39–40, 44–5, 62, 75, 124; *abdal, qutb*, 126; *awliya*, 21; Toynbee, 159
Mythology, science of, 46, 48–50, 52, 62

Naff, T., 178
Napoleon Bonaparte, 30, 32, 82–3, 85, 172
al-Nasiri, A. (*Kitab al-istiqsa*), 162
Nation-state, 51, 136–7, 148, 164, 184
Nationalism, 33, 59–60, 87, 95–9, 102, 156–7, 178–9, 182
Near Eastern History Group, Oxford, 19n
Neologen, 52
Newman, J. H. (*Lectures on the History of the Turks in its Relation to Christianity*), 33–5
Nöldeke, T., 52

Nomadic movements, 32, 64, 68, 94, 140, 164; 'tribal' studies, 32, 188–9
North Africa: Berbers, Beduin, 69; Blunt in, 91; Gibb on, 115; historiography, 163, 165, 167–71, 177–8, 186, 194; *see also* Morocco; West Africa
Nubar Pasha, 169

O'Brien, P., 186
Ockley (*History of the Saracens*), 28
Oral history, 171
Orientalism, 27–8, 59, 104–34, 180, 192
Orientalistische Literaturzeitung, 172
Ottoman Empire: 4, 10, 25–6, 57–8, 63–4, 69; archives, 167–8; Blunt on, 91–2, 94; Gibb on, 117–18; historiography, 171–2, 175–8, 184, 186, 194; Toynbee on, 136, 140; Volney on, 85
Owen, E. R. J. (*Cotton and the Egyptian Economy*), 186, 190
Oxford: Faculty of Oriental Studies, 127–9; Laudian Chair of Arabic, 104, 112

Paganism, 8, 21, 23, 35, 37, 59
Palestine, 84, 115
Pan-Islam, 87, 93, 178
Pascal, Blaise, 27
Periodicals, 174
Persia: language and religion, 67, 111, 161, 173; *see also* Iran
Peter the Venerable, 9, 23
Philadelphia History of the Crusades, 126
Philosophers of history, 20–1, 29–35, 55, 59, 61–5, 69, 72; moral, 107–8
Pococke (*Specimen Historiae Arabum*), 28
Political-institutional historians, 180–1
Political and Social Change in Modern Egypt (ed. Holt), 174
Political relations, 25–7, 85–6, 93–8, 100–1, 114–16
Political theory, 116, 190–1

Positivism, 58–9, 69, 71
Pound, Ezra, 89
Prideaux, Humphrey (*The true nature of imposture fully display'd in the life of Mahomet*), 11, 27
Pringle-Pattison, A. S., 107, 121
Prophetic tradition, 1–2, 4–5, 8–9, 21, 24, 48–50, 65, 70, 74–5
Protestantism, 5, 16, 26, 67, 71; Reformation, 10–11, 25–7, 106
Psychology, 78–80, 121
Publication of research, 173
Pugachenkova, G. A., 170

Qajar State records, 168
Qur'an, 2, 5, 6, 16–18, 21, 24–8, 34, 38–42, 49, 60, 65, 76, 123; *tafsir*, 126; translations and commentaries, 9, 23, 27–8

Rabie, H., 186
Race theories, 13, 33, 52, 61–2, 65–6
al-Rafi'i, 'A., 164
Rahmatullah al-Dihlawi, Shaykh, 6
Rainolds, William (*Calvino-Turcismus*), 11, 26
Rationalism, 158–9
Raymond, A., 167, 177, 188
Records (research), 167–70, 177, 195–6
Redhouse, J. W. (*Lexicon*), 173
Reference books, 172
Religion, 15–16, 32, 41, 44–6, 49–55, 67, 144–5, 150–3, 157–9; science and, 11–12, 98, 154; science of, 2–3, 121–2, 162
Renan, Ernest, xii, 11–14, 52, 61–2; quoted, 48
Répertoire chronologique d'épigraphie arabe (Combe, Sauvaget, Wiet), 170
Research tools, 164–5, 194–6
Reshid Pasha, Grand Vizir, 58
Richards, D. S. (ed. *Islam and the Trade of Asia*; ed. *Islamic Civilisation*), 167, 174
Riza Bey, Ahmad, 58
Robert of Ketton, 9

Rodinson, Maxime (*Islam et capitalisme;* 'The Western image and western studies of Islam'), 14, 19n, 73, 185
Rome, influence of, 37, 56, 59, 61, 67, 182
Roolvink, R. (*Historical Atlas of the Muslim Peoples*), 172
Ross, Sir E. Denison, 108
Rothstein, Theodore (*Egypt's Ruin*), 99
Rousseau, J.-J., 29
Royal Institute of International Affairs, 114, 116
Russia, 141, 157, 168-9, 172
Rustum, A., 168

Sabunji, Louis, 93
Sachau, E., 122
Safavid dynasty, Iran, 167, 176, 184
St Augustine, 21, 192
St John of Damascus (*The Fount of Knowledge; Disputation between a Saracen and a Christian*), 8-9, 16, 24-5
St Paul, 49
St Thomas Aquinas, 9-10, 24
Sainte-Beuve, C.-A. de, 83-5
Saladin, 106, 126, 133
Sale, G., 27
Salibi, K. S., 177, 190
Salisbury, Lord, 101
Sassanians, 61, 182
Sauvaget, J. (*Introduction to the History of the Muslim East; Historiens arabes*), 170-2, 181, 187, 195
Savary, René, 84
Scanlon, G. T., 170
Scarbrough Commission (1947), 127
Schacht, Joseph, 19n, 123, 182
Schlegel, C. W. F. von (*Philosophy of History*), 32-5
Schlumberger, D., 170
Schölch, A., 168
Sciences, natural, 35, 58, 61-3, 66, 142, 144
Scientific disciplines, 46, 58, 61, 62
Seale, P. (*The Struggle for Syria*), 171

Seljuks, 33, 176-7
Semites, Semitic languages, etc., 2, 12-14, 61-2, 123
Seth, James, 107
Sezgin, F., 171
Shaban, M. A., 166, 175
Shafi'i School of law, 124
Shakib Arslan, 169
shari'a (holy law), 2-3, 94, 116-17, 124
Shaw, G. Bernard, 145
Shaw, S. J., 177
Shi'ism, 69, 125, 194
silsila, 125-6
Smith, Adam, 64
Smith, W. Robertson, 108, 191
Smith, Wilfred Cantwell, 16, 54
Social anthropology, 15, 46, 72, 131, 191
Social democracy, 157
Social history, 175, 182-4, 191-9
Social sciences, 72, 131, 157, 191
Sociology, 13, 14, 63-4, 67, 69-73
Sourdel D., and Sourdel-Thomine, J. (*La Civilisation de l'Islam classique*), 167, 170, 172, 175, 194
Southern, R. W. (*Western Views of Islam in the Middle Ages*), xiii, 8, 19n, 22-3
Spain, 10, 176
Spencer, Herbert, xii, 98
Spengler, O., 66-9
Sprenger, A., 52, 59
Spuler, B., 176
Stern, S. (ed. *Fatimid Decrees; Documents from Islamic Chanceries;* with A. Hourani, *The Islamic City*), 166, 172, 174
Storey, C. A., 171
Strachan, J., quoted, 47
Strauss, D. F. (*Life of Jesus*), 48, 49
Studies in the Economic History of the Middle East (ed. Cook), 174
Sudan, 20, 97, 102, 168, 169
Sufism, 6, 124, 126, 173
Sunnism, 69, 122, 124-5
Surveys, 196
Sutcliff, Matthew (*De Turcopapismo*), 11

Svoronos, N. G., 186
Syria, 24, 34–5, 59, 115, 162, 167, 169–71, 176–7; Blunt in, 91; Volney in, 81, 84–5
Syriac civilisation, 68–9, 140

al-Tabari, 165
al-Tabbakh, R., 164
Talmud, 51, 182
Theism, 3–4
Thomist tradition, 41
Thomson, W., Jewett Professor, Harvard, 129
Tignor, R. L., 178
Todorov, N. T., 186
Torah, 51
Toynbee, Arnold J. (*A Study of History*), xiii, 66–9, 116, 135–60; theory of history, 136–42; vision of history, 142–5; future of Western civilisation, 145–7; rhythm in history, 147–50; religion, 150–2; duality of truth, 152–5; technology and Western civilisation, 156–8; mysticism, 158–60
Trade records, routes, 34–5, 64, 166, 177, 186
Tunisia, 4, 92
Turkey, 20, 33, 58, 69; Blunt in, 91–2, 94, 97–8; Gibb's studies, 111, 117; historiography, 161–5, 169–70, 174, 176, 178, 184, 187
Turkish Historical Society, 174
Tyrrell, Fr, 90

Udovitch, A. L., 166, 186
'ulama, 94, 118, 120, 124–6, 187–8, 192
al-'Umari (*Masalik al-absar*), 173
Umayyad caliphs, 8, 24, 35, 175
'umdas, 188
umma, 72, 119–20, 124–7
'Urabi Pasha, Ahmad, 89, 95, 168
Uzbeks, 184
Uzunçarşili, I. H., 176

Valensi, L. (*Le Maghreb avant la prise d'Alger*), 186, 195
van Berchem, M., 170
Vatican Council II, 17, 22, 42–3

Vinet, P., 26
Volney (C.-F. Chassebeuf: *Voyage en Syrie et en Egypte; Les Ruines, ou Méditations sur les révolutions des empires*), 81–6, 142, 177; bibliography, 204–5
Voltaire (F.-M. Arouet: *Le Fanatisme ou Mohamet le Prophète*, play), 11, 28, 30
von Grunebaum, G. E., 72, 181
von Hammer-Purgstall, J., 181
von Harnack, A., 49
von Kremer, A., 59
von Leibnitz, G. W., *see* Leibnitz, G. W. von
von Schlegel, C. W. F., *see* Schlegel, C. W. F. von

Waardenburg, J. D. J. (*L'Islam dans le miroir de l'occident*), xiii, 19n
Wahhabi kingdom, 92–3
Walzer, Richard, 123; quoted, 185
waqfiyyas, 166
Warburg, Aby, xiii
Watt, W. M. (*Islam and the Integration of Society*), 72–3
Weber, Max (*Wirtschaft und Gesellschaft; Gesammelte Aufsätze zur Religionssoziologie*), 14, 69–71, 72, 183, 190
Weizmann Archives, 169
Wellhausen, Julius (*Prolegomena to the History of Israel; The Arab Kingdom and its Fall*), 3, 14, 50–1, 71, 108, 175, 181
Wells, H. G. (*Outline of History*), 135
West Africa, 115, 171
Western Europe: attitudes to Islam, 20, 31–6, 60, 73; Islamic history teaching, 163; national communities, 138, 145–6, 151, 156; Nazism, 156; technology, 156–7; Toynbee on, 136
Whitehouse, D., 170
Wiet, G., 187
Williams, J. A. (ed. *Themes of Islamic Civilization*), 195
Wolff, Sir Henry Drummond, 97
Wood, A. C., 190
Wyndham, George, 101

Yeats, W. B., 89
Yin and *Yang* doctrine, 137–8, 142, 149
Young Turk revolution (1908), 58

Zaehner, R. C. (*At Sundry Times*), xiii, 17–18, 74–5
Zaghlul Pasha, Sa'd, 169
Zambaur, E. de (*Manuel de généalogie*), 172
Zeine, Z. N., 178